Acclaim for Linda Schierse Leonard's Books

Meeting the Madwoman

"Through her splendid examples from literature, history, movies, and dreams, Linda Schierse Leonard allows us to see both the destructive and creative fire of the Madwoman within. An intense and thought-provoking book."
  —Marion Woodman, Jungian analyst and author of *Addiction to Perfection*

"An authentic rendering of the energies of the madwoman in our daily lives by an author of profound insight."
  —Robert Johnson, author of *He, She,* and *We*

"Richly evocative . . . Leonard provides a new perspective on how women can break out of culturally imposed roles."
  —*Publishers Weekly*

The Wounded Woman

"Every woman will find insight here and the immense comfort of understanding herself. I cannot recommend it too highly, a splendid addition to our growing need to come to terms with womanhood, and to rejoice in it."
  —May Sarton

"The book's great strength derives primarily from its elegant and profoundly original vision of feminine psychology. . . . I urge everyone to read Linda Leonard's book. A revelation for men, an inspiration for women, it offers all of us the chance to break the bitter cycle."
  —Alan Rinzler, *San Francisco Chronicle*

Witness to the Fire

"The most perceptive and compassionate study I have yet read of the problem of addiction. Essential reading for anyone who has dealt with or is dealing with addiction."
  —Athol Fugard, director, actor, playwright, and author of *Master Harold and the Boys*

BANTAM BOOKS

NEW YORK   TORONTO   LONDON   SYDNEY   AUCKLAND

MEETING

THE

MADWOMAN

AN INNER CHALLENGE FOR FEMININE SPIRIT

Linda Schierse Leonard

MEETING THE MADWOMAN

A Bantam Book

PUBLISHING HISTORY
Bantam hardcover edition published February 1993
Bantam trade paperback edition / April 1994

For permissions, please see page 315.

ISBN 0-553-37318-8

Published simultaneously in the United States and Canada

PRINTED IN THE UNITED STATES OF AMERICA

BVG   0 9 8 7 6 5 4 3 2 1

For my grandmother, Ida M. Klipple, who was deprived of the formal education she wanted, and who shared with me her heart and soul, her love of nature, poetry and literature, and encouraged me to study and to write.

CONTENTS

ACKNOWLEDGMENTS

MY DEEP APPRECIATION AND GRATITUDE GOES TO ALL THE women and men who encouraged me to write this book through their support, suggestions, and creative dialogue: participants in workshops, hiking friends, and especially all those who generously shared their stories and their dreams.

In particular, I would like to thank: Leslie Meredith, my editor, for her vision and wisdom, astute, creative ideas, and editorial expertise in the final shaping of the book; Diane Guthrie, my typist, for her enthusiasm, intuitive insights, dedication to the manuscript, and emotional support; and my agents, Katinka Matson and John Brockman.

Special thanks also to those colleagues who read the entire manuscript in its final stages and offered extensive suggestions: Betty Cannon, Keith Chapman, Lynne Foote, Ellen Fox, Gloria Gregg,

Cathleen Roundtree, and Karen Signell, and also to those colleagues with whom I consulted extensively on particular issues: Noni Hubrecht, Phyllis Kenevan, Peter Rutter, Myra Shapiro, Suzanne Short, Elaine Stanton, Peggy Walsh, Robert Wilkinson, and Steve Wong.

Thanks also to Karina Golden, Micah Monsom, Cathleen Roundtree, and Mary Elizabeth Williams for their poems.

INTRODUCTION

Much madness is divinest sense.
. . . .
Much sense the starkest madness.
Emily Dickinson

MANY YEARS AGO, I FELT HAUNTED BY A FRIGHTENING FIGURE whom I now call the Madwoman. My initial reaction was fear. A series of Madwomen appeared in my dreams at night, threatening or taunting me. In my outer life, bullying women bothered and harassed me. During this period my life seemed like a living nightmare. Plunged into chaos, I knew I had to delve deeply within myself in order to discover the meaning of this figure, to encounter and work with this psychological and emotional energy.

One night I dreamed that a beautiful Madwoman stood above me as I slept, ready to plunge into my heart a jagged dagger of stained glass from an ancient cathedral. When I awoke, I knew that if I did not face this inner feminine force, her madness would destroy me. The rich, multicolored stained-glass dagger from the cathedral suggested that be-

hind the Madwoman's murderous, crazed nature was an ancient
spiritual and creative energy that could be mine if I were bold
enough to confront her and consciously use her active—and my
potential—inner power.

This dream also triggered me to remember a series of other
dreams in which Madwomen had tried to trick me in order to steal
my opals, my precious birthstones. For me, the mysterious opal symbolizes my mystical feminine self and my intuitive way of knowing.
The Madwomen who were after them were actually shamanic healers who wanted to alert me to rely on and use my instinctive self
more fully and responsibly. I also remembered periods in which I
had had beautiful but overwhelming visions while I was hiking in
the mountains, but had fought against their power, afraid they
might mean I could go crazy. This fear also kept me from going into
the furthest, ecstatic depths of my creative and spiritual self and
kept the feminine in me partially buried. My suppression of these
dreams and impulses, my attempt to deny the more assertive aspects
of my natural feminine makeup, caused these energies to demand
my attention in my dreams and manifest in my inner life as
Madwomen. For in my external life, I tended to retreat from confronting more aggressive women and men. This shy introversion
kept me from sharing my wisdom and knowledge forcefully and
effectively in the world. Although I wrote books, taught, and practiced Jungian analysis, I still was not using the *full force* of my knowledge and power. Because I denied myself the expression of my own
assertiveness, I came up against the need to exercise it more and
more frequently in the outside world.

Through workshops I was giving around the world on feminine
psychology, I began to see a common theme in the dreams and
creations of participants that reflected my own dreams of the Madwoman. Women artists, for example, were spontaneously painting
and sculpting huge powerful female figures, dark and bloody, sometimes dismembered or dismembering others. Poets had put similar
images into verse. Both men and women told of frightening Madwoman figures appearing in their dreams. The Madwoman was also
a frequent figure in many of my clients' dreams.

The Madwoman demanded my attention over and over again. I
saw her appear in film after film. Pondering these cinematic
Madwomen, I suddenly realized that many women characters in literature were also Madwomen of various kinds. Powerful female fig-

ures from mythology and fairy tales came to mind—Medea, Cassandra, Artemis, Inanna, Kali, the Ice Queen, and other feminine forces—many embodying paradoxical powers of creation and destruction.

I also saw the Madwoman manifested in political events. Case after case of a woman fighting for her rights against sexual abuse and harassment in the workplace appeared in the news media. Most often these women were labeled hysterical females, victims of their own fantasies, denigrated by men but also ridiculed by other women.

In the center of these puzzling events was the mysterious Madwoman: a feminine figure in the psyche, universal to most cultures, fearsome to many, acted out destructively by others, appearing in public and private life, and plaguing me personally. I decided to confront her by writing about her and focused a chapter on the Madwoman in my book *Witness to the Fire*. While this chapter became my first step into this feminine mystery, however, I had not gone far enough.

As a result, I had more dreams of Madwomen and suffered additional abrasive attacks from the Madwoman part of the psyches in otherwise normal women and men in my outer life. And I continued to see her manifested more powerfully in the arts and in social affairs. *She* even interrupted a book I was writing on the gentle mystical feminine healing in Nature. I began to recognize an inner urgency to deal with this mad feminine energy more effectively. My own anger began to surge to the surface. After I saw a German film, *The Nasty Girl,* which depicted Justice as a big-breasted, fierce Madwoman, I felt intensely the Madwoman's constructive and creative side. The next morning, I gave in to her demands for attention, and as I sat down to write, the chapter titles for this book flowed out fast and furious onto the page.

This book is a result of my ensuing dialogue with the Madwoman. Writing it brought up childhood memories—memories that participate in the greater feminine memory of all women, personal experiences with which all women can resonate. I remember, for instance, how much my maternal grandmother, who loved learning and desperately wanted an education so she could become a teacher, suffered when her father took her out of school when she was ten years old to make her work on his farm. She was forced to do housework and was never able to forge another identity in the world outside of the home. I wondered if my paternal grandmother, who suffered from rheumatoid arthritis and spent most of her later life in a wheelchair, was really a victim of repressed rage, physically crippled and martyred by the abuse she suffered from her alcoholic husband. My own mother, a strong survivor, went to work to support our family, but she did so at minimum wages and felt like a second-class citizen most of her life. She, too, had married an alcoholic and only in her sixties was she able to enjoy herself more freely. Caught by the expectations and rules of her generation, her spirit was harnessed. What wonders might these and all women have accomplished in their lives, had their energy been freed from external patriarchal proscriptions as well as their inner fears of their own power and nature?

It is amazing to me sometimes that I was able to succeed professionally, since my own natural temperament inclines toward receptivity, gentleness, and peace. In general, I have tried to be "too nice." Underneath that, of course, lies my shadow sister, the Madwoman. Now in my fifties, I finally have turned to face her inner energy. I have tried to sort out her destructive from her constructive sides and to point to the ways we can consciously use the positive side of anger, frustration, assertiveness, tension, and other shades of feminine madness for creative ends rather than acting out in unconscious or destructive ways. To this end, each chapter in *Meeting the Madwoman* delineates traditional life patterns in which women can get caught and become inwardly angry, depressed, consciously or unconsciously frustrated or blocked, or even actually mad because they cannot express themselves or live according to their natural or creative impulses. Modes of expression and being that are uniquely feminine or simply unconventional and therefore potentially creative are often disparaged by patriarchal cultures, and when women try to live them, they are often labeled crazy or eccentric.

In each chapter of this book, I paint the portrait of a female character who exemplifies a different face of the Madwoman. To describe each pattern, I draw from universal (archetypal) literary and cinematic examples in the art of our culture as well as mythology and fairy tales; I offer examples of historical women whose lives show in dramatic form our own collective, cultural heritage; and I share the personal stories of individual women confronted with these problems now.

Women from history catch our imagination because they have

lived out before us some patterns we may be trying to change. By understanding their dilemmas and how they dealt with them, we can better understand our own. The characters from film, literature, and mythology reveal the universal dynamics we all must face in our lives. We will see how others learned to relate to the Madwoman in productive ways and to set effective limits and boundaries on her influence over them. Sometimes they have had to struggle with the Madwoman, perhaps in a psychological dance or even in the form of a metaphoric duel, or a battle in a court of justice. In the film *Misery,* for example, a male romance novelist who needed to break into a new form of writing was followed by a Madwoman fan who didn't want him to change. She held him captive and tortured him so he would write the endings she wanted. This outer Madwoman symbolized an inner destructive Madwoman whom the writer had to battle in himself in order to break through to a new creative form, for the Madwoman romanticized misery and held the writer hostage to his old endings. In contrast, in *Thelma and Louise,* the protagonists have to embrace their inner Madwoman as sisters to become free spirits. Men, too, need to befriend their inner Madwoman, their own disowned and rejected feminine self, so they can reel in their negative attitudes toward women, have access to the feminine creative energy within themselves, and relate to women in a mature way.

Through these literary and historical characters, a contemporary woman who personally faces the same problems they so dramatically portray can find solace in her predecessors' stories and can see the Madwoman patterns more clearly in artistic expression. By getting to know these female characters, we can learn to recognize how they operate in ourselves and to identify the unique cluster of feelings they present. These women from literature and film can become our friends; they can help us on our own feminine paths.

The stories of the living women who are dealing with these issues now also attest to the fact that we can face the Madwoman energy and transform it. From them we can learn some of the ways women have misused their energy, and the real-life solutions they discovered to improve their lives. In each chapter I identify everyday behavioral emotional patterns of "madness" that can help us see the forces that have been governing our lives. When we can identify and understand these forces, we can break through them, take control of them, and release ourselves from them and make free choices about how we want to live. These female models who have passed through some form of madness before us and transformed it into creativity can be our guides to hope, even though our own journey will be unique. These expressions of the feminine can help free women into a spirited and creative life.

The last chapter, "Through the Madness," brings together all the patterns and explores ways of using the Madwoman's energy as a positive force for change. Every woman experiences the need for change and transformation in the course of her life. This process of change can itself feel like a kind of madness, like being eaten alive by life. The process is not clear, nor can we control it. Each woman has to go through her own metamorphosis, her own madness in her own way, and getting through it combines struggle, surrender, and a commitment to endure with belief in the process as one that will ultimately yield miracles. Meeting the inner Madwoman is just such a process.

Virginia Woolf once said that our problem in recognizing our true selves lies in the idealization of woman as the "angel in the house." We need to acknowledge the dark side of women, too, so that we can release the Madwoman in her creative aspect, yet be aware of her destructive side. We need to heal this internal split. When the Madwoman's energy is not acknowledged, when she is not "invited to the table to eat," like the neglected thirteenth fairy godmother in the story of Sleeping Beauty, she can curse us with unconsciousness, as symbolized by Sleeping Beauty's one hundred years of sleep. But if we become conscious of her presence and power in our psyche, she can give us remarkable creative gifts. By identifying how she manifests in your own life, and where you fit into the cast of characters described in the following chapters, you will be able to invite her to your table and meet and partake of her transformative presence.

1
MEETING
THE MADWOMAN

I saw you once, Medusa; we were alone.
I looked you straight in the cold eye, cold.
I was not punished, was not turned to stone.
How to believe the legends I am told?
. . . .

I turn your face around! It is my face.
That frozen rage is what I must explore—
Oh secret, self-enclosed and ravaged place!
This is the gift I thank Medusa for.
          —MAY SARTON, *The Muse as Medusa*

A STRANGE AND UNSETTLING FIGURE HAS INHABITED A CORNER of the minds of both women and men since the beginning of time. She emerged in ancient Greek drama and world literature, in fairy tales, in the Bible, and in the myths and songs of various cultures. She is a frequent character in the dreams of modern women and men. She frightens us; she fascinates us; she threatens and intimidates us. She can destroy us, and she can transform us. Complex and compelling, the uncanny face of the Madwoman stares at us from contemporary films, art, and literature, from our dreams, and from the traumatic experiences of our waking lives, reminding us of her energetic presence. If left in the shadows of our unconscious, she wreaks havoc. Our task as conscious human beings is to acknowledge her and learn to use her energy constructively in our lives.

The word *madness* has a vast array of meanings. Madness encompasses a wide range of states, from the extreme of insanity, to fury, anger, and moodiness. We can recognize it in confusion, frenzy, foolishness, recklessness, and impulsiveness, as well as infatuation, passion, enthusiasm, divine ecstasy, and spiritual awakening. When we are confronted with the archetypal figure of the Madwoman (an archetype is a universal energy or pattern of experience in the human psyche) it is important to remember that her energy represents a paradox. She can entice us to destructive actions against ourselves and others; she can entrap us in negative behavior patterns and experiences of victimization; or she can lead us to use her energy—our energy—creatively to change our lives for the better.

Who is this Madwoman? Where is she? Why does she haunt us? Why do we need to face her *now*? What are the forms in which she appears? Let us look around and find her in images in our daily lives. Perhaps she crouches in a corner of your mind. Is she an angry housewife in a loveless marriage, sitting in the kitchen, feeling trapped and bored? Is she a woman who has just been rejected by her lover? Is she despairing or furious? Is she lonely, a woman drinking by herself in a bar? Has she been abused? Perhaps she is a fierce lawyer or a politician, fighting for women's rights. Or she might be a homeless woman on the streets with her bags. Is she a working woman, struggling under a male-dominated business structure, harassed by her employer? Is she marching defiantly in public demonstrations, defending her belief in human rights? Maybe she sits alone in a garret, writing or painting, portraying women black with rage or passionately alive. Is she a nun struggling with the Church patriarchy? Is she intuitive, feeling crazy because she sees what others cannot envision? Or is she a woman walking alone in the wilderness, ecstatic with her love of Nature's mysteries? Does she disturb the men in her life who are frightened of feminine forces in themselves and in women—forces they can neither control nor understand? Perhaps she is a woman locked away in a mental institution, deemed mad because she refuses to conform to the patriarchal status quo. Perhaps she is a rebellious daughter, an angry sister, or a mother maddened by her plight in life. The Madwoman can be all of these women and others. Since the Madwoman's energy exists in all of us to varying degrees, we need to look at some of these forms she takes most frequently in our ordinary, modern lives.

MODERN MASKS OF THE MADWOMAN

So many women say in their therapy sessions, "I am not seen for who I am. No one really listens to me." Our dominant culture prescribes how women should be seen. It praises women for living out certain roles while rebuking or punishing them for others. Frequently, the very roles the culture expects women to play make them mad. We often see women rebelling against these roles and acting as Madwomen in literature, for instance, *The Madwoman of Chaillot* and *Antigone,* and in movies such as *Thelma and Louise* and *Fried Green Tomatoes.* Through these outer Madwoman figures, we learn to recognize and get in touch with our own rebellious nature.

In our patriarchal society, women often have negative characteristics and fears projected onto them by both men and other women. When we ignore, suppress, or fear a quality in ourselves, we tend to see it elsewhere—to project it onto others—and judge these other people negatively for displaying this very quality we share with them. We often project characteristics of the feared and rejected parts of our feminine self. For instance, a career woman may deride the value and pleasures of motherhood because of her fear of becoming submissively entrapped in a marriage and in other traditional roles. A homemaker and mother may devalue the working woman's spirit of independence as aggressive, unfriendly, or argumentative. Conversely, we also tend to project positive qualities that we wish we had ourselves onto someone who attracts us. We then may try to possess that quality through that person. For example, the expected images of femininity in our culture have been determined in large part by the desires and needs of men. Men raised with traditional values tend to want women to be soft and caring, instinctual, "good," and "nice." Yet women are not necessarily what men imagine or want them to be. A woman can become confused about her identity in a culture that prescribes and rejects certain roles for her, especially if her natural way of being is one that is rejected by men or women who disown or disparage that feminine part of themselves. She may be labeled a bitch if she is assertive, abnormal if she is unmarried, a slut if she is sensual, cold if she is smart, an airhead if she is funny or easygoing, an unfit or selfish mother if she tries to develop interests outside the home, and a woman who is wasting her education if she stays at home. Even the wives of presidents and presidential candidates are stereotyped: One is criticized for living in her husband's shadow, another for overshadowing her spouse. A woman can become trapped and enraged by this limiting stereotyping when all she wants is to be and act as an individual. Even if a woman fits a culturally desired feminine image and is happy with her life in a traditional role, parts of herself that she has denied eventually will cry out to be seen and heard, and she will feel the urge to change. Ignoring these vital parts of herself, her various desires or needs, can make a woman act or feel crazy.

In my work as a therapist I have observed women suffering from a variety of conflicting feelings and suppressed desires, many of which are expressions of the Madwoman. In our culture, women are usually rewarded if they live the roles of mother, wife, and helpmate, or even mistress and the passively inspiring Muse. While many women find these roles meaningful, to others they can become limiting and debilitating. A woman's psychological development requires integration of many facets of her self in order for her to become a whole and healthy human being. When a woman is limited to only one or two roles, she can feel or act mad because the unactualized parts of herself are struggling to express themselves. If she is not aware of her frustration, her anger at her unlived life is likely to be directed unconsciously at her children, her husband, her parents, her friends, or even herself. This accounts for the inexplicable moodiness of many mothers who seem "mad" to their children.

The need to understand how our mothers may act out their madness is important, since to the extent that we don't understand our mothers, we won't understand ourselves. It is especially important to understand the sides of our mothers that we ignored, disliked, rejected, or feared, for this is often the first face of the feminine—and so the first face of the dark, mad side of the feminine—that we experience. Our mothers' madness is likely to be internalized by us in some form when we are children. To some degree, we cannot help but become like our mothers. If we understand how we formed these patterns of thought, behavior, and emotion in ourselves, however, and see how we reenact them through the expectations and prescriptions of our mothers and our culture, we can change them and free ourselves of their uncontrolled, "mad" aspects.

Each chapter in *Meeting the Madwoman* describes a different mask that the modern Madwoman may wear. The chapter "Mad Mothers,

Mad Daughters'' describes four basic character patterns of relating or acting that daughters (and sons) are likely to recognize in their mothers or in managerial, working women who dominate, reject, withdraw from, or disappoint their children, peers, or employees due to their frustration with their own lives. These negative patterns often intermingle. For example, the freezing treatment of the "Ice Queen" mother can turn in an instant to the explosive fiery tongue of the "Dragon Lady." "The Saint" and the "Sick Mother" may be the martyred, mirror images of the Ice Queen and the Dragon Lady. While mothers today continue to be scapegoated by many psychiatrists and other "experts" for the injuries they inflict on their children, it is important for us to remember that they themselves have been wounded and maddened by their own families' and culture's expectations and by their own mothers, who also were forced into stultifying roles. In order to break the chain of "Mad Mothering," we need to recognize and understand the limits that these false expectations and patterns of behavior impose upon women and to imagine and strive for the freer feminine ways of being that we require.

Many housewives who feel trapped in their marriages experience the feelings of the "Caged Bird," which we look at in Chapter 3. Men, too, experience being caged in their jobs and family life and in the role of provider. Although the Caged Bird syndrome was more prevalent for women in previous generations, it still exists today. Look at the many Caged Bird characters who appear in modern films: *Alice, Fried Green Tomatoes, Ordinary People,* and *Kramer versus Kramer,* to name only a few. Getting to know how we are trapped and the various guises these cages take will help us free ourselves to lead more genuine lives.

Many women have idealized the role of the "Muse," which we examine in Chapter 4. The woman who inspires a man to creativity or public prominence and is rewarded with riches, love, and security, has been glamorized by Hollywood. To live out their lives as a beautiful inspiratrice may seem an easy path for some women. But traditional Muses, such as Zelda Fitzgerald, Alma Mahler, or Camille Claudel, the latter two whose lives we look at in this chapter, often became mad and sick, consciously or unconsciously resenting the sacrifice of their own abilities to create, their illness a misplaced attempt by their neglected inner energies to demand expression. The traditional Muse is often rejected as she ages and is readily replaced by a younger version of herself, as the Bette Davis character found out in *All About Eve*. Seeing the forms in traditional and contemporary roles in which the Muse can lose herself—from the wife who bolsters up or takes care of her husband's feelings, to the secretary, graduate student, performer, or junior business partner—can help us choose to be free to express and live according to our own creative impulses.

In the above patterns—mother, housewife, Muse—the Madwoman is usually denied, covered over, excused, or repressed because any indication of her dark and active power contradicts our cultural expectation of the gracious way a woman should appear. Usually consigned to the cellar or the attic, allowed to express itself positively only rarely in the occasional, unusually passionate night of married lovemaking or through some inspired but culturally acceptable artistic hobby or a talent for being superorganized, a Super Mom, the Madwoman's energy occasionally erupts in extreme expressions of creativity or vision or revolutionary activism that are at variance with women's usual behavior. Women who express and yield to this energy sometimes become confused, not understanding that creativity and growth are essential to their health. Or they may feel guilt and shame at their secret desires to break free of their normal existence. They may try to suppress their anger or impulses, believing their captors or family or society or doctor is right in their criticism of them. They may compromise themselves, caught between desires they cannot express and images of femininity they are unable to accept any longer. In extreme cases, some are abandoned, sent away, or committed to asylums, deemed mad and "uncontrollable" by the men who run their families, communities, or culture.

The Madwoman may also emerge when a woman is rejected in love. How many women have felt the shame of rejection and the rage and desire to wreak revenge upon the one who abandoned them? This occurs especially when women have no other outlet for their creative energy except in relation to a man. The newspapers and other media are full of reports of women who live as victims of rejection, acting out their anger in vengeance toward others or themselves and who fail to transform their anger into a constructive energy for a meaningful life. Chapter 5 deals with the jealousy, revenge, and destructive dependency that "the Rejected Lover" feels, and it tries to show other ways to fulfillment.

Other manifestations of the Madwoman that are punished or

ridiculed by society are those that represent the shadow of a patriarchal culture. The shadow side of a culture is the aspect or characteristic that the culture most fears. Take, for example, "the Bag Lady," a dropout who brings up our fears of loneliness, insecurity, and homelessness in old age. Most people turn away or avert their eyes guiltily from the bag ladies on the street. Yet the Bag Lady, discussed in Chapter 6, represents a feminine side of ourselves that can mutter crazy wisdom. As a survivor of the streets, she possesses a certain feminine strength that has no need of patriarchal values. In our psyche, she can symbolize freedom; in our external life she needs to be acknowledged and helped.

Another rejected female shadow figure is "the Recluse," who we look at in Chapter 7. Many people view the Recluse as a Madwoman. The aging single woman is often considered eccentric and sometimes even crazy. We tend to be suspicious of any woman who is alone. Culture dictates that something is awry in her life and denigrates her solitude. A single woman is often made to feel ashamed or paranoid, an object of disdain, stared at when she is by herself. The culture's negative projection upon the Recluse often will make the solitary woman question her own normality and may keep her from letting herself be alone, even though she needs her own time, space, and rhythm to find and understand her unique feminine independence. Because our culture devalues solitude and silence as experiences important to personal development, communication problems often arise between men and women who have not learned to listen to each other because they do not know how to listen to themselves and understand their own inner needs and promptings. Far from being a pitiable figure, the Recluse may be an independent woman who hears and understands her own voices, who finds time for her creativity, enjoys solitude, and knows how to *listen*. Her aloneness may actually be indicative of a healthy self-respect and feeling of wholeness in herself. She is a model we need to value and understand.

"The Revolutionary," a rebellious woman who refuses to be overlooked or ignored, has learned to transform her fiery energy and use it to effect social reform, as we will see in Chapter 8. Because she threatens to change the status quo, however, she is often feared and accused of madness. By partaking of her courage to confront injustice and demand change, we can make needed changes in ourselves as women—we can refuse to allow everyday injustices in our homes and offices, we can speak out against pollution and choose not to buy the patriarchy's wasteful products, we can choose to work for health and freedom from addiction and from restrictions on our reproductive rights—and bring feminine values to the world to make it a more human place to live. One way the Madwoman's energy can be a resource for social transformation has emerged in the feminist movement's rage and action against patriarchal abuses.

"Feminine intuition" has been ridiculed for its sensitivities and accurate prophecies. A particularly sensitive woman, "the Visionary," is often considered mad by those who need to hold on to conventional ways of understanding or living the status quo, as we will see in Chapter 9. In past centuries, the Visionary was persecuted as a witch by patriarchal governments and religions when she opposed societal norms and rules or practiced family or folk medicine. Society still today often denigrates the mystical person as impractical and foolish, or even crazy. Yet the inner light of the Visionary can lead us into our own spirituality and guide us through the wilderness of our unknown inner lives. In our technological age of conquest and control, we need the Visionary's insights more than ever, to see a way to rebuild our society, now on the brink of destruction, in accord with the ways of Nature. Indeed, many of the Madwomen of mythology are Nature goddesses who warn of the dire consequences of living out of balance with the natural world and of disrespecting its procreative, destructive, and regenerative powers.

THE MADWOMAN IN MYTHOLOGY

The mythologies of many cultures are replete with archetypal images of the creative and destructive Madwoman, showing the universality of her presence in the human psyche and of our experience of her forces. In the Hindu pantheon, Kali, the great mother of time, is the goddess of both creation and destruction. Black as night, illuminated by the moon, blood upon her lips, Kali dances wildly on the corpses of the dead, surrounded by wailing female spirits. In her four arms she holds the sword and trident, a lotus, and a pot of honey, while she wears a necklace of heads and a belt of human hands. Kali chooses the souls who will be released to know eternal bliss. And she gathers the seeds for creating new life.

The Tlingit-Haida Indians also acknowledge the power of the Madwoman. They revere the Earth Mother, Volcano Woman, who demands respect for living creatures, cherished objects, and tribal tradition. If people are sacrilegious and fail to observe the correct rituals, Volcano Woman will destroy the village, sparing only those who try to observe and protect her rites. Another of their honored Earth Mothers, Fog Woman, gives salmon to the natives of the North Pacific. When her husband, Raven, abused her and arrogantly claimed her power by bragging that the salmon came from him, Fog Woman punished him by leaving, taking the salmon with her to the sea. Potentially destructive but also life-giving, once a year Fog Woman calls the precious fish back to the streams where they were born, so the people can have food and the salmon can reproduce.

The Rainbow Serpent of Australia is honored by many of the Aboriginal tribes as the feminine creatrix. She travels over the earth in "Dreamtime," creating beings as she journeys. But just as she "dreams" creatures into being, she will devour those who are irreverent toward her creation.

In the Talmud and the Kabbalah, Lilith was reputed to be the first wife of Adam, made not from her husband's rib but from the same dust of the earth as he. Refusing to be regarded as inferior, Lilith would not lie beneath Adam when he insisted, and she left to live her own life. She would have only a love born of mutual respect. Angered at her independence, the Talmudic patriarchs wrote that Lilith was a demon of the night who tempted men to spill their seed. To this day, some men have trouble separating their own sexual impulses from women who attract them. They demonize women who appeal to them as "asking for it" and, unable to tolerate women who say no, may abuse them physically or emotionally.

In Sumer, Ereshkigal was the great goddess of the underworld. Ereshkigal could kill by staring with the eyes of death. When her sister, Inanna, queen of the upper world, dared to enter her realm, Ereshkigal turned her into a rotting corpse hanging upon a peg. But when Inanna's androgynous helpers, created by Enki, god of the waters, empathized with Ereshkigal, she gave life back to Inanna, who returned with knowledge and power from her dark sister's realm.

The goddess Hecate was worshiped by the Greeks and in Nubia and the Sudan as well. Hecate was a goddess of witches and magic and was associated with the dark side of the moon. She had the power of ancient spells, and the amphibian power to swim in water and walk on land. As holy enchantress, she was the mother who renewed the cycle of life and guided transformations. Guardian of the crossroads, where decisions of life and death are made, her sacred caldron was consulted for ancient and oracular knowledge.

The Greek goddess Artemis was the guardian of young maidens, and she taught them to be independent and true to themselves. She was also protectress of the animals and the forest, provider of medicinal herbs, and an aide to all those giving birth. Artemis protected all to be free to follow the rivers and the winds, to enjoy the forests, and to honor the women of the woods. Artemis could give life, but she could also take it away from those who broke the laws of Nature. Above all, she demanded respect for Nature and the inviolable integrity of women. Artemis could become a Madwoman, enraged at anyone who defiled her integrity or her laws. When the hunter Actaeon overstepped the boundaries of sexual propriety and spied at the naked Artemis one morning as she bathed in a clear stream in her forest, she was angered, changed him into a stag, and turned his own hunting hounds against him to kill him. Nowadays we see Artemis' demand for respect of feminine integrity in women's outrage at child abuse and sexual harassment, and in their demand for the right to live in accordance with their own nature.

Demeter, goddess of grain, became a Madwoman when her daughter, Persephone, was abducted and raped by Hades, lord of the underworld. Hades wanted to keep Persephone in the underworld and make her his queen. When all peaceful attempts to retrieve her daughter failed, Demeter, maddened by grief, threatened to withhold all growth from the earth. Finally, a bargain was made between Zeus and Demeter. Persephone could be with her mother half the year, when things grow in spring and summer. During the other half, when things lie dormant, she remains in the underworld with Hades. Persephone's separation from Demeter symbolizes every young woman's separation from her mother to enable the awakening of her own sexuality and distinct individual life. Her return to Demeter for part of the year symbolizes the new relation she can build with her mother, enhanced by her own experience.

The Polynesian volcano goddess, Pelé, becomes enraged when she is dishonored, stamps her foot in anger, and releases fiery lava, causing the earth to tremble and volcanos to erupt. Legend reports this happened when converted Christians defied Pelé by throwing rocks into her sacred crater. When an elder princess recited the ancient chants to honor the fiery goddess and offered gifts at the edge of the molten lava, Pelé was appeased and stopped the lava flow.

The witches in fairy tales are another manifestation of the Madwoman. Russia's Baba Yaga is one of many. Often by confronting the witch, fairy-tale heroines are transformed into mature young women of great power who have faced the darkest parts of themselves, who have recognized their inner Madwoman and integrated her energies into their lives in a conscious, active way. In the Middle Ages and later, Christian patriarchs projected the witch onto women who didn't conform, burning them at the stake, as they did Joan of Arc.

These are just a few of the powerful Madwomen valued through the ages in cultures worldwide.[1] Most hold in common the mysteries of life and death, light and dark, creation and destruction. When life is not honored, when Mother Earth is not revered, when the feminine is defiled, they warn us with natural cataclysms, disasters, and physical and environmental punishments, as well as emotional and psychological storms and upheavals in the psyche. But at the same time they are creators, renewing the cycle of existence, transforming old life-forms into new. Besides these ancient archetypal figures who can help us identify mythic patterns of behavior in our own lives, we also have our own unique, contemporary cultural expressions of the Madwoman.

THE MADWOMAN AT THE MOVIES, THE OPERA, AND IN LITERATURE

Today, films confront us with many recognizable Madwomen and their paradoxes, including women going mad, women on the "verge of a nervous breakdown," women killing the lovers who reject or mistreat them, women terrorists, women trying to break free of stultifying everyday lives. These images of the Madwoman have been unleashed in today's cinema and in contemporary literature. The heroines of these films rebel against their Caged Bird existences and the abuses of women in contemporary society. In *She-Devil,* a rejected wife seeks revenge on her arrogant, betraying husband. The Chinese film *Raise the Red Lantern* shows different ways women go mad and turn against each other when they are allowed to exist only in the role of concubine, subjected to a husband's domination. The tendency of the oppressed to turn against each other, instead of against the power figure who threatens and abuses them, is a tragedy true in the lives of most minorities. *An Angel at My Table* portrays the true story of a New Zealand writer, Janet Frame, an introverted poetic woman who was misdiagnosed as schizophrenic, hospitalized, and given shock treatments to "cure" her of her shy and reclusive nature when she could not speak before a group of judging supervisors. Using her creativity saved her life; in the hospital, she wrote short stories, which were discovered and published, a testimony to her sanity and her talent. *War of the Roses* especially shows a pattern of behavior and interaction that I call the confrontation of the Madwoman and the Judge—which we look at in the next section—a wife and husband whose unchecked energies finally destroy each other. Films like *Fatal Attraction* and *Presumed Innocent* show the fear men have of the Madwoman, of the destruction that their own ill-considered actions can set in motion. Some films with the Madwoman motif show creative women being locked away, while others show women trying to break free, including *Woman on the Verge of a Nervous Breakdown, Misery, Sheer Madness, Thelma and Louise, Fried Green Tomatoes, Postcards from the Edge, Camille Claudel, Looking for Mr. Goodbar, Persona, The Glass Menagerie, Housekeeping, Frances, Mommie Dearest, Terms of Endearment, The Hand That Rocks the Cradle, Sybil, A Woman Under the Influence, The Diary of a Mad Housewife, The Three Faces of Eve, La Femme Nikita, High Heels,* and *Who's Afraid of Virginia Woolf?*

Throughout the ages the tragic power of the Madwoman has appeared in literature and song. We know Medea killed her children in revenge at her lover's betrayal, and Anna Karenina, confined in a loveless marriage and a society that allowed her no creative outlet or freedom to be herself, committed suicide. In world literature, she is also represented by Clytemnestra, Electra, Antigone, Ophelia, Lady Macbeth, Madame Bovary, the Madwoman of Chaillot, and the mad Mrs. Rochester, locked away in the attic in *Jane Eyre*.[2] In opera there is Lucia di Lammermour, Madame Butterfly, Norma, Elvira, Carmen, Salome, Turandot, the Queen of the Night in *The Magic Flute*, the gypsy mother in *Il Travatore*, and countless others.

The various forms of the Madwoman in these artistic works correspond to a real and powerful force in the human psyche—one feared by men and women alike. They show a frightening face of the feminine, revealing the potential wrath and power of women who are abused, trapped, and disrespected. If we are to transform this wrathful energy into a usable, creative force, we need first to examine it carefully in ourselves and others. We cannot and should not simply dismiss it as abnormal or "just crazy."

THE MADWOMAN AND THE JUDGE: *THE BACCHANTS*

One of the greatest conflicts in our culture today exists between two archetypal energies—the Madwoman and the Judge. We see this struggle in films as well as in our family and political lives. Contemporary Western culture has repressed and suppressed the archetype and psychological energy of the Madwoman. It clings to order and control and stresses the suppression of genuine feeling in favor of rational formulas for success. It avoids deep thought and reflection in favor of quick and easy, superficial solutions. The Madwoman threatens all of these attributes of the status quo of traditional patriarchal authorities and especially threatens the Judge in our own psyches, the rational, controlling part of our mind and being who wants to be in power at all costs and at all times.

Whether these two forces are at war within one individual, or are struggling for influence between friends, neighbors, and couples, or are acted out in the battle of the sexes or in violence between nations or countries, the Madwoman and the Judge are at odds. The unbridled self-expression of the Madwoman is an affront to the heartless, rational Judge who wants to restrict and subjugate her. Conversely, the rigid rules of the self-righteous Judge can drive the Madwoman into demented fantasies of revenge. When the Madwoman energy is rejected by the rational, judgmental patriarchal powers and locked away in prisons or dark corners of habit and thought, then the "crazy feminine" turns on men in wrathful indignation.

Yet the Judge is as crazy in his extreme of rigid righteousness and self-justification as the Madwoman is in her chaos.[3] The dementia of the Judge can be seen in "witch hunts" as dramatized, for example, in Arthur Miller's *The Crucible,* in which good-hearted men and women alike are persecuted when suspected of resisting the controlling powers in the name of God, the Father.

This conflict between the Madwoman and the Judge is older than the Christian era and is beautifully and timelessly illustrated in an ancient Greek play, Euripides' *The Bacchants,* a haunting warning to both ancient and modern Judges who contemptuously reject the Madwoman energy as irrational, unworthy, and dangerous.

The Bacchants depicts a confrontation between a rational Judge, Pentheus, King of Thebes, and a group of "irrational" Madwomen, the Maenads, whose very name means Madwomen. Devotees of Dionysus, the Maenads danced in frenzied ecstasy to his music, nursed the young god, and suckled wild animals at their breasts. As nurturers, the Maenads possessed the magic of boundless motherhood. But when forbidden to dance in honor of Dionysus, they became maddened and bloodthirsty and could tear their young to pieces. Pentheus forbids Dionysus in his kingdom because he wants to rule by reason alone. He plans to capture and imprison all the women who leave his city to honor Dionysus with ecstatic dancing and reveling in the woods. With their wild ways of rejoicing and dancing barefooted in nature, these Madwomen threaten the king. Pentheus judges their ecstasies a sham, their priestess rites a pretense. According to the dictates of *his* reason, women belong at home with their husbands. Planning to "catch them in iron traps and put a quick stop to this immoral revelry," Pentheus blames the stranger Dionysus for bringing this bizarre madness upon the women of Thebes.[4]

Pentheus sends the townsmen to interrupt the Bacchants' joyful movement, laughter, and singing, which honors the life-force, by ambushing them to bring them home. But the Bacchants, enraged at this attempt to control them, go on a rampage. They wantonly tear bulls to pieces, pillage homes, and wreak confusion everywhere. The men cannot control them. To stop this chaos, and because he cannot tolerate the disgrace of women defeating men, Pentheus makes further plans to bring the women under his control. He is advised to dress as a Bacchant so he can spy on them. When the Maenads see this impostor, they descend upon him in fury at the order of their leader, Agave, Pentheus' own mother who is under Dionysus' spell. Not recognizing her son, Agave leads the charge upon this intruder. She and her Bacchant sisters pelt him with stones and attack him so he cannot reveal the secrets of their rites. Pentheus cries out to Agave that he is her son, but it is too late. Possessed by Dionysus, she and the other Maenads tear him apart, limb from limb, digging into his bloody flesh. His mother even keeps the head, putting it atop her shaft, believing it to be the head of a mountain lion. When she returns to the city, Agave awakens from her madness and learns she has killed her son. In grief, she leaves in exile.

The drama of *The Bacchants* shows the tragedy that occurs between men and women and within a culture where the Judge suppresses the Madwoman, when the rational and the irrational are not integrated or allowed to coexist side by side. Pentheus' rigid, rational need for power is itself "mad" in its refusal to honor the irrational forces of Nature or to believe in the power and mystery of the divinities. When the Madwoman's ecstatic dancing energy is denied expression, it takes destructive form and can unknowingly hurt or kill her own children, as Agave did Pentheus, a potent example of a woman unwittingly destroying one of her own, most precious parts of herself, or her own work of creation. It is also a vivid example of the patriarchy's inherent self-destructive and victimizing tendencies.

In our time and society, too, the archetypal energies of the Madwoman and the Judge are dangerously out of balance and in opposition to each other. When we split apart these energies in our psyche and behavior, we lose the inherent connection between discriminating judgment and instinct. Conflicts arise when people, acting as Judges and patriarchal dictators, prescribe rules of order for each other and for women. To be put under external, unnatural rules of thought, values, duties, and structures that are not his or her own can throw any person off balance. The person expected to conform to these restrictions and models of behavior will inevitably fall short and be victimized by the authority figure's negative judgments. If a woman is forced out of her own natural rhythm or is unable to find her own place in the world, and if she does not accept her own inner feminine powers and try to correct her personal and social situation, she will become and remain victimized. Once a woman identifies with the victim role, she can become trapped in a kind of negative, noncreative madness. This destructive struggle between Judge and Madwoman energies has resulted in a widespread pattern of victimization behavior throughout our society. In this book, we will see the Madwoman confronting the Judge in the lives of historical, fictional, and contemporary women.

How can we check or avoid the destructive aspect of the Madwoman? The first step is to confront and accept the dark, chaotic intuitions coming from our innermost selves. We need to confront our inner fears, our forbidden desires, and our urges for ecstasy and to celebrate the Madwoman. By viewing ordinary life through her unique vision, we can see things freshly and differently, with "creative madness." Out of our inner Madwoman can come growth into the kind of "crazy wisdom" that Buddhist and other mystical traditions describe. By accepting this challenge, women will find new ways to communicate with each other as well as with our husbands, sons, and lovers.

THE PATRIARCHY . . . THE MADWOMAN . . . AND FEMININE SPIRIT

Before we go on, I should explain what I mean when I refer to "the patriarchy." Essentially, the patriarchy, to me, embodies the Western principles of linear rational thought, with its emphasis on order, abstractions, and judgment from above. Both women and men are influenced by our patriarchal culture, although the patriarchy is experienced differently by men and women and women's experience is different based on their race, class, and color. Through the centuries, women as a gender have been especially oppressed by the patriarchal hierarchy.

Patriarchal thinking and principles narrow our human existence to only part of what we are by nature. As humans, we live in the paradox of having consciousness and the freedom of choice to express the greater mystery of Being; yet we must also order and control our lives to a degree if we are to survive. Patriarchal thinking —Western rational linear thought—tends to reduce our existence to one extreme: order and control. When we succumb to this reduction of our lives, we lose contact with the reality of our greater human mystery as well as that of the entire cosmos.

The Madwoman rises up inside us when we are oppressed by rigid order and control. Carolyn Heilbrun has pointed out that in Greek drama, the Furies' "bloodiness and revenge were reserved only for those who denied the feminine powers. These raging females were not sackers of cities, nor despoilers for gain of others' homes or homelands. The Furies represented the strongest deterrent against the male usurpation of female rights and powers. . . ."[5]

I should also discuss more particularly what I mean by "the feminine." The feminine is part of the human dimension and is manifested in both men and women, as is the masculine. It is a mistake to identify feminine with female, or masculine with male. Our feminine side emphasizes caring, responsiveness, receptivity, and relatedness. Feminine concerns and values focus on the process of human interaction. Although rooted in the feminine, these concerns are manifested in both men and women. Psychologist Carol Gilligan's studies of ethical values point to a feminine focus on the network of relationship, responsibility, and caring in contrast with a masculine focus on separation, autonomy, principles and rights, and hierarchy. Masculine insecurities arise through intimacy, in contrast to the feminine side, which is threatened by isolation. The Madwoman is an archetypal energy within the feminine side of the psyche of both men and women. When the Madwoman energy breaks through our usual suppression or ignoring or denial of it, she does so to challenge us to live in the whole of our human existence, to acknowledge all facets of our personalities and psyches, not just part of them. The Madwoman dares us to acknowledge and live with our inner feminine spirit as an essential part of being human.

Feminine spirit connects us with each other through caring. I see feminine spirit as a human energy that compels us to quest, to engage in the psychological process of self-discovery; it is an impulse toward freedom.[6] Feminine spirit is beyond definition, to a degree. It is an energy that is felt and intuited in images. We know the feminine spirit through the way we feel about ourselves, each other, and the way we feel together. Earthiness, spontaneity, flexibility, emotional vitality, compassion, warmth, merging in a network of caring—all are aspects of feminine spirit. The power that enables grass to grow and push up through rocks and concrete, the energy that flows through our bodies and rejuvenates us every spring, the reverence for life, for planting seeds, for the cycle of the seasons, and the courage to endure the pain of labor and giving birth, all are expressions of the feminine spirit that enlivens and moves us, inspires and breathes life into us, and links us to the earth. When we do not feel a connection to the growing earth, the feminine in us feels betrayed. Feminine spirit has an innate assertive strength that is nonaggressive, nonmartial in quality. It is an energy that we can tap that is a creative alternative to the regimented patriarchal spirit in which our culture and society are fixed.

THE MADWOMAN'S PARADOX: CREATION OR DESTRUCTION

At the deepest psychological level, the Madwoman holds the birthing connection to creativity. Out of inner chaos and emotional upheaval can come creative, energizing visions that bring new life to the individual and the culture. But chaos can also 'become destructive and turn inward to insanity, paranoia, and isolation. While we sometimes speak positively about madness as a characterization of different kinds of carefree or impulsive behavior in every person's life, madness in its most degenerate form stultifies creative life. The novelist Joanne Greenberg, who, writing under the pseudonym Hannah Green, fictionalized her experience of entrapment in insanity in *I Never Promised You a Rose Garden,* points out the danger of romanticizing madness. At its worst extreme, madness isolates us and cuts us off from the "real" world. Greenberg describes a hallucination as "a metaphor for some inexpressible anguish. It says, 'I am adrift, I am bereft. I am somebody for whom gravity and the laws of the universe do not apply.' " Speaking of clinical insanity at the extreme end of the spectrum of "madness," Greenberg maintains that mental illness is the opposite of creativity; it is a boring, unproductive state in which no fertile interaction between imagination and the world takes place. She says: "Creativity and psychosis are about as far apart as two experiences can be. Creative things learn and grow. In psychosis, there's no meaning, no future, the world is senseless. The whole thing is stuck. Mental illness is boring in a way that's inconceivable. If there's no learning, all there is is reacting. It's boring because there's no place to go."[7]

Yet some types of mental disturbances, upheavals, breakdowns, and psychological and emotional storms can trigger creative and spiritual awakenings. Artists speak of the divine madness inherent in the creative process, for they must descend into a kind of chaos in order to give new and vital expression to their creative experience. Mystics describe their encounters with the transcendent as "god-intoxication" or "divine madness"—an ecstasy that defies description except through imagery. Literature describes numerous mystical, chaotic, and religious experiences in dramatic terms of descent and isolation. Saint John of the Cross called this "the Dark Night of the Soul," Kierkegaard called it "despair," Jung the "night sea journey" or "defeat of the ego." A classic image for this deep, personal, inward journey is the wandering into the wilderness, a period of feeling lost and disconnected from others, a time of alien-ation and isolation. At the seemingly darkest hour, divine nourish-ment or inspiration or integration or insight suddenly manifests itself and the person feels miraculously reborn.

Socrates said that madness was of divine origin and that the madness of poets, seers, lovers, and prayers contains wisdom higher than worldly knowledge. Some psychiatrists distinguish between "a madness of the left, full of ecstasy and terror," which entails a "be-wildering encounter with the spiritual and demonic powers in the psyche," and "a madness of the right," which is "hollowed out in bland impoverishment and narrowness in which conventions and concreteness of the mundane world are taken for self-evident real-ity."[8] Madness in its destructive aspect is a madness of the right that isolates and impoverishes us, as Greenberg describes. But "divine madness" can lift us into the ecstatic state that mystics describe, give us superabundant creative energies, and release us to imagine bet-ter lives and act to improve society. As Evelyn Underhill describes in her book on mysticism, genuine mysticism is active and practical and transforms our personality so we can be at one with all cre-ation.[9] And most modern mystics and teachers would emphasize that genuine mysticism frees us from our limited visions of self so that we can work with compassion to communicate with and help others.

Both women and men need to confront the divine madness in themselves and to differentiate it from destructive craziness on both the individual and the social level. We need to bring "creative mad-ness" into both our personal and public life to deal with the issues of our time, such as the threats of modern warfare and of modern technology to life on the planet. To meet the Madwoman, we must learn to relinquish the destructive aspects, her self-referential and self-absorbed anger, and mobilize her energy for positive action. We need to learn to live within her creative tension and to find ways to approach her and learn from her.

BEFRIENDING THE INNER MADWOMAN

When the Madwoman emerges in our lives, we are usually over-whelmed by fear, and we try to assassinate her in ourselves or in others. However, as frightening as her crazy energy and images can be, my experience as an analyst is that the Madwoman can be transformed when she is befriended. Once I consulted a shamaness in Bali about a series of Madwoman dreams I was having. The Balian shamaness sat chewing seeds and cackling, looking like a Madwoman herself, as she described an exact image of the events that had occurred. Then, grinning, she turned to me and said, "Invite the Madwoman to lunch. She only wants to be your friend." For a long time, I puzzled over this strange advice. When I finally understood it on the symbolic level, I realized that my way to befriend the Madwoman inside me was to understand her images so I could integrate her various forms of emotional and psychological energy into my life. My befriending of my inner Madwoman led to writing about her in this book.

Sometimes befriending the Madwoman is as simple as expressing one's anger or just confronting a parent or a lover, a friend or a boss —telling them how you feel and what you need. It is our fear of being angry—even crazy—that makes the Madwoman into a truly frightening monster. Anger and other unacknowledged or denied feelings, when split off from the rest of our lives, fill the Madwoman with poisons that feed destructive acts. Unexpressed fear and anger build up inside us and can make us feel crazy. In order to deal with these feelings, we need to differentiate them, to give them forms we can see and understand, as our dreams do when they present us with figures such as the Madwoman. Her images move us and help bring feelings, ideas, and patterns that are at work in our minds at an unconscious level up to our consciousness, where we can deal with them. Her images and many guises help us identify, remember, and recognize what we are about, who we really are, and what we mean to become. We need to get to know the Madwoman in her manifold forms, to recognize her presence within ourselves, and to befriend her rather than isolate her and cut her off. When we try to separate ourselves from her, we suffer the consequences.

Most people are not likely to choose to address their Madwoman. Life inevitably brings her energy to us, nonetheless. She barges in upon our lives, defying logic, bringing chaos, usually just when we are trying to control our lives in a rational way. So we tend to try to continue to avoid her. We stress order and routine. We dismiss psychological problems such as anxiety, depression, phobias, low moods, or sadness. We may further suppress our emotional difficulties, which causes additional suffering as they affect us physically

through psychosomatic symptoms and illness or resurface as intensi-
fied anxiety or depression.

When we repress or suppress the Madwoman's energy in our
lives, she will often appear in a startling dream or even manifest
herself to us in an event in our everyday lives. Like dutiful daughters, many of us try to lead tidy, unchallenging lives in keeping with
the culture. We often seem to be rewarded with material comforts
and success, and sometimes even with fame and power. But in or-
derliness we can lose our connection to the process of life, the con-
tinuous flowing river of energy and change. Our days are often dull,
our relationships dry, our minds bored and restless, our lives empty.
Something in us secretly cries, "There must be something more to
life than this!" Seemingly successful and content as we skim the
surface of existence, a crisis is often necessary to shake us up, to
make us look and explore within. In crisis, the Madwoman appears
to shock us out of our complacency, to shake us up with her chaos.
Because we can no longer ignore her or our need to change or our
inability to control our lives, we have to enter into her chaos and
deal with it, one step at a time.

The Madwoman cannot be described with quick and easy con-
cepts. Her essence is chaotic. To find her, we must look inside to our
feelings and our dreams, where we have encountered her many
times. Since the Madwoman appears in many guises, the images in
our dreams help us better see her presence and roles in our lives.
Images move us. They help us bring a pattern that is working in our
minds at an unconscious level to our consciousness. They help us
identify and remember what we need to recognize and deal with in
our lives. The following dream of a successful businesswoman at the
top of her career shows one way the Madwoman can confront us in
our dreams.

Outwardly prosperous, inwardly this professional woman felt
confused. Her life had lost its meaning and zest. She had a dream in
which she was desperately boarding up her father's house to protect
him against an invading Madwoman. Dressed in tattered clothes,
with wild, unkempt, and dirty hair, the Madwoman broke into the
house in spite of the dreamer's efforts and attacked her father. This
woman was being confronted with an interior Madwoman who was
trying to break up the judgmental, patriarchal structure in which
she had become trapped. Once she started to face the Madwoman
by looking at her anger and her fears, which she had suppressed in

deference to her family and in service to a proper public image, this woman was able to live in accord with her own emotional and spiritual needs.

Men, too, have dreams of the Madwoman. One man dreamed he was at a party, hosted by a woman dressed in a low-cut black gown. When he looked closer, he noticed she had bared her breasts. In horror, he watched the nipple of one breast grow so large that it turned into a huge red mouth with gnashing teeth. Realizing she was a Madwoman, he and all the other guests tried to escape. But looking back, he noticed that the Madwoman was about to attack an innocent four-year-old girl standing in a corner. He decided to return to try to save the little girl. The dreamer's personal associations indicated that the Madwoman symbolized a sex addiction that was threatening the little girl, who represented his capacity for love and genuine feeling.

This man's dream may have had a larger meaning as well. According to Jung, dreams sometimes reveal meaning for an entire culture as well as the dreamer's personal life. On the collective level, this man's courageous and compassionate decision to return to face the Madwoman and save the little girl may have symbolized our culture's need to face the Madwoman and to acknowledge our culture's abuse of the gentle, vulnerable feminine side of life and our society's abuse of women. Men need to listen to and try to validate women's feelings and ideas. Some men may devalue women and harass or run away from them because they have projected their inner vulnerability onto the outer woman. If men would also validate themselves as men who are not afraid of women's powers or the feminine in themselves, they could then meet women in genuine respect and equality.

These dreams are examples of ways the Madwoman can confront us and ask to be integrated into a personal life or into the social sphere. Besides working with dreams to face the Madwoman's energy,[10] we can also meet her through the use of "active imagination," a consciously focused dialogue with an inner symbolic image.[11] This can be done through writing, painting, dancing, psychodrama, or any mode of expression that can bring unconscious material out and give it more form. Throughout the book, I present examples of working with dreams and active imagination in the stories of real contemporary women who had to face the Madwoman's destructive force in their lives and identify the negative emotional and behavioral patterns that were holding them hostage in order to gain access to their creative energies.

Identifying a pattern in which you are living unconsciously is the first step in freeing your feminine energy. Because we are often unconscious in our actions and reactions, we can actually initiate the process of overcoming or transforming negative forces in our life by identifying a behavioral pattern and bringing it to our consciousness. Then we must struggle—wrestling with the pain and anger and finding original ways to re-vision and re-create positive uses for that neglected energy in our life. Finding the original, conscious ways of changing yourself and of living is the uniquely human challenge that we face as a species.

2

MAD MOTHERS,

MAD DAUGHTERS

I stand in the ring
in the dead city
and tie on the red shoes . . .

They are not mine,
they are my mother's,
her mother's before,
handed down like an heirloom
but hidden like shameful letters.

—ANNE SEXTON

MY MOTHER AND I WERE ABLE TO FORGIVE AND MAKE amends to each other when we finally realized and accepted that we were very different people. This happened when I was in my forties and she was in her sixties. Our reunion was one of the greatest growth points in both of our lives. Opening up to each other took a lot of honesty and courage. We had to acknowledge our anger toward each other for not being the person the other wanted us to be, and we shed tears for feeling deprived of the close bond we originally had shared.

Traditionally, mothers have been blamed for their children's ills. Feminists, rightly, have objected to this scapegoating. We need to remember that the mother herself is a wounded woman, often limited, hampered, and frustrated by dysfunctional cultural conditions. Our mothers have enormous influence on our worldviews as the first human beings upon whom we depend, and their pain is passed down to daughters and sons for generations until that wounding is confronted and dealt with consciously. The severe wounding that affects both mothers and daughters is shown in the following dream:

> I see my father lurching down the street and want to get away.
> Then I see my mother's severed head growing out of the side
> of his neck. Her head is only a bloody protrusion of my
> father. My mother is not a person in her own right.

The dreamer, named Maria, was so shocked by this image that she started therapy. Maria realized that her mother was living as a mere appendage of her father and not as a whole person. Angry at her mother for her lack of responsibility for herself and for having put Maria's father's needs before her own need for maternal nurturing, Maria realized that this image reflected the way she had been living, too. Maria saw the dream as symbolic of the patriarchal destruction of the feminine—in her mother, in herself, and in women on a cultural level.

When mother and daughter clash, an element of madness is present in their entangled feelings. Even when relations appear good on the surface, conflicting emotions are concealed that complicate the interactions of this intimate pair. Mothers and daughters not only have to deal with the personal and familial factors that confuse their relations; they also have to deal with generational and cultural projections on women, expectations coming from the patriarchy. But what is more urgent for every woman to face is a powerful and fearsome inner feminine energy—the archetypal Madwoman—that dwells in all of us. Mothers and sons, fathers and daughters, husbands and wives, even fathers and sons—all must contend with the Madwoman's emotional and psychological presence. In this chapter, I will describe four common patterns in mother-daughter relationships that the Madwoman energy can take when its forces are pushed aside and not confronted directly.

The stories in this book come from the daughter's point of view since every mother has also been a daughter. Although I describe this emergence of the Madwoman in the context of mother-daughter relations, men will find themselves embroiled in these patterns as well. Few of us live out only one role in the course of a life. Most likely, you will find a little of each pattern in yourself, just as I have.

The Mad Mother cannot talk with her daughters on a feeling level. She dominates her daughters through her particular form of behavior, whether she is an Ice Queen with frozen feelings, a Dragon Lady with so much emotion that genuine feelings and their nuances are burnt up in her volcanic explosions, a Sick Mother who controls everyone around her with the threat of her frailty, or a Saint Mother who, needing to be "good," maintains a superficial and martyred personality, expecting her children to follow suit. A daughter's emotions and psychology are subjugated by the Mad Mother, and she needs to learn to separate from the Mad Mother's enforced behaviors in order to recognize her own feelings and inner self. Otherwise, she may repeat her mother's patterns.

For example, if her mother lived and acted like a martyr, serving her husband and family at the expense of her own self-expression, the daughter may repeat this role in her own life and feel martyred in her work, even if she is a success in her profession. Another daughter, however, may rebel and try to be the opposite of her mother. If her mother constantly acted out unbounded feelings that overwhelmed everyone in the family, a daughter might withdraw and encase her feelings inside a tight shell to protect herself. Whether by repeating or by reacting to their mothers, the daughters then affect their mothers, who are further hurt in a sad feedback loop. This is illustrated in the film *Autumn Sonata,* which we will look at in detail later in this chapter. Fathers, husbands, children, friends, and colleagues are also affected by this chain of injury between mother and daughter. For example, a mother who retains unresolved anger toward men is likely to pass on her accumulated distrust to her daughter, who then may vent this anger on her husband, son, or male co-workers. Woody Allen's film *Interiors* is another popular expression of the different patterns daughters develop as a result of Mad Mothering.

THE SAINT (OR THE TOO-NICE MOTHER)

As we discussed in Chapter 1, many women deny the archetypal energy of the Madwoman in themselves because it can be so potent and threatening. Of course, any unacknowledged energy in the psyche functions like a ghost in the house. It frightens from behind and unconsciously affects behavior. Women who have been indoctrinated in the prevailing views from the patriarchal culture—for example, that they should be nice and nurturing, obedient, supportive of men, and of service to their husbands—may try to act that way on the surface. But in the hidden recesses of their psyche, the shadow of the Madwoman will be lurking. Sometimes very kind and positive women, consciously meaning to do well by their daughters, actually hurt them by instructing them to repress their natural feelings, especially if the emotion is dark or angry or if the daughter is intuitive and has felt the hidden anger raging unconsciously in her mother. Daughters often carry their mothers' unacknowledged anger, and they can be conscious of the anger but unconscious of the cause. In the film *Class Action*, the daughter seethes at her father for having affairs while her saintlike mother forgives and forgets and eventually drops dead from a heart attack, symbolic of a broken heart. The daughter, who is burdened with her mother's unconscious rage, has had no feminine model to help her learn how to channel this energy. If her mother's rage is unconscious, a daughter may even think she is to blame for her mother's anger, anxiety, depression, guilt, shame, or confusion. A daughter may also share these dark emotions with her mother. As the daughter matures, she must strive to become increasingly conscious of her psychological ties with her mother and also of where her mother ends and her own psyche begins.

When I asked one young woman, Anna, about her mother, she described her as kind and generous—a saint. Her mother was a hard-working nurse who never got angry and never cried. Anna's father was an alcoholic who disrupted family life with his drunken rages. Believing that any expression of anger or painful feelings was self-indulgent, Anna's mother told her never to say angry things because one can't take them back. Her mother's unconscious anger and emotional turmoil emerged at certain times in cynicism about other people's motives and in bitterness about not getting ahead in life. She was particularly resentful toward men, dismissing them as "out to take advantage and get you." As a nurse, she served others but rarely got thanked and so developed a martyred, tired response and a belief that the world grinds people down. She was passive and didn't protect or defend Anna, who was left with the enormous shadow of her mother's unexpressed and unacknowledged rage.

As a child, Anna wanted to emulate her mother, but her natural assertiveness was unconsciously turned against herself as self-blame, and she suffered from severe depressions. Like her mother, Anna was self-sacrificing, giving, and generous, but when others took and didn't give back, she too became resentful. As she became more conscious of her own behavior, she realized she was sometimes angry, but she didn't know how to express negative feelings and felt guilty for having them. Because of her father's uncontrolled rages, Anna was afraid of angry people; she didn't know how to protect and defend herself. This interfered with her relationships with other people, particularly her intimate ones with men.

When she met a man whom she wanted to marry, Anna realized she needed to do some inner work and went to a group specializing in communication techniques. During this process, she was able to understand that her mother had a lot of repressed anger, and to recognize her own as well. Anna's unexpressed rage revealed itself in dreams in which mean, angry figures threatened to hurt her. One sadist, wearing a rubber mask that completely covered all his facial expression, cut into her skin with a knife, saying, "When you fear, it doesn't hurt." To Anna, this symbolized her mother's teaching that she should smile and cover her feelings. By telling her daughter never to be angry or let people know when she was hurt, her mother had programmed her into the fearful role of victim who would have trouble stopping her own victimization because she was denying it was even happening!

Women whose mothers have repressed their own rage and have instructed their daughters to be and act as they themselves do often have dreams in which sadistic figures, particularly men, abuse or torture young girls or women. If the father has been violent or abusive in any way, this compounds the issues of anger and love, since the daughter is dependent on her father and mother for love and support, yet suffers because of it. Many such women dream of Nazi officers who brutally terrorize the dreamer. Sometimes the Nazi officer is linked up with the Madwoman, as in the dream of another woman, Grace:

My mother runs a whorehouse for SS officers in Nazi Germany. I am a little girl, prepubescent, and horrified at their joking and boasting about their atrocities against the Jews. I have Jewish girlfriends and feel totally helpless and tormented that I can do nothing. Each day my mother, who is mad, injects me with a small amount of something that numbs my emotions. As I reach puberty I am now expected to sleep with the Nazi officers. I run away but end up writhing in pain in a ditch—I need another injection! I make my way back, totally sick at the thought of returning to that hell. But without the injection I will die. The officers laugh at me in my futile attempt to escape. How could my own mother do this to me?

In the dream Grace's mother always had her head down, bent over some work such as laundry or preparing food. She never looked at her daughter, although the young girl desperately wanted contact and communication. Watching her mother work and interact with the officers as a servant, not a bawdy madam, she could feel her mother's rage, like acid flowing through her veins. When her mother came after her to give the injections, it felt like being struck by high voltage.

This dream recurred for Grace from the time she was seven until she was fifteen. These Mad Mother dreams continued to haunt her until she worked to understand them so that she could integrate their message and become a whole and wiser woman. Grace had perceived her mother as an all-forgiving saint who gave unconditional love to her abusive and alcoholic husband. Her mother was not able to deliver Grace from her father's painful spankings, made more frightening because of his rage. Her mother could not deal with Grace's anger about the unfair spankings, even though she had tried to intervene to stop them. She gave her daughter the message that she should be a good girl and submit, thus confusing Grace about what kinds of behavior she had to accept from other people and where she could draw the line.

Grace's mother had tried to be the best mother she could be, but she was limited by her perception of womanhood. Grace's mother was physically affectionate and tried to listen to and be helpful to her daughter, but due to her own lack of consciousness and growth, she could not give Grace wisdom or a sense of feminine empowerment. Grace's maternal grandmother had been a devout Christian who idealized self-sacrifice and suffering martyrdom as good and who harshly judged anyone who fell short of this goal. Abandoned by her father in childhood, Grace's mother naively tried to live her own mother's model of femininity. She also feared having a fatherless family, vowing never to leave the man she would marry.

Conditioned to be unable to listen to Grace's feelings when she complained about her father, her mother would excuse him, saying: "He doesn't mean it. He loves you. He just doesn't show it." Afraid of a beating if she challenged him, and afraid of leaving him if she really faced the situation, Grace's mother tried to keep peace at all costs. She had no time to share feminine activities with Grace, and she was exhausted from working, most of her energy devoted to keeping house and caring for her alcoholic husband, a "son" for whom she was the martyred mother. Grace eventually wondered whether her mother actually got a "high" from being the martyred saint, a *mater dolorosa,* an image that she kept despite the cost—a hard and lonely life and alienation from her daughter. Grace saw her mother act out the role of "the sweet loving woman married to the abusive adolescent alcoholic father," and she saw others living this way in neighboring households as well. Grace suffered from the crazy confusion of being loved yet terrified at home, and she unconsciously understood that her mother's weak, dependent relationship with her father was dangerous for them both. By acquiescing to her husband's addiction and abusiveness, Grace's mother was actually hostage to the form of addiction that today is called codependency.[1]

After much inner work, Grace began to realize that her recurring Madwoman might be her own internal rage at her mother for subjecting her to "life with father." Through the dream she saw that her mother had been trying to numb her daughter's emotions, as she had repressed her own, thereby subjecting Grace to the same fate the mother felt she had to bear. Grace's dream imaged this situation as a "house of prostitution" in which women were forced to subjugate themselves to the abuses of sadistic men in command, symbolized by the Nazi officers. The threatening atmosphere of her parents' addictive relationship, and in particular her mother's severe codependency, were symbolized by the numbing injections inflicted upon Grace by her mother, making her so dependent that she had to return to the hell of her household.

Very often, Grace would wake up depressed, even though by nature she was a warm, vital, and energetic person. In therapy, she decided to do some active imagination work with the Mad Mother figure. In an imaginary dialogue, Grace talked to her "depression," saying, "Tell me who you are." When she asked this question, the figure of a Madwoman appeared. Almost dead, the woman looked like a mummy (dreams often make bad puns for us), with only a few live strips of skin showing on her face. The Madwoman's eyes rolled wildly back and forth in her head. She rasped out weakly, "I want to die." Later, in a psychodrama session, Grace recognized this decaying Madwoman as an aspect of the mother in her recurring dream. When she asked the mother figure why she was prostituting herself, the mother, full of remorse, confessed that she felt incapable of helping Grace and saw no way to survive but to prostitute herself and run this house. Expressing her sorrow, the mother said she hated what she was doing to herself and her daughter. But she felt she was *"too weak and without a vision of change."* She felt exhausted and guilty, and her nerves were on fire with the anguish of their suffering together in that place. The violence she had brought on her own soul and that of her daughter made her long for death, and she asked to be buried—Grace saw she had to bury her mother symbolically in order to free herself from the internalized Mad Mother who was inhibiting her life.

Daughters who have been raised by mothers who are unconsciously angry or disturbed—even if they consciously experienced their mothers as loving and affectionate, as in Grace's case—frequently dream of Madwomen. Sometimes these Mad Mothers take the form of witches who threaten their lives or try to imprison them, like the witch in "Hansel and Gretel," or sometimes the mother appears in their dreams as cold and rejecting. Sometimes the mad side of the Saint Mother appears as a devouring beast, like the wolf in "Little Red Riding Hood." A daughter may have to kill off and bury the internalized rage and resentment that she shares with her mother, in order to be free and to be herself. Novelists, poets, and artists of all varieties frequently do this in their creative works by writing, painting, or dancing out the character that needs to be dispelled in the psyche. While a daughter may not be able to have an effective confrontation with her real mother—who may be unable to hear or understand her daughter's viewpoint, or who may be too sick, or dead—she can confront the internal Mad Mother, recognize the dark emotions that are working to dominate her, and consciously determine how she will choose to behave.

Grace purged herself of the Mad Mother by paying attention to her dreams, getting bodywork to help her become more physically conscious of her feelings, working with her feelings through active imagination, and enacting them in the contained and safe therapeutic environment of psychodrama sessions. In the psychodrama sessions, supported by the therapists who were present, Grace was able to forgive the decaying Mad Mother and allow this figure in her psyche to die and be buried. Supported by her therapists, Grace allowed the mad, sick daughter from the recurring dream to die as well, and she gave her a proper burial in this psychodrama. Symbolically, this freed Grace from the negative energy of these internalized figures and released her to be reborn with a stronger feminine commitment to herself. Emotionally, Grace felt a great sense of relief, accompanied by an energy shift in her body. She said it felt as if the rage and shame had been held in her abdomen, like a contained cyst. When the healing occurred, the imprisoned energy was released and available to be used positively. This new energy enabled her to work on her rage at her abusive father in subsequent psychodrama sessions, and eventually Grace and her father reconciled with love before he died.

After high school, Grace had left her unhappy and conflicted home life and entered a spiritual retreat, where she worked with many women who were independent, strong, powerful, loving, and spiritual. They had become the positive, motherly mentors she had lacked at home, and they passed on to her their womanly wisdom and sense of feminine empowerment. Grace regarded one woman, Sarah, as her "adopted mother." Sarah appreciated Grace's artistic and mystical nature, helping her learn about the positive Madwoman who could howl at the moon and shriek in delight about the exquisite flowers in the garden. "If you have yourself, you have everything," she often told Grace, and Grace has said, "To this day, the very thought of Sarah lights my inner being up. Her madness modeled reveling in love and waking others up to ecstasy." This help from Sarah and other women enabled Grace to internalize a strong, loving mother that could eventually replace the buried, negative Mad Mother. And it helped her to value the spiritual aspect of madness. Grace expressed this as follows: "My own madness, when allowed to enrich my creativity, gives me independence and detachment from the criticism of others. I revel in the energy I feel from the earth. I revel in the storms of Nature, in the lightning bolts in the sky, and I allow its energy to pass through me. My madness allows me to touch my spiritual ecstasy. I now see the mad part of me as the spiritually aware part of me. Nature is my 'good mother.' "

In her twenties, Grace repeated her mother's mistake by marrying a dominating man similar to her father. She gave birth to a son. Early on, she recognized that her marriage was dysfunctional and began to train for a profession so she could become independent and divorce her husband. Later, as a single mother, Grace made a conscious effort not to repeat the mistakes with her son that she felt her mother had made with her. She provided him with a safe and nurturing environment and good community, shared her love of Nature with him, and played with him creatively. During his early adolescence, when he felt conflicted and depressed, Grace listened to him and talked to him without fear or defensiveness. She told him about the suffering inherent in every hero's journey, as in the story of the Holy Grail, and this universal mythic tale helped him feel less isolated. She also shared with him her own times of confusion and how they had led her to search for her spiritual path.

Grace was thus able to transform the legacy of madness passed down from her mother and grandmother. Because of the inner work she did, she was able to have empathy for her mother rather than blame her and perpetuate her role as a victim. Now, in spite of their differences, they can talk to each other with more understanding. While it is important for a daughter to identify and acknowledge the particular kind of madness that her mother has passed on to her so that she may recognize how it has affected her, she must get beyond the stage of identification and blame in order to change the pattern in her own life. Becoming conscious of the inner Madwoman enables a woman to invoke her energy for positive creative acts such as self-assertion, becoming a better mother to her own children, and improving social conditions to help other women grow. Only in this way will she be able to stop the chain of destructive and debilitating behavior and refrain from passing these behaviors down to her own daughter or to other women of successive generations. In later chapters, we'll see the Saint, or the Too-Nice Mother, reappear in the behavior patterns of the Caged Bird and the Muse—both roles that can lead women to live as passive victims—and learn to unmask the Madwoman in them, too, in order to free ourselves for fuller lives.

THE ICE QUEEN

One of the maddest of mothers is the Ice Queen, an imperious, power-hungry woman who often has an underlying sense of inferiority. Although secretly she craves emotional warmth, she pushes people away by her cold responses to their feelings. The Ice Queen mother withdraws, rejects, and abandons. Often she freezes herself into a position of superiority with a cold rationality, placing supreme value on order, cleanliness, and perfection. If her daughters fail to have her sense of discipline and need for perfection, the Ice Queen will often punish them through sharp demeaning remarks that humiliate and shame them. An Ice Queen tends to prick at any good feelings, because she is afraid or jealous of the warm, enveloping emotions of others. One woman described her mother as jabbing at her with icy words anytime she felt expansive, enthusiastic, or ecstatic, to bring her down to earth and "responsibility." The Ice Queen mother feels uncomfortable with gifts or generosity and often returns a gift with an icy remark—a sharp stab of an ice pick to the heart. She wants to be heard but does not want to listen to others, especially about their feelings, and she may cut off the conversation. But when the Ice Queen is ready to relate, she expects complete attention.

Some daughters of Ice Queens fail to receive warmth from other sources and, already chilled by their own mothers' frigidity, become Ice Queens themselves. Because these daughters learned that any warm feeling their mothers deigned to give them often came with an emotional or psychological price tag, they frequently find it hard to receive the gift of love, and they constantly look for hidden motives. The Ice Queen's daughter who repeats her mother's pattern often wants love and adoration from friends and partners but cannot return these feelings in kind. Other such daughters, seeking to melt the glacial atmosphere passed on by their mothers, long for the warmth they did not receive as children and sometimes become overly dependent, always searching for the nurturing that their mothers didn't give them.

The Ice Queen mother can be very controlling and tends to be ambitious. Often she is an expert at manipulating to get what she wants. Since she tends to be impervious and insensitive to feelings, she can maneuver and promote herself more easily than her more sensitive sisters. Frequently politically astute, she knows how to take care of herself in the world and to sell herself; she has an angle on everything.

Films abound with the character of the Ice Queen. Many of the characters played by Bette Davis and Joan Crawford in the Hollywood films of the forties and fifties depict Ice Queens—often rich, ambitious young women in New York. The mother in the 1980 film *Ordinary People* and the protagonist played by Glenn Close in *Dangerous Liaisons* are other examples. Rich women often end up as Ice Queens; metallic jewelry surrounds their necks and wrists like armor, the gleam of the dollar sign in their eyes. Sometimes these women, realizing that money cannot bring them the love they really crave, put themselves in a stupor with alcohol and drugs to escape their feelings. The film *Reversal of Fortune,* depicting a true story, shows the pathos behind the cold demeanor of a wife and mother who went into a coma via alcohol and drugs to avoid her feelings. Yet even in the coma, she holds power over others.

The way women are wounded by a patriarchal culture, often to become Ice Queens, is shown in Rainer Werner Fassbinder's film *The Marriage of Maria Braun.* Just before the war, Maria, a young German woman, marries Hermann, the man she loves. He goes off to war and the family suffers from poverty. When the war ends and he doesn't return, she believes he is dead and has an affair with a kind and loving black man, Bill. Hermann returns home unexpectedly while Maria and Bill are making love, and in the ensuing fight and confusion, Maria accidentally kills Bill. Hermann insists on confessing to the crime in her stead and goes to prison. Maria, still in love with Hermann, waits for his release, but she has become cynical and angry and, tired of poverty, strives to become a businesswoman. She begins to manipulate men sexually to advance her career and to gain money and power. She follows masculine rules, becomes a cold opportunist, and, succeeding, becomes the power behind an unscrupulous corporation. She is the mistress to the boss, Oswald, and holds the power in this relationship. Behind her back, however, Hermann has agreed with Oswald to keep out of the way during Oswald's lifetime, upon whose death he will inherit one-half of Oswald's estate. So although Maria appears to hold the power, she is actually the pawn of these two men.

In the process of her power-building, Maria, like so many Ice Queens, uses the patriarchal system for her own ends and fails to question it. She betrays herself spiritually through her dependence on competition and material success. She becomes a chain-smoker, symbolic of her contribution to pollution. When, after Hermann returns, she finally learns of the secret agreement between the men, she is thrown into confusion. Feeling betrayed, unable to surrender her power for the sake of love, she "accidentally" blows up their house, forgetting she had turned on the gas when she lights her cigarette (symbolic of her cold distancing from others). The house exploding symbolizes how destructive the unconscious energy of the Madwoman can be and how quickly one pattern can turn into its opposite. In this case, the frozen feelings of the Ice Queen explode into the violence of the Dragon Lady. The film is a symbolic treatment not only of the woman who becomes an Ice Queen, still ruled by patriarchal power, but also of the entire German nation driven by icy perfectionism to the brink of destruction.

The depth and violence of the anger that can be passed down to the daughter of an Ice Queen mother is reflected in the following dream of a daughter named Irene:

> While passing a house I look through the kitchen window and see a woman working mechanically. She reminds me of my mother. I become a monster. I am a wooden, wormlike creature. With superhuman energy, I wrestle with the woman, throw her to the floor, and choke her. She turns into twisted wire. Madly, I thrust the wire up my vagina.

Irene's mother was an angry Ice Queen who ruled the house with the efficiency and order of a military officer, constantly criticizing her daughter. A perfectionist, the mother also controlled the family through her attitudes toward food. The result for Irene was an eating disorder. The dream shows the cold control around food via the image of the mechanical mother in the kitchen. In later life, Irene encountered another Ice Queen mother—a teacher who was a famous Ice Queen of the dance world. This teacher was cold and brutally perfectionistic, demanding that her dance students be wiry, to a twisted extreme—one of Irene's associations to the "wire mother." When, in the dream, the daughter becomes a monstrous Madwoman and chokes her mother, she also hurts herself in the process by thrusting the "wire mother" into her vagina. This suggests the woundedness of her feminine sexuality as well as a destructive feeling toward her feminine ability to bring life into the world.

An extremely creative writer, Irene had difficulty getting her best work published. Acknowledging the internal and external value of their own creative work is a frequent problem for women who suffer the cold criticism of Ice Queen mothers.

THE COLD CHAIN OF INJURY: *AUTUMN SONATA*

Ingmar Bergman's film *Autumn Sonata,* which we'll now look at in some detail, shows the story of the painful confrontation between two Madwomen—a mother and a daughter. It reveals the difficult and complicated relationship that can drive women to a form of madness in which both are wounded in the process. As the daughter, Eva, observes,

> A mother and a daughter—what a terrible combination of feelings and confusion and destruction! Everything is possible and everything is done in the name of love and solicitude. The mother's injuries are to be handed down to the daughter, the mother's disappointments are to be paid for by the daughter, the mother's unhappiness is to be the daughter's unhappiness. It's as if the umbilical cord had never been cut. The daughter's misfortune is the mother's triumph, the daughter's grief is the mother's secret pleasure.[2]

The mother, Charlotte, is an Ice Queen, whose feelings are frozen, while the daughter, Eva, suffers from the belief that no one can ever love her—a typical reaction for daughters of Ice Queens. Eva feels she does not know and cannot even risk knowing who she is. Believing she is unlovable, she fears she may discover something awful about herself. If only someone could love her truly, she thinks, she might be able to risk looking at herself. Eva is unable to see that her husband genuinely loves her in this way; she cannot believe it and cannot return his love. With him she too is an Ice Queen, like her mother. Eva has loved only one person fully—her son, who died young. Secretly, she still hopes to receive such wholehearted love from her mother, but she is also nursing bitter resentment at her mother's aloofness and critical judgment, which hurt her as a young girl. Harboring this anger and confusion most of her life, in her heart Eva has accused her mother of abandoning her and her younger sister, Helena, who suffers from a degenerative illness, for her career as a concert pianist.

Eva invites her mother to visit, hoping on the conscious level for reconciliation. But Eva has brought Helena to be with them without telling her mother. Guilty over the way she has related to both daughters, Charlotte doesn't want to face her feelings. She, too, longs for a rapprochement with Eva, but she does not know how to talk to her and is unwilling to undergo the suffering this self-examination would entail. Charlotte is lonely and confused from the recent death of her husband and has not seen Eva for seven years while traveling on international concert tours. During this time she has also been ill and suffered from a nervous depression, which she has concealed from Eva.

Soon after her mother arrives, Eva cannot suppress the terrible anger over the wounds she received from her mother's cool indifference. When Eva plays the piano at her mother's request, she feels her mother's condescension—Eva has been too emotional in her playing of Chopin, her mother finally says. The piece technically requires restrained emotion.

Told of Helena's presence in the house and confronted with her sick daughter, Charlotte, angered, nonetheless acts the kind and smiling mother. Charlotte hurts inside—both at the pain of seeing the sick girl and from her guilt at having handed her over to a nursing home. But Charlotte's tears are frozen and she covers them over by putting on a gay red dress for the rest of the day and makes plans to shorten her visit. Eva's bitterness leaks out. To herself she thinks: "Does one never stop being mother and daughter? . . . It's like a heavy ghost that suddenly falls on top of you when you open the door to the nursery, having long since forgotten that it *is* the nursery door after all."[3]

Eva is like many daughters of Ice Queen mothers—confused and unable to speak or express her feelings. Charlotte has been unable to tolerate tears or emotion of any kind and has remained distant from Eva, always covering her own feelings under a smiling veneer of tolerance. In order to confront her mother, Eva drinks too much, then blurts out her madness—what she has been afraid and ashamed to say to Charlotte. Eva confesses how she always felt ugly and awkward, even repulsive, to her tall, regal, beautiful mother, and how she cried in secret because she knew her mother detested tears. Before this cool, composed mother, Eva had always felt speechless, even when Charlotte deigned to talk to her. Eva tries to tell Charlotte what it was like to be a daughter faced with such an aloof, assured mother who treated her daughter like a doll for whom she occasionally had time.

> Then my cheeks flamed and I broke out in a sweat but couldn't say anything—I hadn't any words because you had taken charge of all the words at home. I loved you, it was a matter of life and death—I thought so anyway—but I distrusted your words. I knew instinctively that you hardly ever meant what you said. You have such a beautiful voice, Mother. . . . I didn't understand your words—they didn't match your intonation or the expression in your eyes. The worst of all was that you smiled when you were angry. When you hated Father you called him "my dearest friend," when you were tired of me you said: "darling little girl." Nothing fitted.[4]

Continuing, Eva tells her mother that, as a child, she loved her and was convinced Charlotte was always right and she was always wrong, a frequent legacy of lack of self-esteem felt by an Ice Queen's daughter. Although Charlotte never criticized her directly, Eva always felt her mother's insinuation that she was wrong. The consequence, she tells her mother now, is that she felt she had no identity of her own.

> I felt paralyzed, but one thing I did understand quite clearly: there wasn't a shred of the real me that could be loved or even accepted. You were obsessed, and I became more and more afraid, more and more crushed. I didn't know who I was any more, because at every moment I had to please you. I turned into a clumsy puppet that you worked. I said what you wanted me to say, I made your gestures and movements so that you would approve of me. I didn't dare to be myself for one second, not even when I was alone, because I violently disliked what was my own.[5]

It was a nightmare, Eva confesses, because she thought they loved each other and didn't realize how much she actually hated her mother. Her unconscious hatred turned into a crazy fear that

came out in horrible dreams, as well as in habits of pulling out her
hair and biting at her fingers. Because Eva couldn't cry out her
despair or scream or otherwise articulate her feelings, Charlotte
sent her to a psychiatrist. Eva now accuses her mother of breaking
up a love relationship and of brainwashing her into having an abortion while pretending sympathy. She rebukes her mother for wanting to possess her, even though she had abandoned her.

Shocked, Charlotte asks Eva why she had never talked to her.
Now Eva finally releases the rage she has been hiding. She describes
the way she experiences her mother. She hates her

Because you never listen. Because you are a notorious escapist,
because you're emotionally crippled, because in actual fact
you detest me and Helena, because you're hopelessly shut up
inside yourself, because you always stand in your own light,
because you have carried me in your cold womb and expelled
me with loathing, because I loved you, because you thought I
was disgusting and unintelligent and a failure. And you
managed to injure me for life just as you yourself are injured.
All that was sensitive and delicate you bruised, everything alive
you tried to smother. You talk of my hatred. Your hatred was
no less. *Your hatred is no less.* I was little and malleable and
loving. You bound me, you wanted my love, just as you want
everyone else to love you. I was utterly at your mercy. It was
all done in the name of love. You kept saying that you loved
me and Father and Helena. And you were an expert at love's
intonations and gestures. People like you—people like you are
a menace, you should be locked away and rendered
harmless. . . . We lived on your conditions, on your mean
little marks of favor. We thought life was meant to be that way.
A child is always vulnerable, can't understand, is helpless. It
can't understand, doesn't know, nobody says anything.
Dependent on others, humiliated, and then the distance, the
insurmountable wall. The child calls out, no one answers, no
one comes. Can't you see?[6]

Eva expresses the rage a daughter feels at the distance, the rejection, and the humiliation of an Ice Queen mother. When the
daughter cries out, no one responds, so she remains speechless most

of the time. This emotional illiteracy and inarticulateness are usually passed on from mother to daughter. Sometimes the Ice Mother becomes withdrawn in reaction to a Dragon Lady mother, a woman who overwhelms her daughter with so much emotion and force that the only way to survive is to escape by retreat. Or as with Charlotte, she may repeat the pattern of her own mother, an Ice Queen who never showed warmth or attention to her daughters. Charlotte's parents had been distinguished mathematicians—totally involved with their work and each other. While they were kind to their children, they were not really interested in them. Charlotte couldn't remember ever being touched by her parents. She was neither caressed nor punished. Her one emotional outlet was the feeling that she was able to experience when she played the piano. Through her performances she knew she could make others happy, but she remained isolated, feeling shut out of life. She felt *"squeezed out of my mother's body. It closed and turned at once to Father. I didn't exist."*[7] Unwilling to look within herself to acknowledge or try to heal her injuries, Charlotte passed down the madness of the Ice Queen pattern to her daughters.

Charlotte tries to defend herself to Eva. She admits that she had a bad conscience about leaving her family and that she suffered from excruciating backaches that prevented her from practicing. Since her performances were going downhill, she began to feel that life was meaningless. She decided to spend time with her family, but then felt that she was a burden to Eva and her father, she says. Charlotte confesses to her daughter that she felt inept as a mother and that several years ago she became ill, then suffered a depression. Astonished that she is saying things she hadn't even known about herself, she tells Eva that underneath she had been afraid of her daughter and her demands. Charlotte even had wanted Eva to comfort and take care of her. The mother wanted her daughter to put her arms around her. Feeling crippled and awkward herself, Charlotte felt too helpless and frightened to be a mother. Her daughter always seemed the stronger one to her. Desperately, Charlotte pleads with Eva to forgive her and to teach her to relate.

Eva cannot accept the excuses, however, and continues to accuse Charlotte, telling her that children are not supposed to be caretakers for their mothers. Refusing to forgive her mother for deserting Helena and herself, Eva's raging voice wakes Helena, who cries out for her mother. Both Eva and Charlotte rush to her, but Helena wants her mother's arms. At this moment, Charlotte puts her head in Helena's lap, as if to be healed by her sick daughter.

Charlotte is overwhelmed by a need to escape. She cannot bear the suffering of her sick child and wonders how Helena can bear to live with her illness. She thinks Helena would be better off dead. Nor can she stand the emotional confrontation with Eva. After she leaves, Charlotte acknowledges to herself her feelings of isolation and homesickness. She realizes she longs for something greater. But she is unwilling to look further within. Admitting her depression, she still pushes it aside, thinking to herself: "I can't be bothered about self-knowledge. I'll have to live without it."[8]

Eva recognizes she has driven away her mother. She realizes that Charlotte is frightened, tired, and aging. Alone, Eva mourns and goes to sit by the grave of her dead son, Eric, for consolation. She cannot sleep and suffers from the knowledge that she has expected too much from this meeting with her mother. Instead of affection, she has met her mother with demands. She reflects that even though Helena was sick, she had given love to her mother while she, Eva, has held on to her sour resentment, keeping Charlotte at a distance. Feeling she has wronged her mother, Eva writes to Charlotte, telling her of this discovery, and asking for another chance. The daughter has learned that the most important thing is ". . . a kind of mercy after all. I mean the enormous chance of looking after each other, of helping each other, of showing affection."[9] Knowing that the letter may never reach her mother or that Charlotte may not even read it, Eva nevertheless promises herself she will not give up trying to reach her mother. Eva has learned that love is the only chance for future transformation and for humanity's survival.

Eva is ultimately able to transform her anger to compassion because she is able to give up her own clinging to the Ice Queen. She lets go of being her mother's victim when she is able to forgive her. In order to do this, however, she first has to feel the full suffering of her pain and her rage at her mother. She has to go through chaos and confusion, descend into a mad desperation, and express it. In this case, Eva expresses it to a mother who ultimately cannot tolerate the suffering and consciousness required for mutual transformation. The mother's madness remains frozen; unwilling to look within, she cannot change.

DAUGHTER OF AN ICE QUEEN: VICTORIA'S STORY

The fictional Charlotte is like the adoptive mother of Victoria, one of my clients. Victoria's mother is an Ice Queen who had always remained aloof and condescending toward the younger woman's enthusiasms and emotional expression, repeating the pattern of repression and icy judgments and rejection she had experienced with her own mother. She never freely shared her own life experiences to help her daughter learn about feminine life. She criticized her daughter for wanting her attention, yet whenever Victoria expressed feeling bad or inferior, the mother empathized with her, thus unconsciously encouraging her to remain weak and dependent.

When Victoria, hungry for love, turned to sex as a substitute for the love she wasn't receiving from her mother, her mother judged her immoral. Even so, her mother listened to Victoria's accounts of her erotic affairs with a vicarious pleasure that encouraged her daughter to "live her mother's life for her." Victoria was living out her mother's repressed sexuality, her shadow, which accounted for her mother's disgust at Victoria's promiscuity. This mixed message left Victoria feeling confused and crazy, and a victim of her own sexual obsession. Victoria recognized this as an addiction and went for help to a twelve-step group, where she received nonindulgent love and worked on these issues. Afterward, she began to feel free of this obsession, fell in love with a man, and was able to commit to this relationship.

When Victoria became healthy and strong and could relate to a man in a committed way, her mother stopped responding to her letters. On the telephone, she was curt and noncommittal and would only talk about the "good daughter," Victoria's much younger sister, also adopted, who had stayed with her. With this she insinuated, of course, that Victoria was the "bad daughter." When Victoria married, the mother refused to visit. Finally, she cut Victoria off completely by writing her a letter and telling her never to write or visit her again.

Luckily, Victoria was well on her way to recovery when this final rejection came. Moreover, she had received many warnings in dreams: she dreamed that her mother led her to a half-frozen river and told her to cross it and go on her own. After she crossed the icy stream, she found herself suddenly in the underworld with a rowdy group of men, all trying to seduce her. Her mother's brother, who symbolized her mother's seductive masculine side, urged her to join the men. At the time Victoria did not understand this dream, for in reality, she liked her uncle.

Victoria also had several dreams that her mother had died and disinherited her. As she went through recovery, her mother failed to respond to her letters, and she had many recurrent dreams in which her mother rejected her in various ways. In these dreams, the mother was supercilious, flip, patronizing, haughty, and imperious, often throwing her sister in her face as the good, dutiful daughter. Sometimes in the dreams, when Victoria would try to visit or write her mother, the sister would intercept the letters and the calls or tell her that their mother was not at home. Sometimes when she phoned, there would be no answer.

Often Victoria's dream mother appeared in a cold climate. Once she threw a bunch of packaged irises in the snow on Victoria's doorstep; they lay like a wet and damaged newspaper on the icy steps, half frozen. In another dream, she shamed Victoria in front of the "good daughter." In still another, she talked to Victoria as if she were a sick mental patient whom she might or might not treat. In this dream, the mother was cool, aloof, and condescending and got a "high" off Victoria's dependency. This dream was a clue that Victoria's mother really wanted her to be a sick patient.

In some ways Victoria felt as though she had never had a mother, as though the relationship had never existed. How had she come to be? Then she had a dream that she should try to contact her mother one last time to try to reach a reconciliation. But she wasn't sure whether to do it. In the dream, she consulted a friend who was a very grounded person and a psychotherapist. Her solid friend told her (in the dream) that the dream was trying to show her that she needed to let go of her attempts to reach this rejecting mother and focus on developing her inner nurturing mother. In the end of the dream, Victoria met a prominent woman therapist who had written many books on feminine transformation. The older therapist said she knew who Victoria was and wished they could have known each other better. As the dream concluded, Victoria was walking in the forest with her down-to-earth friend, feeling good to be with this life-affirming friend. The two positive women healers in this dream —the older woman teacher of her mother's generation, and the warm friend who was her own age—symbolized Victoria's positive feminine sides.

Victoria had one last dream about her Ice Queen mother that confirmed without a doubt her own capacity for motherly nurturing that had been developing within.

With an icy, queenlike gesture, the woman, whom I loved dearly as a mother, banishes me from her kingdom. Exiled, I leave in confusion and have to climb up a steep, wide green hill. From behind the forest, gigantic, primeval animals enter the clearing—huge horses and woolly mammoths from the Ice Age. In awe and fear, I awoke, wondering whether to retreat to the kingdom of rejection or to brave the great ancient animals and go forward into a new life. I decided to go forward.

When Victoria researched mammoths, she learned that they were reputed to be huge gentle creatures, especially nurturing of their young. This image confirmed Victoria's knowledge that she had the ability to take care of herself. She now knew consciously that she was able to respect herself and her own instincts.

HEALING THE ICE QUEEN: A FAIRY TALE

The healing of the Ice Queen requires thawing frozen feelings. In nature there is an analogy to this melting process: Icy glacial fields support very little vegetation. But gradually, as glaciers melt, life begins to appear again, first small green tufts, later bushes and trees, then flowers and animal life returns. If you have had a chance to travel up the fjords in Alaska's Glacier National Park, you can see this happen before your eyes. Bordering the great glacier is rock and rubble. Next, as you leave the glacial area, a black crust forms that is mostly algae; then come some tufts of moss, then fireweed flowers and bushes of alder and willow and finally small trees—spruce and hemlock—that turn to mature forests. You can see the gradual transformation from bare rock to revegetation as you travel along the fjord from the glacier's farthest reaches to the land where things are growing.

Ice Queens and their daughters can take heart from this process of Nature. If they can leave the icy atmosphere—the freezing external environment of the mother and the internalized icebergs that have formed in the psyche—growth will happen naturally. A dramatic thaw is often needed to start this process. Some women caught in the Ice Queen syndrome try to achieve this thawing unconsciously through consuming too much alcohol (firewater) or through repeated sexual encounters, seeking an obsessive and unfulfilling passion. Still others seek warmth and love through food, or they try to compensate by buying clothes, trying to be glamorous.

Because these ways of seeking warmth are external and often destructive, they do not really satisfy or bring lasting change. A productive, positive melting of the Ice Queen must come from an inner heat and conscious, internal healing. The Ice Queen needs to accept the suffering and deep wounding that led to her formation and to diminish the shame and sense of inferiority that she secretly feels. Since the Ice Queen tends to be embarrassed by tears, equating them with weakness and imperfection, she needs to learn that a deep cry from the heart can melt her frozen feelings. Tears of empathy for herself and all those who are caught in this cold pattern can help heal the Ice Queen. Humor is also healing for the Ice Queen, for she must learn to laugh at herself and her human imperfections.

"THE SNOW QUEEN": A HEALING

In fairy tales, as in dreams, different characters can be seen as parts of ourselves. "The Snow Queen," a fairy tale by Hans Christian Andersen, shows how an Ice Queen wounds others and what is needed for healing. The Snow Queen of the title is a beautiful empress of the north polar region who flies about but never remains on earth. Made of ice, she can freeze things with a look. A young boy, Kay, whose eye and heart have been pierced by fragments of a broken mirror belonging to the Devil, loses his good feelings and becomes mean to his friend Gerda. Seeing everything as ugly, he becomes fascinated by the perfect Snow Queen, who takes him as a hostage to her Ice Palace. This can be interpreted to mean that women caught in the Ice Queen pattern of behavior are like boys, frozen and held captive in an immature armor of icy, artificial masculinity.

To save her friend, Gerda journeys to the Snow Queen's realm with only her spontaneity and good, warm feelings to help her. Because she is vulnerable and open and listens to Nature, people, flowers, and animals help her on the way. Healing the damage that the Ice Queen wreaks in people requires this vulnerability. When Gerda offers her favorite red shoes to the river in exchange for her friend, she shows she values the flowing waters of life and is willing to make the necessary sacrifices for love. Sacrificing the red shoes may symbolize the surrender of obsessive and imprisoning standpoints handed down from mother to daughter, as is expressed by Anne Sexton's poem in the epigraph to this chapter. The Snow Queen, whose feelings are frozen, needs to learn exactly this—to let go and surrender to the flow of feeling. The Snow Queen's position of power and control from high on her icy throne isolates her and is in sharp contrast to the vulnerability and innocence of the young girl within. She has lost access to the young, gentle feminine side of herself, represented by Gerda in the fairy tale.

The young heroine makes her journey with bare feet, symbolizing her humility and closeness to the earth. The danger she faces is that she might forget her goal due to her sweet nature—her wanting to please others—and that she might be waylaid by her love of play and beautiful and magical things, as when she is detained in the garden of a strange old woman who causes her to lose her memory. The old woman, who wants to possess Gerda's sweetness, actually is another aspect of the Ice Queen mother who wants to hold onto her daughter, even while rejecting her. To do this, she may entice her with beauty and a kindly facade, like the mother in *Autumn Sonata*, or with attention only when the daughter is sick or feeling inferior, as in the case of Victoria. The Ice Queen's devouring and possessive aspect is often concealed under her mask of perfection, and the woman who seeks to save herself from the Ice Queen needs to be alert to the danger of these glittering seductions.

Warm tears are the saving grace for Gerda. She cries as she is searching for roses, symbolizing the love of her friend Kay, and her tears water the ground, causing the roses to bloom again, reminding her that she must continue her journey to find him. Her tears are not the drowning tears of a victim but the heartwarming tears of natural feeling that can begin the thawing of an Ice Queen.

Even though Gerda's feet become sore and she is tired, she does not give up her journey. Giving up is one of the ways women fail to transform the Ice Queen. If you are on a hike in a cold, snowy area and you stop due to exhaustion, you are likely to suffer frostbite or freeze to death. So too you must persevere on a journey to face the

Ice Queen, or perish, unconscious of the freedom you might have ultimately gained had you persisted. There is always a danger of giving up, of becoming paralyzed by her icy demeanor. Sometimes, to continue on your own path, you have to break off a destructive relationship, as Victoria let go of her obsessive relation with her rejecting Ice Queen mother in order to continue her life. When she left her mother's icy kingdom she encountered the warm and woolly mammoths, symbolic of an enormous interior nurturing energy.

In the fairy tale, as Gerda continues her journey, she meets many characters who help her. She has the help of a royal couple, who invite her to stay in their castle. They symbolize the future possibility of inner royalty, but Gerda has farther to go before she can achieve this. Accepting their help—a carriage, food, and a fine muff— Gerda continues her search.

An encounter with a Robber Girl suggests Gerda's encounter with her shadow side. Gerda is sweet, but she needs a little of the Robber Girl's trickery and cleverness to succeed in her quest. Since the Ice Queen presents a perfect image, her transformation requires finding her dark side. So Gerda exchanges her pretty fur muff for the muff of the Robber Girl's mother. The exchange of muffs symbolizes this exchange of knowledge and acceptance. The Robber Girl's mother also drinks too much, suggesting the ineffective use of alcohol by some Ice Queens to melt their armor. The muff symbolizes both a connection with the dark mother and a warning.

The Robber Girl also gives Gerda a helpful animal, a reindeer, that enables her to complete her journey. A gentle yet wild animal, the reindeer can survive in freezing arctic regions (home of the Ice Queen). It is a nomadic animal that annually migrates to give birth. In shamanic cultures, the reindeer symbolizes the capacity to journey between the human world and the spirit world. Just as we must bridge the personal and archetypal realms by understanding how the universal dynamics of the Ice Queen function personally in ourselves in order to transform ourselves or be free of her, so the reindeer helps Gerda bridge these realms and takes her to seek help from two old women.

Representing two aspects of the wisdom of the nurturing mother, the Lapp woman feeds and shelters Gerda, and the Finnmark woman provides the spiritual power to harness the winds. The Finnmark woman lives in a hot chimney where she gets dirty from the soot and heat (or emotions), suggesting that the spiritual mother with wisdom and power does not look perfect as the Ice Queen does but is affected by feelings. The Finnmark woman or spiritual mother does not need a beautiful, finished facade. Most important, she has the wisdom to recognize Gerda's power and to know that Gerda must recognize her own power in order to complete the journey herself. She is a transforming mother figure who does not hold on to a young woman to keep her dependent but urges her to take the crucial next step while offering a safe station on the way.

Gerda must go by herself into the land of the Snow Queen; the reindeer takes her to its borders. Although she is afraid and overwhelmed by this vast icy kingdom, she fights her fear of facing the formidable Snow Queen. Knowing when to pray for help, she receives it. In this way she finds Kay and hugs him, and her hot tears melt his frozen heart. Her power is her love, courage, and innocence and her ability to weep. Gerda's weeping enables Kay to cry, too, and his own tears wash out the splinter in his eye that had obscured his vision. Just so, any rescue from the Snow Queen requires grieving for the pain needed to loosen the feelings that were paralyzed and inaccessible.

Weeping with another human being can be a most healing event, as my own mother and I discovered in our interpersonal healing. When Gerda and Kay weep together, their joyful tears cause the ice to dance merrily. The ice forms the word that solves the icy puzzle that the Snow Queen had assigned Kay to solve if he wanted to be free. The word is *Eternity*, suggesting a divine love that is greater than ours, and the children return home understanding the value of innocence and childlike faith and love.

The Ice Queen freezes our childlike nature within us. In our modern-day lives the child needs to be freed. In contemporary life, the frozen boy, Kay, might correspond to a woman who assumes that being masculine is superior. The tale shows us that the heroine who melts the Ice Queen's frozen feelings is full of youth and vitality, spontaneous, warm, and unarmored, symbolizing the gentle, vulnerable *feminine* strength that is frequently abused, denigrated, or ignored in our culture. Yet a uniquely feminine strength is needed to meet and unmask this icy version of the Madwoman.

THE DRAGON LADY

The mother who intimidates her children through unpredictable emotional explosions is a common kind of Madwoman. Such Dragon Lady mothers intimidate their daughters through fear and overwhelm them with their rage. When opposed, these mothers overreact with extreme emotion—sometimes tears, sometimes anger—in this way ruling the family with an iron hand. Dictating how things are to be done, how a daughter should act, and what she should think or feel, the Dragon Lady is certain she is always right. Determined to have her way at any cost, she screams and shouts and uses scare tactics and threats to dominate, and she is always on the attack. If the daughter is gentle, she feels terribly humiliated and ashamed of her mother's insensitivity toward others. Up against such a constant display of power, the daughter often feels as if she doesn't have a chance. One adult daughter dreamed she was a little girl again, trying to leave home to go out on her own, when she saw her mother driving a huge red tank, aiming to run over her. Although the dreamer was a grown, independent woman and her mother was by then old and sickly, she was still dominated by this internalized image of her mother.

Some children actually refer to their mothers as "the Dragon Lady" to their friends and other family members. Always breathing fire and anger, she seems like a huge monster to them. Just as fire depletes oxygen, leaving no air to breathe, a Dragon Lady seems to take up all the space when she enters a room. Obsessed with having the last word, she shouts down others to get it. She is a bully and a tyrant, bossing her children around with critical judgments and bulldozing them with her anger. She can be so barbaric and savage that no one in the family, not even her husband, wants to cross her. Shame and humiliation are two of her major strategies, and she knows how to make her children feel guilty. Insulting or seducing with words to manipulate the family for her own ends, she is expert at making people feel helpless.

With this woman you cannot win, no matter what you do or say, for the Dragon Lady must always be in charge. Often spiteful, vicious, vindictive, devious, devouring, and sinister, she hurts and criticizes and drives away people who happen to get in her way. Examples of Dragon Ladies in films include Martha, played by Elizabeth Taylor, in *Who's Afraid of Virginia Woolf?* and the pathetically abusive mother, played by Joanne Woodward, in *The Effect of Gamma Rays on Man-in-the-Moon Marigolds.*

Unlike Ice Queens, Dragon Ladies are passionate, but their ardor turns around themselves. Their passion is not a warm feeling but is cold at its core; it burns like dry ice. The Dragon Lady seldom extends true empathy or understanding to others, for she doesn't try to imagine how other people feel. She cannot let others live their lives or honor what is important to them. Often these mothers are jealous of their daughters and vengeful, intolerant of their daughters' differences from them. Daughters of Dragon Ladies are so busy trying to defend themselves that it is difficult for them to relate humanly to their mothers.

Underneath the explosive power of a Dragon Lady may be a woman who had been a sensitive and frightened little girl, or one who was abused or abandoned as a child. In her fear of being hurt again, she attacks first. Because she suffers from the memory of real or imagined slights or injustices, any attempts to soothe her feel like criticisms. Often she feels martyred. Rage governs the Dragon Lady's life, and if her rage were to somehow be removed, she is likely to lose her identity, for she feels most alive when she is angry or emoting, the center of others' attention. If she isn't in the limelight, she often storms away. Hurt herself, all she knows is how to hurt others. Having learned that her explosions intimidate, she rules by her anger, which she projects outward against others. Ultimately, however, the Dragon Lady hurts herself most of all. Wanting to escape her rage, people avoid her, leaving her to relive her original wound, lonely and isolated. Underneath her explosive temper, she is excruciatingly vulnerable. Like a small child consumed with rage at her own impotence, she screams her furious hatred of the world.

Some Real-Life Dragon Ladies

Janet, the daughter of a Dragon Lady whose madness was fueled by alcohol, felt she was unable to express her own anger after growing up in a violent, raging atmosphere. Her mother's fury was so all-encompassing that it had excluded and submerged Janet's own feelings. After many years of therapy, however, Janet did gain access to her own anger and powers of expression. As though to help her in this process, her dreams began to reveal all the things about which she was angry, and they became a veritable inventory of her rage. Night after night she dreamed of various times in her life when she had been angry but had not dared to express it. In her dreams Janet could say everything she had ever wanted or needed to say. In one dream, for example, she berated her mother for drinking and for her incompetence in dealing with the details of everyday life, such as cooking and cleaning. In another dream, when she was criticized for being overweight, Janet stood up for herself and said, "I'm a decent human being!" Dreaming that her boss at work demeaned her, she affirmed herself by replying that she was a competent worker. The dreams showed her that daring to assert her own authority was exhilarating—a wonderful release from her usual self-destructive ways, being obsequious or getting on her high horse.

One Dragon Lady mother, Anita, had a recurring dream throughout her life. She had always wanted to be a lawyer, but she had grown up in the early part of this century, when women were expected to be wives and mothers. Anita had a brilliant mind and was a master in arguments. Her husband, a businessman, wanted her to use her brilliance for his work. So she worked as his accountant, totaling debits and credits for his business, while the greater part of her intelligence lay dormant. Anita's enormous energy was turned to bossing those around her, especially her children. Everyone in the family capitulated to her demands. If they resisted, she exploded, made a scene, and punished them in various ways. She especially bossed her son and raged at him. Her husband always did what she wanted and supported Anita in her commands to her children. Her children were brought up to be nice and never to be angry or hurt anyone. In return, Anita told the children never to hurt their father, for a nasty retort might cause him to have a heart attack. Instead of standing up for themselves against their dominating Dragon Lady mother, both son and daughter obeyed, repressing their own anger.

Despite Anita's power, she actually felt helpless. Her children withdrew from their Dragon Lady mother as they grew older, and she felt abandoned. After her husband died, she felt alone. A recurrent nightmare that she had had throughout her adult life showed her difficulty: In her dream she was a lawyer who had collected all the evidence for an ironclad case. It was definite that she was right. Each time she presented the case in the courtroom, however, the judge, without fail, shook his head no. When she protested with all her evidence, she was ignored. She would wake up from this night-mare in great frustration, and during the years when her children were at home, she took it out on them. The dream underscores the irony of this Dragon Lady's situation. On the one hand she always thought herself perfectly justified in whatever she did. Of course, this both intimidated and alienated her children. On the other hand, she was truly a Madwoman up against the patriarchal Judge. The real tragedy was that the culture of that time had not nurtured her innate talent. Denied the development of her ability, she was relegated to commanding a small area of her home, where she and her children suffered from her madness.

If a woman fails to overcome her intimidation by confronting the Dragon Lady in her mother, she may discover other Dragon Ladies in her life whom she must learn to deal with. Marriage often presents a pattern of behavior similar to the dynamics in the part-ners' families of origin. Unable to express anger, a daughter of a Dragon Lady may link up with a man who has more than enough anger for both of them. Daughters of Dragon Ladies often marry men who are the male counterparts of a Dragon Lady—possessive, jealous, and abusive. One woman, Jennie, whose mother was a Dragon Lady, married a man who was so obsessively fixated on her that he was jealous of all her friends. Jennie felt trapped in this marriage in much the same way that she had felt trapped by her mother. One night she had a dream that her mother was lying in bed behind her, and she was afraid her mother would make sexual advances or smother her or both. Gathering her courage, she turned, in the dream, to face her mother and saw with horror her husband instead. When Jennie woke up, she realized that she had escaped one Dragon Lady only to end up with another. In another nightmare she dreamed she had married her mother—a frequent motif in the dreams of daughters of Mad Mothers.

Jennie's husband would blow up at her for no reason, in scenes such as she had suffered many times as a child in her family home. Jennie had often felt as though her parents acted like children, while she and her brothers were the adults. Now married to a man much like her mother, she felt trapped in an abusive and unfulfill-ing relationship. Typically, her husband became furious behind the wheel of the car, and she would become afraid because she was trapped in the car. Once while he was driving, his face reddened, swollen with a sudden temper tantrum, and she saw him as a big, fat, red-faced man in a baby's body, dressed in diapers. This humorous waking image helped Jennie to see the bluff behind the bully and enabled her to laugh at her inflated Madwoman image in both her husband and her mother. Gradually, as she began to accept her own anger at being bullied, Jennie was able to confront both mother and husband when necessary.

The story of another daughter of a Dragon Lady is typical of women who have grown up with this kind of Mad Mother. Julie's Madwoman first appeared in her dreams, but after diligent inner work, she became a helpful figure to Julie in both dreams and actual life:

Julie grew up with an overworked mother in a household without masculine models. Her father had died before she was born. Working to support the family, her mother was gone most of the time and came home tired and exhausted. Julie's mother disciplined her daughter by yelling at her until she obeyed. She would also use guilt to control her, reminding Julie of her martyred life. This misuse of her emotional power over Julie worked during childhood when Julie was so afraid of her mother's yelling that she acted the "good daughter." At fifteen, however, she started to fight back, ineffectively, exploding in anger at her mother, who just laughed at her and didn't take her seriously.

Julie's mother was herself the daughter of a happy-go-lucky alcoholic father and an Ice Queen mother who was cold, critical, and unforgiving. Without a good model of the feminine, Julie's mother reacted in the opposite mode to her own mother, breathing fire instead of freezing with ice, and she passed the madness she felt from her mother down to her daughter. Both the mother and grandmother did share overly critical personalities. Julie's mother was concerned with appearances and constantly criticized Julie about her weight and the way she dressed. Later, when Julie married and had a child, her mother also criticized her about the way her house looked and the way she was bringing up her son. Somewhat paranoid about how she herself was being judged, Julie's mother turned her paranoid projections against her daughter. Like many mad and narcissistic mothers, Julie's mother was unable to see that Julie was a separate person. She could only see her own face in the mirror. Thus, she was unable to allow Julie to develop in her own unique way.

In adolescence, Julie obsessively sought the love her mother never gave her from boyfriends who eventually rejected her, a common pattern of experience for daughters of rejecting mothers. When the hippie movement emerged in the sixties, Julie finally felt at home with the unconditional love of this group. She liked being accepted and understood by all. Since she was a warm and loving person herself, she became the nurturing mother, cooking for everyone, but still often neglecting herself.

Besides being intensely insecure about her looks and about how other people, especially women, saw her, Julie was also extremely fearful—typical for daughters of Dragon Ladies, who yell and abuse them. Julie was so afraid of her mother's unpredictable reactions that she did not tell her about the three times she had been molested: at four by a baby-sitter's son; at nine by an evangelist; at thirteen by a music teacher. Her fear of authority figures became so severe that Julie developed debilitating symptoms: phobias, panic attacks, and migraine headaches. She had no energy, and she became so anxious and depressed that she was afraid to get into her car and go anywhere. This interfered with her profession as an artist. She had to force herself to go to art shows, overcoming her fear of critical judgment. She also felt she was somehow a fraud and was admitted to art shows by some bizarre mistake, even though she was actually an accomplished artist. Finally, at thirty-nine, she sought help from a therapist.

Julie was aware that, although her mother was not physically affectionate, she loved Julie in her own way. Julie grew up feeling very much alone, trying to escape by reading. Her mother, who was not intellectually inclined, saw Julie's reading as "a waste of time." In an attempt to heal herself, Julie had studied metaphysics. Her mother couldn't understand and was even embarrassed by Julie's lifelong interest in mysticism and spirituality, because she was unable to look inward.

Julie had been intrigued by dreams even before she started therapy and remembered and recorded them in a journal. In therapy, she had a startling series of dreams of Madwomen who were trying to kill her. The Madwoman was usually thin and glamorous, dressed in red or black and wearing spike high heels. She reminded Julie of the way her mother dressed. And just as Julie's mother had manipulated her emotionally, so the Madwoman in her dreams usually worked behind the scenes, directing a man to do the violent killing, showing the negative animus of her mother.

The first two Madwoman dreams reminded Julie directly of her grandmother and her mother. Julie said the first dream reflected the way she felt about her grandmother, the cold and critical Ice Queen:

> A woman is chasing a little girl around the house trying to cut her and kill her with a razor blade. I watch in horror, feeling helpless.

The second dream showed that Julie experienced her mother as devouring, a recurring feature of Dragon Ladies:

> In a jungle swamp, I see a strange creature—a cross between a hippo and a huge swamp fish. She is a mother who is smothering her baby girl.

Then Julie had a dream that helped her deal with her own internalized Madwoman, imaged as the wife of a serial killer but also someone who was sick and needed help.

> I am with others in a city ghetto. A serial killer is chasing us. The only way to escape is to descend into a sewer filled with vomit and filth and swim in it. I see a dead black man floating in this vomit, but he seems to be coming back to life as I swim near him. Back at my apartment, the phone rings. It is a man who appears friendly, but I know it is the serial killer trying to track me down. He arrives at my house with his wife, a severe but glamorous woman dressed in black and wearing high heels, which remind me of my mother's shoes. I know this woman is mad and is directing the serial killer to attack me with a knife. Suddenly the Madwoman vomits. There is a child in her lap now and I see she is sick. As I try to help this sick Madwoman, the dream ends, and I wake up.

This dream was a turning point for Julie. She became aware of both the danger and the sickness of the Madwoman. By recognizing the Madwoman's vulnerability and trying to help her, Julie not only diluted the power her mother held over her but recognized her mother as an internalized part of herself, a crazy woman who was trying to kill her but who was also sick and needed Julie's help.

The child on the Madwoman's lap symbolized new life and potentiality and the inner child Julie had never been able to be when young.

The dream showed that Julie first had to go down into a sewer of vomit and filth, symbolizing a descent into darkness in which she had to face many things in her life that had been repressed and were hard to "stomach." Every woman must make this descent in order to encounter the Madwoman and her attendants—the shadowy fears, memories, and miseries that we have to acknowledge and transform. The dark man, coming back to life, symbolized an important, instinctual masculine energy she needed to retrieve, one that had been denigrated by her mother in real life and that was needed to counter the Dragon Lady. At the time of this dream, Julie was becoming aware that she was repeating the Dragon Lady role with her son, and she knew it was imperative to understand this dark feminine aspect of herself. She was suppressing her feminine power and anger, which she feared because of her mother's dominating behavior, and this suppressed fury was beginning to tyrannize her. At any time, she felt it could erupt toward her child. Julie also suffered when other people were angry at her because she did not know how to respond to their anger effectively, having been squashed by her mother in her early attempts to respond to her mother's unjust and manipulative rages.

Other dreams continued to link the Madwoman with her mother. In one dream a young man, unhappy in love, turned into a glamorous Madwoman who fired a gun at Julie, missing her. Then the Madwoman shot Julie's sleeping mother in the head. Julie grabbed a gun and shot at the Madwoman, who laughed at her, for she had tricked Julie by putting blanks in her gun. Originally in the dream the Madwoman had been a young man disappointed in love, which Julie associated with her mother's own unhappiness in love and her Victorian disapproval of sex. Her mother had tried to pass on her prudishness to her daughter and criticized Julie for any sexual behavior. The dream showed Julie she had to be aware of the Madwoman's many guises and dangerous tricks. But when the Madwoman aimed at the sleeping mother's head, it also helped to awaken Julie to the relation between her mother's domination, her own fear of anger, and the power of the Madwoman.

About the time of this dream, Julie's mother had hurt her in a cruel telephone conversation. Julie could see the connection between the way the archetypal Madwoman hurt people, the way her mother hurt people, and the way she had internalized this Mad Mother and projected her onto other people who hurt her. Still another dream showed the Madwoman trying to get power over children. In this dream Julie was aware that two children in a dilapidated house had killed their parents. There was a movement afoot among the rest of the children to kill their parents too. Behind all this was the Madwoman again. Beautiful, dark, and wearing high heels, she was trying to get power over all the children by getting them to kill their parents. Aware in the dream, Julie tried to phone for help, but she couldn't get through. Finally, a benevolent man in the dream helped Julie trick this manipulative Madwoman.

The dream showed that the child side of Julie was so angry at the parental power that had subdued her that killing seemed the only solution. The Madwoman was operating behind the scenes, to direct the children to kill off the parent side. To avoid the extreme of killing—an urge that frequently surfaces when one feels like a helpless child before omnipotent parents—Julie needed to confront her mother directly with her anger. She also needed to look at her own rage that had been suppressed. The dream showed she had the aid of an interior benevolent masculine energy to help her; this may have corresponded to the help she was getting at the time from her male therapist.

Finally, Julie had the last of her Madwoman dreams and was able to gain constructive energy from this inner figure. This helped her make some important changes in her life.

It is after Armageddon—the end of the world—and I am with friends in a cabin in the mountains trying to survive. The scene changes and I go to a Chinese restaurant with a friend, similar in temperament to my mother. An exotic waiter brings a menu and tells me I'm in a temple. Running his hand up and down my body, he says this is a ritual. When he takes my order, I think he has misunderstood me but I decline to say anything. To everyone else he brings a good Oriental meal, but he gives me a plain American breakfast. Then the hostess, a beautiful Oriental woman in a long red Chinese mandarin dress, her hair piled high on her head with ornamental sticks through it in the Oriental fashion, enters and questions the waiter. She pulls out a dagger and gives it to the chef, directing him to stab the waiter who had brought the wrong order. Frightened, I try to escape with my son to save him.

With this dream, Julie understood the paradox of the Mad-woman. On the one hand she seemed evil by stabbing the waiter; on the other hand she was actually trying to help Julie, who had not received what she ordered and was served up plain, distasteful food. In some ways, "the waiter" in Julie needed to be stabbed for she had been waiting on other people all her life while neglecting herself. About the Madwoman, Julie reflected: "As evil as you seem, you also have my interests at heart." Julie began to understand that the Mad-woman had the power to help her. At this point, Julie did an active imagination dialogue with the Dragon Lady, who told Julie she had to own her positive power.

Julie began to see that her archetypal feminine power (both dark and light) had to be given expression, or it would continue to poison her internally and externally. She said, "I could no longer avoid the issue of power and anger and had to face my fear of confrontation. I had come to the point of no escape. I was damned if I didn't. In the abyss, you either die, go mad, or discover the strength and power to survive and transform." Accepting her power, Julie began to allow her anger to appear. She confronted her mother when necessary, and she also began to let other people know when they upset her. By allowing her anger its natural expression and by facing women and men who tried to intimidate her (her neighbor, sales-women, bank clerks, waitresses, teachers, and anyone who treated her rudely), she asserted herself and began to do what she needed for herself. She now felt she no longer had to take care of everyone else. Instead, she was integrating the positive side of the Dragon Lady (confidence and self-assertion) and using it for herself and her creative ventures.

Today criticisms from her mother and others do not upset Julie as much as they used to. When people say hurtful things, she tells them how she feels. The fact that she changed and stood up to her mother helped her mother change too. Like a typical Dragon Lady, her mother was addicted to power and needed to see that trying to overwhelm others with power ultimately doesn't work. When Julie finally stood up to her mother, her mother backed down in her demands and criticisms. This was living proof to Julie that individuation in oneself transforms others and can even heal family curses.

Once Julie started using her power, the Madwomen in her dreams were replaced by huge snakes that were her friends and protectors. Julie felt aligned with the transformative power of the ancient instinctual feminine snake goddess. In her professional life, she cut down on her secretarial work, in which she served others, and devoted herself more to her artwork.

In dealing with a Dragon Lady externally, one needs to call her bluff and to set boundaries. One Dragon Lady refused to go to her granddaughter's wedding because she disapproved of the groom. So her daughter decided not to invite her to the engagement party. The old lady wanted to come to the engagement party and demanded to come. But the daughter held her ground and said no. She refused to tolerate her mother's bad behavior. Remaining consistent, the daughter said, "No wedding, no engagement party." The Dragon Lady was shocked at her daughter's strength and refusal. But she backed down, apologized to her daughter and granddaughter, and said she would go to the wedding. By using some dragon fire herself, as Julie had in the previous story, this woman was able to be consistent, strong, and true to herself in calling her Mad Mother's bluff.

To heal herself, a Dragon Lady must realize what she is doing to others. She also has to glimpse that there is more to her than her rage. If she can see the consequences of her rage and acknowledge that she has contributed to the problems, the Dragon Lady can change. For example, in the film *Postcards from the Edge,* Shirley MacLaine plays an aging actress who is a Dragon Lady mother. She bosses her beautiful but unsuccessful young daughter who has taken to drugs to fend off her mother's domination. At the film's end, when the Dragon Lady mother, an alcoholic, is sick in the hospital, she is visited by her own mother, who had always criticized her. The Shirley MacLaine character's daughter, now in recovery, takes her grandmother out of the room, since she sees history repeating itself —she sees her grandmother criticizing her mother in the way she was criticized—and she knows her mother needs nurturing. Now vulnerable and humble, the mother acknowledges her faults to her daughter. She admits she has always been jealous of her and that she has been treating her daughter as her mother treated her.

When a Dragon Lady realizes that her interventions make things worse and that "Mother doesn't always know best"; when she can be vulnerable and humble and let go of her false need to be "right" all

the time, then the Dragon Lady can recover other aspects of herself
and use her energy to create instead of control.

THE SICK MOTHER

Many women inherit an inner Madwoman who had tortured
their mothers and made them sick. Sometimes the sickness is physical and the mother is an invalid and unable to be active. Some
invalid mothers, however, use their sickness as a power to bind their
children to them emotionally and psychologically. For example, in
the movie *Moonstruck,* an "ailing" mother calls her son back to Italy.
Complying with his mother's request, he loses his lover. Such a
mother's sickness may be emotional and result in a nervous breakdown or insanity, or it may be a drug or alcohol addiction.

In many of these sicknesses, the mother's ego is fragmented. She
throws her daughter into confusion because she lives in chaos. Split
into pieces herself, she tries to divide the members of her family so
that she can be the center. Because her personality is independent
and unhealthy, she needs her daughter to mirror her in order to
feel secure and centered.

Growing up, the daughter of a sick mother often feels she has to
live ultracarefully, for she has been made to feel guilty and uncer-
tain and is afraid of triggering her mother's medical problem or
nervous condition. She must tiptoe timidly around her mother, so
as not to upset her, and so she has to suppress her own natural
feelings, particularly the angry ones, which might provoke her
mother. Even worse, she lives with the fear that she might end up
crazy or addicted or sick like her mother.

One woman, Claire, had a dream image of walking through exploding land mines that jolted her mother's house. She saw her
mother, who suffered nervous breakdowns, hanging upside down
on a picture window as it was shattered. Claire's mother's breakdowns were characterized by flashes of transrational knowledge and
intuition. Her mother was frightened of these insights and had denied them in herself. Claire herself was also extremely intuitive and
often had precognitive knowledge of the way things were likely to
turn out. Her almost prophetic feeling and knowledge of people
often frightened and confused her. Her mother feared and criticized her daughter's intuitive nature and unconventional perspec-

tive, which mirrored her own shadow side, and Claire came to feel that other people mistrusted and feared her visionary nature, too. This made her wonder whether she, too, was unbalanced like her mother. Yet more often that not, her intuitions turned out to be correct. How could she have this kind of foreknowledge, and what was she to do with it? Claire often felt like the Greek prophetess Cassandra, gifted with prescient knowledge but disbelieved by all around her. After much therapy and inner spiritual work, Claire finally could believe that it was really her mother who was mad and not herself.

As a child, Claire was confused by her mother's moody projections—the unpredictable outbursts of angry criticism hurled at her, followed by her mother's self-recriminations, brought on by fear, guilt, and her paranoia that her daughter was judging her. A sensitive girl, Claire intensely *felt* her mother's fragile psychological constitution, but she could not comprehend why her mother saw her as a severe judge. She turned to her father for help. He was a kind man whom she loved and idolized, but he had devoted his life to accepting his wife's condition and protecting her. He loved his daughter very much, feeling the innate strength and instinctual wisdom that she manifested even as a child, so he shared with her his worries about his wife's fragility, asking his daughter to assist him in his caretaking role. The result was that Claire became a dutiful daughter—adult before her time: her father's companion and her mother's caretaker.

Claire viewed her mother as a Caged Bird. Because her mother had been afraid of her own innate intuitive nature, complicated by her tendency toward nervous breakdowns, she had never actualized the creative potential that her intuition promised. Undeveloped, her mother's intuitions turned into large, looming fears that kept her trapped in her home, afraid to venture into the world. They also deteriorated into ungrounded opinions and criticisms with which she aggressively battered her daughter. Her husband's protectiveness allowed her to remain home, but this made her feel more insecure. Her insecurity led to enormous resentment and anger, which she took out on her daughter in the form of cynical judgments about her character and the world. Claire did not want to be imprisoned in the cage of protection that marriage had become for her mother. So she avoided long-term relationships with available men for most of her adult life, until she was in her forties.

At about this same time, Claire went into therapy, and the figure she feared most—the Madwoman—began to appear in her dreams. Much of her inner work involved coming to terms with this terrifying interior figure, for her feminine legacy was to heal the sick Madwoman to whom her mother had fallen victim. Claire's task was to transform the Madwoman's destructive energies into creative forces.

The Madwoman first appeared to Claire in the following dream:

> With a friend who is driving the car, I go to the beach to take a walk. I try to show her the dunes where I once made love with a man long ago, but the ocean water is too high to reach this place. Because there are police in sight we decide not to go on the forbidden pathway that might yield access. To avoid more police, my friend decides to drive up a hill on a driveway which turns out to be a private road to a very large estate. There is a guarded, thirty-foot metal gate and guard post at the top of the hill. The gate begins to close as we approach. This makes me anxious that I am being watched and I want to get away from here quickly. Even though there is just room enough for the car to slip through and turn around if the gates close, I am afraid we'll get locked in on the other side. My friend is hurrying to get us out of this scary situation when a crazy woman walks up from behind the hill to my side of the car. The woman looks hostile and cackles at us. My friend is afraid, and I am uncomfortable but also curious. When the woman stops cackling, I applaud her. Surprised at my response, she smiles, stops being crazy for a moment, then walks back in the direction from which she came with a pleased rather than hostile countenance. Then we hurry to get out of this place.

Claire was surprised and relieved to see how the Madwoman could change from hostile to friendly "if she responded to her without fear," as she had done in the dream. When Claire recognized and acknowledged the Madwoman's presence by applauding, the woman stopped being crazy and left the two friends alone. To Claire this meant that by recognizing the Madwoman in herself, she might at least bring about a standoff between them, if not a transformation of the mad energy. She decided to confront and talk to this inner figure. Claire said that applauding the Madwoman contrasted with the way in which the seer Cassandra had been treated: Her talents were never recognized and accepted.

In reflecting on the dream, Claire realized she was afraid of being locked in the estate on the hill because it was being used as a mental institution. It also corresponded to a fear of being trapped in her head. The presence of too much ocean water in the beginning of the dream suggested the overwhelming power of being caught unconsciously by the mother, which could prevent a love relationship with a man. Too much water preventing access to the site of past lovemaking also suggested a connection between love relationships and the danger of the Madwoman who evoked too much emotion, including the risk of being imprisoned in a relationship by yielding to love. Claire had experienced the Madwoman in her mother as a lack of boundaries: Her mother was unable to contain her feelings, and they spilled over onto her daughter, frightening her and threatening to overwhelm her. Claire was held hostage by her mother's uncontrolled emotions, "too much water." This affected Claire's own ability to express angry feelings and stood in the way of her relationships with men.

Although the Madwoman had walked away in the previous dream, she soon returned in another dream.

> I am standing outside of a house, in the front yard, preparing to fix a picnic meal. I do not recognize the meat that I am about to cook. There is a "larger-than-life" leg of mutton and also some ground meat. A crazy woman comes out of the forest that borders the side of the house. She grabs the mutton leg and devours it raw with such intensity that I am frightened and disgusted. I consider killing her by breaking a glass jar over her head. I pick up a glass jar and get so close to her that we are staring at the whites of each other's eyes. She reaches for a jar, too, and I realize she could kill me. I decide not to take that risk and back away from her. She walks back into the forest. I worry that she will return and do greater harm sometime in the future. I fear that I should have killed her, even though I didn't really want to.

In this dream, Claire came face to face with the fierce, devouring power of the Madwoman who once again comes from the dark, thick forest, symbolizing the darkness of the unconscious. Appalled and disgusted by her intensity and abandon, Claire considered killing her but didn't know whether the Madwoman might not kill her first. Her gut feeling was not to kill the Madwoman, for despite her repugnance, she was aware that the Madwoman could have something to teach her. Like the Greek Maenads, the crazy woman tears flesh from the bone. And like the Maenads, she can't be controlled but must be accepted and acknowledged—incorporated into ourselves, as a meal is incorporated and made part of us.

The devouring Madwoman in the dream symbolized the way Claire had experienced her mother. She had seen her mother consume others with her demands, and she did not want to be like her. Since Claire's mother's needs had been devouring, her father had asked Claire to sacrifice her own desires in order to administer to her sick mother's demands. Thus, taking what she needed looked like primitive gluttony and seemed disgusting. Hence, in the dream, the decision to take what she needed appeared as a grotesque form of grabbing and devouring. In actual life, Claire needed to be more accepting of her own needs. Captured in the caretaker role, she felt overly responsible and tended to give everything away to others, to the extent that she did not leave enough time and energy for herself. She had to learn to say no to others and to acknowledge that she couldn't take care of everything. The Madwoman represented the power that Claire had denied in herself, as a reaction to her mother. Claire needed to integrate the Madwoman's energy and strength into her life.

As with many women, one of Claire's greatest conflicts was between two archetypal combatants—the Madwoman and the Judge.[10] Whenever she followed her intuitive visions, her inner Judge, a rational perfectionist, criticized her and denigrated her desire for a more integrated and spiritual way of life. When Claire recognized that this inner war was a result of behaviors that had developed from the dysfunctional family dynamic to which she had been subjected in childhood, she began to heal the Madwoman's legacy. Brought up to be an adult child, Claire had developed an inner controlling critic that made her restrain her feelings. Because her father had been so "saintlike" (much like the Too-Nice Mother), she had difficulty getting angry with her father and with other men. Her mother had passed on to her daughter many taboos—for example, not to hurt her father. "Men are really sensitive, they just don't show it," her mother would lecture. In this way, Claire was cast as a caretaker for her father's feelings, too. Claire had many dreams in which she was not seen by other people. Not being seen is a frequent motif in the dreams of women whose genuine feelings and feminine ways of perception have been demeaned. Knowing that her experience was like that of many women, Claire was angry at the male naiveté of her father and of many men for not "seeing" who she was, and also at the patriarchal culture for discounting the importance of certain feminine experiences and visionary modes of perception.

This male presumption was also imaged in her dreams as rude, staring redneck men, whom she wanted to avoid, and as male sadistic killers. Although Claire had tried to express her anger with her father, with the managers at work, and with other men, she felt that she kept coming up against a blank wall. After she developed an inner relationship with the Madwoman, Claire began to feel hopeful that she could use her anger effectively when she needed to confront men. Toward the end of her therapy, Claire said, "I feel a relationship with the Madwoman opening, and I'm hopeful that she won't need to attack men without my permission, or if she leaps out, that I'll better understand her voice and be able to maintain the *human* connection with the man." Claire was also beginning to be able to relate to *herself* in a human way, to surrender to her physical and emotional limitations, to say no to others, and to confront them when they transgressed her boundaries.

Through inner work Claire was beginning to befriend the Madwoman. Then she had a very healing dream:

> I am walking down the street when I notice a woman babbling to herself. She is sitting on the sidewalk and is clearly "out of her mind," yet is well dressed in a business suit for office work, acceptable by society's standards. I am drawn to her and wonder if there is anything I can do to help. Then I notice that two women are preparing to heal her. One helps the Madwoman to kneel so that her third eye can focus on a building while the other woman prepares to channel the healing energies. The channeler is a spiritual healer and artist whom I admire and I feel honored to be present at this ceremony. Suddenly, I realize I am in the ceremony, too, and have been chosen to be the grounding force for the healing, channeled from the prime healer to the kneeling Madwoman.

As the healing energy passes through me via a triangular
circuit, I start sobbing and cannot move. Then the energy
connection breaks and the chief healer says to the
Madwoman, "You are filthy," and walks off with her assistant.
My crying stops and I am confused about what has happened.
I feel empathy for the kneeling Madwoman. Although I
understand that the remark had to do with the Madwoman's
sexuality, I don't understand why the chief healer had to be
so harsh. I take the Madwoman home. We interact like
teenage girl friends and try on clothes. I put on a colorful
Mexican shirt and wear it like a minidress, pulling it over my
body in a revealing way, showing her how this dress is meant
to be worn. We laugh together at how silly it is. I learn that
she was once a prostitute and see that she is a beautiful,
healthy woman.

The dream reveals that Claire can now channel healing to the
Madwoman. After the healing, the Madwoman is no longer threatening but is instead a beautiful and healthy woman who is fun and
playful. The incongruity of the Madwoman's "third eye" with her
office business suit illustrates the conflict in which Claire often
found herself: that of the Madwoman and the Judge. She had
worked in an office requiring business dress. The men in charge
were patriarchal, invested in maintaining the "good old boy" rules
of business. They were threatened by her perceptions, symbolized by
the third eye, and she often found herself up against a wall. The
Madwoman's prostitution symbolized Claire's own sacrifice of her
third eye when she tried to please her employers or conform to her
parents and the patriarchal culture in her role as the good daughter, but she managed not to prostitute herself fully by internally
affirming her vision. The beauty and health of the Madwoman in
the dream showed that Claire had not suffered permanent damage.
The dream revealed the conflict between the practical, rational order ordained by the culture, and the mystical, spiritual world in
which Claire felt at home. To express her visionary spirit, the Madwoman needed to wear a sexy, colorful ethnic dress, not a business
suit.

The healing really occurred when, in the dream, Claire befriended the Madwoman and took her home, showing her the beautiful, unconventional Mexican dress in which she could express her

colorful, earthy self. After reflecting on the shocking judgment of the chief healer, Claire felt she had been awakened into befriending the Madwoman, much in the way a Zen teacher uses a paradoxical koan to reprimand and shock the student out of a state of paralysis between two seemingly conflicting opposites. In Claire's case, the opposites were the Madwoman and the Judge, which, when integrated, could be used for creative action. Unreconciled, however, they kept her caught in a state either of paralysis or of battle, which on the personal level can make us mad and on the cultural level can destroy the world. By ferreting out the value in each one—the creative chaos of the Madwoman and the discriminating judgments of the Judge—we can create ourselves anew and make the world a better place to live in; we can transform our dysfunctional society into a healthy and creative one.

By the time of her third Madwoman dream, Claire had done a lot of intensive work in therapy: recording and working with each of her dreams, seeing the family dynamics that had shaped her in ways that were not her own, trying to understand the parts of herself that needed development, changing the behavior that worked against her, and most important, learning to be and express herself in accordance with *who she* really was. She was able to differentiate herself from her Mad Mother and embody her intuitive, creative self in both work and relationships. Leaving her office work, after several years of training to be a psychotherapist, she took the risk of starting a private practice. Not only was she successful, she found her intuitive nature to be an asset in healing others. Soon after this dream she met a man and entered into a relationship that was healing for both of them.

At last, Claire felt confident of her imagination, of the images of her psyche and the truths they revealed. She felt sure of herself as a creative and intelligent woman who could revere and reveal her genuine self, having transformed the crazy, threatening Madwoman into beautiful and healthy feminine energy.

UNDERSTANDING THE MAD MOTHER

All of us, to some degree, are affected by the wounds of a Mad Mother. Reconciliation with the mother is essential to our healing. It is not always possible, however, as I mentioned earlier, for you to do this with your actual external mother, for she may be caught in her own madness and unable to listen; she may be too sick or even dead. In these cases it often helps to write a letter to your mother, for in the writing you can heal the hurt within yourself. After my father died, I chose to write to heal the injured relationship with him. This project resulted in a book, *The Wounded Woman*. Although it took me seven years to complete this painful work, I was able to process my rage and tears and finally feel compassion for my wounded father. This freed me to move on to other areas of my life. Later, I was able to heal the relationship with my mother in real life as well.

Another way to restore harmony with our mothers is through ritual. For example, one group of women who had been meeting weekly to work on feminine issues decided to devote a day to do a ritual, thinking they would be able to release the stored-up anger at their mothers in this way. Each woman came dressed as her own mother and tried to tell her mother's story. By doing this, these daughters were surprised at how little they really knew about their mothers. By speaking in their mothers' voice, they became aware of how trapped their mothers had been. Hearing their mothers' early messages—"Don't grumble," "Do what is expected of you," "Don't waste your time on self-reflection," "You made your bed, now lie in it"—helped them realize how hard it had been for women of the previous generation to break free. The ritual helped these daughters release their pain and anger, but not in the way they had expected. It also enabled them to sacrifice their boxed-up memories and projections onto their mothers. By meeting their Mad Mothers in this way, most of these women gained more compassion for their mothers and were able to heal the mothers in themselves.

Reparenting via therapy can also heal the mother wound. Working with dreams gives us images and stories about the inhibiting patterns we have inherited from our mothers and often reveals a guiding path to follow on the feminine journey that is unique for each woman. Painting the images, dancing them, making masks, singing songs, dialoguing with the mother figure revealed in dreams —all are ways to get in touch with the inner negative mother that needs transforming. Body work, which tries to release traumas stored up in the body, can take us back to our very origins and is also helpful in finding and healing early wounds.

Ultimately, healing the wound of the Mad Mother requires some sacrifice, letting go of resentments, surrendering our victimization, and owning and embodying our unique feminine power. A step in healing for daughters is to accept their mothers' love, even though their mothers may show that love in outmoded or awkward ways. At the most fundamental level, we can appreciate our mothers by thanking them for giving us life. This honors the mystery of motherhood while allowing for individual differences and difficulties. It may be the daughters who can give to their mothers by reaching higher levels of consciousness and showing them another way. For the Mad Mother is herself a wounded daughter who needs empathy, understanding, compassion, and love. By healing ourselves, we have the best hope for healing our Mad Mothers and the vicious circle in which all wounded women are caught. Reconciliation cannot occur by overlooking the pain and anger that is there. But having faced it, we can proceed beyond it to forge a new path.

On a spiritual level, many of us have forgotten to thank Mother Earth for her gifts. On the global and ecological level, we are feeling the Madwoman's fury at the way the earth has been mistreated. As one woman expressed it, we are experiencing "Mother Earth's revenge" in the form of various cataclysms, the greenhouse effect, endangered species, disease epidemics verging on plague, and the possibility of destroying the earth. We need to listen as individuals and as a collective group to the Madwoman without the defensiveness and self-justification of either the victim or the Judge, and to act responsibly at a personal and community level.

Some wisdom from the ancient Sumerians, who told the myth of Inanna and Ereshkigal, can enlighten us here. When the great mad goddess of the underworld, Ereshkigal, was enraged and held the upper world goddess, Inanna, captive and threatened to kill her, two tiny androgynous creatures descended to meet Ereshkigal. They did not argue with her, or plead with her, or trick her, or fight her. They simply cried with her in empathy, sharing her grief. Grateful for their kind compassion, their sharing of her painful rage, Ereshkigal heaved a sigh of relief and released the goddess Inanna to bring her dark sister's knowledge and power back to the world. If we could try to meet the Madwoman in ourselves and others and listen to her with understanding, perhaps we, too, could pave the way for a separate and universal peace.

THE CAGED BIRD

The caged bird sings
with a fearful trill
of things unknown
but longed for still
and his tune is heard
on the distant hill
for the caged bird
sings of freedom.

—MAYA ANGELOU,
"The Caged Bird"

MANY YEARS AGO, THE POET MURIEL RUKEYSER SAID:
"What would happen if one woman told the truth
about her life? / The world would split open."[1]
Rukeyser helped many women realize they were
caught, like birds in a cage, and she voiced their
need for freedom.

Today, although women are beginning to speak
assertively for their rights so that they can live according to their natural rhythms, needs, desires, and
abilities, the social structures in which we live still
make it difficult for us to actualize the full range of
our creative abilities. In *The Politics of Reality,* Marilyn
Frye points out that women's mobility is reduced by
a systematic network of barriers and forces, just
as the many wires of a bird cage imprison the
bird, preventing full freedom. The wires of the cage,
which together constitute the barrier to freedom,

vary from external legal restrictions to social expectations of what women can and cannot do, to internalized adaptations to these constraints by women themselves.[2]

Our fantasies of women, too, constitute some of the wires of the cage. In fairy tales, Sleeping Beauty was trapped inside a hedge of thorns, Rapunzel was imprisoned in a tower, and Snow White was poisoned and put inside a glass coffin. In each case, a Madwoman plotted the caging—a neglected fairy-godmother, a devouring witch, a mad and jealous step-mother. In these tales, rescue occurred by virtue of outside masculine forces. As young girls, we are shown these examples of men rescuing the captive maiden from the Madwoman, often from the cage of the Mad Mother. Yet these maidens move on to another cage, often a cultural or patriarchal one, thus perpetuating the Caged Bird pattern.

Today, women have to open the doors of their own cages. To do this we need to meet and identify the Madwoman who tries to cage us, to try to understand why she is mad, to free her energy for constructive ends, and to see if we can help her to help ourselves.

Before the 1960s, in our mothers' generations, the Caged Bird was one of the prevailing patterns of feminine existence. The good woman was a submissive wife who stayed at home, cleaned the house, and took care of her husband and children. This ideal imprisoned many women and their daughters, who had to accept and adapt to this model of femininity and suppress their anger at their limited roles in life—or rebel against the cages that the patriarchy had built for them. Many of these Caged Birds went mad in one way or another, as their freedom to lead an authentic life was constrained. Some lost their sanity by sinking slowly into a boredom and passivity that masked depression or that turned into psychosomatic symptoms. Others tried to escape themselves through addiction to alcohol, pills, eating, shopping, or watching television. Women who tried to break free of the status quo or simply be themselves within it were often diagnosed as mad and put in mental institutions, like the New Zealand writer Janet Frame, the French sculptress Camille Claudel, and the American actress Frances Farmer.[3] But some women struggled and, through their persistence, were able to get out of the cage. The American writer Charlotte Perkins Gilman is an example. Although many contemporary women are still caught in the cage of the family's or society's expectations, many others are changing their lives, becoming strong, independent beings and inspiring other women who meet them, thus creating an ever-widening circle of hope and healing.

CAGES

What are some of the ways we are caged? The Caged Bird can be a wife trapped in a stifling marriage. She can be a secretary or executive director trapped in a supportive role, doing all the work while the boss gets all the credit, and getting all the blame when things go wrong. She can be a daughter dominated by possessive parents. She can be imprisoned in an abusive relationship or by addiction. She can be caged as the status symbol of a husband or lover. Or she can be a celebrity ensnared by the projections of the public and the narcissism of the culture, like Marilyn Monroe. By remaining a bird in a gilded cage, a woman colludes with her jailers, obstructing her potential to be free.

The cage can be the conventions of society that keep us from growing into the fulfillment of our unique personality or form of maturity. It can be our own rigid ideals or perfectionistic standards or ways we think we have to do things. Today, the cage is often material possessions or the desire for material things, security, fame, or fortune. It is whatever we use to fill our inner emptiness instead of facing the challenges life presents us. The cage is any mental structure that becomes calcified, rigid, absolute, that has no openings and allows no journeys through its doors.

One commonly experienced cage is the one constructed out of the projections our mothers and fathers, relatives and culture, children and friends impose upon us.[4] For example, many young girls, upon reaching the teenage years, find their mothers—often Caged Birds themselves—want them to mirror their own lives. If the daughter is different from the mother, she must rebel to get out of the "cage" into which her mother has placed her. If the mother is herself a Caged Bird, the daughter will typically resist following her mother's example; the daughter of a stay-at-home mother may remain single and career-oriented, while the daughter of an overworked mother with a career may choose motherhood over a professional life. One woman's mother became a war bride to escape her ravaged country after World War II and suffered in an abusive marriage because she wanted security. Her daughter was unable to bear her mother's martyrdom and has remained single.

The cage that a mother may try to impose on her daughter may also consist of the mother's own unfulfilled dreams and desires, which she hopes her daughter can realize in her stead. Or the cage may be made of negative ideas or images the mother has about the daughter. While some daughters do rebel successfully and assert their independence over the years, the cost to the mother-daughter relationship can be high, with tensions and pain, dire predictions, and conflict predominating. It is no wonder, then, that some daughters become timid and stay in the cage.

Quite often, husbands take over the role of cage-keeper from women's parents, and the daughter, who may have thought she married to escape an imprisoning role, continues to have another limit her life. One woman, Elsa, told me her mother had wanted her to be a good and dutiful daughter and imposed on her a Victorian model of sexuality. Elsa rebelled and married early to get away from her mother. Elsa and her husband, who had always been proud of her intelligence, were students together, and both went on to graduate school. Then Elsa began to surpass her husband in her scholastic achievements. While he had been her superior, he had encouraged her, but now that she was successful he tried to sabotage her efforts and limit her to a role wherever he could control her identity and her achievements. Since Elsa was committed to her own growth and achievements, however, eventually she had to break out of that marriage. She remarried later to a man who valued her professional actualization.

Artists often struggle within the constraints of family expectations or work to transcend physical or mental confinements through their art. The poets Anne Sexton and Sylvia Plath are examples of creative women who felt entrapped and mentally disturbed by their roles as housewives and mothers. Both women struggled to transform their madness through writing. In their poetry they gave us all a great gift of inspiration and insight, even though they themselves were tragically lost to suicide. The actress Liv Ullmann writes how she became a Caged Bird in her relationship with Ingmar Bergman. To become her own woman, she finally left this relationship. Her struggle for integrity provides a hopeful model for women needing to change their lives.

Literature and films, opera and ballet—all abound with the image of the Caged Bird. Nora, the heroine of Ibsen's *A Doll's House,* is adored and protected but also stifled by her husband. Nora is a Caged Bird who manages to break free. Tolstoy's protagonist in *Anna Karenina,* however, does not escape. Anna is trapped by the stifling conventions of her time and culture, by her rigid husband, and by her own bondage to an addictive love relationship. Her only solution becomes suicide. A similar example is *Madame Bovary,* whose heroine is caged in a boring marriage and by her longing for glamour and romance. Many women today still feel their despair at their unsatisfactory lives, and they fill their empty days with shopping, with aimless visits to malls, or with the fantasies of movie magazines, romance novels, or movies and television soap operas. Addictions such as eating disorders and substance abuse can also be misguided attempts to escape from the cage, leaving a woman even more dangerously trapped, as the film *A Woman Under the Influence* illustrates. The films of the post-World War II years—a time in which women who were "different" automatically were considered mad— feature many Caged Bird protagonists. *The Diary of a Mad Housewife,* which was made in 1970, just as the culture of the late Sixties began to wrestle with its perceptions of women, is one example. Many of these tragic figures simply lived out lives of quiet desperation, remaining passive, subjugated by their spouses, parents, and culture. The housewife trapped into passivity by convention is shown in the contemporary film *Mr. and Mrs. Bridge,* based on the novels by Evan S. Connell.

Modern films, such as *Desperately Seeking Susan,* show a Caged Bird trapped by marriage but challenged to become free through the energetic figure of the Madwoman (a free, revolutionary spirit portrayed in the film by Madonna). *Thelma and Louise* demonstrates the liberating action of anger as two women escape from their dull careers, and abusive husband, and fear as rape victims. But the cost of freedom for women in a patriarchal society can ultimately be death, which in the end Thelma and Louise choose willingly over imprisonment. Illustrating ways to break free of the cage and transform the Caged Bird, these modern films portray women consciously choosing to leave the cage. In *Shirley Valentine,* the protagonist gets so angry at her insensitive husband that she starts talking, even shouting, to the walls. Deciding to take a trip to

Greece, she meets a man who helps her enjoy who *she* really is. Transformed in this way, she finds she can return and change the constricted patterns of her marriage. Woody Allen's film *Alice* shows the metamorphosis of another housewife who leaves a lifeless marriage to live out her dream to visit Mother Teresa in India. By getting in touch with her fantasy life, Alice chooses to leave her safe but boring New York City Upper East Side married life to work with children in the East Village.

All of us—women and men alike—suffer from the Caged Bird syndrome in a patriarchal culture that has fixed and rigid ideals and rules. The traditionally minded man who "protects" his wife, wanting to keep her home, is actually constructing a cage for her and himself, binding himself to support her and a certain life-style. Today, many men are realizing that they have been caught in the role of a provider. Often themselves captives of the cage of corporate structure, they can lose their passion for life, for freedom, and for independence. If they try to free themselves from their company's, society's, or their family's expectations about men as success objects, they may feel guilty, as if they had failed to be real men in the eyes of others. Women complain about men's lack of feeling, yet they do not necessarily want men to give up status-conferring jobs and identities and the security that comes with these roles, and they often fear the expression of the freed personality of the man who breaks out.[5]

THE SYMBOL OF THE BIRD

Why do humans want to catch and cage a free bird? Why do some people want to be caged themselves? What does the free bird symbolize? In the legends and fairy tales of many cultures, the bird represents the possibility of a spiritual pilgrimage; it can guide us to transcendence. The bird is seen as a mediator between earth and heaven because of its ability to fly. In Hindu tradition the bird symbolizes higher spiritual existence. In the art of ancient Egypt, the bird symbolizes the human soul. In Africa birds symbolize vital power. The mythical phoenix symbolizes immortality and rebirth of the soul, rising from its own ashes. To the Sufi mystics the bird in flight was on the long journey to unite with the divinity. Freeing the bird in ourselves means that we open emotionally to spiritual experience, to begin our inner journey to self-knowledge and integration. The poet Rumi expressed this transcendent flight in verse, in which love and freedom are equated, as follows:

> This is love: to fly toward a secret sky,
> to cause a hundred veils to fall each moment.
> First to let go of life
> Finally to take a step without feet.[6]

In Russian legend, the beautiful Firebird is honored as the source of creativity. Igor Stravinsky, among others, celebrated this famous fairy tale in his ballet *The Firebird*. An early form of the story is as follows:

A simple orphan girl, Maryushka, can embroider so beautifully that people marvel at her creative work. Merchants who want to profit from her work and creativity try to lure her to work only for them. But she always refuses, for she wants to be free. An evil sorcerer who wants to cage her and possess her talents changes her into a Firebird when she refuses to marry him. According to some versions of the legend, the Firebird even sacrifices her life rather than marry the demonic sorcerer and lose her freedom. In her death, she allows her beautiful rainbow-colored feathers to fall to the earth, where humans who can recognize their transcendence may be inspired by them to create beauty. In later versions of the fairy tale, a king wants to own the Firebird and sends his son to capture her and put her in a cage. The prince who allows her to be free, recognizing that the Firebird's nature is transcendent and cannot be possessed by human power, is able to find a beautiful princess and marry her, symbolizing the divine and sacred wedding that occurs within the human soul. Those who try to cage her, like the evil sorcerer, are condemned to madness and death.

Stravinsky's *Firebird* ballet dramatizes the futile attempt to capture the Firebird and her creativity. A simple prince, Ivan, is hunting for beasts in the forest, where he is surprised to see a shimmering Firebird dancing joyfully, ready to fly away at any moment. Dazzled by this magnificent creature, with the face and arms of a beautiful woman and the brilliantly colored feathered body of a bird, Ivan wants to capture her. When he catches her by surprise, the frightened Firebird dances frantically to fly free, pleading that he release her. Realizing that she is a supernatural being, Ivan allows her to go free. The Firebird thanks him by giving him a brilliant red feather from her breast, a magic charm that he can wave in the air if ever he needs her help.

The forest is actually ruled by the evil sorcerer, Kaschei, who has captured beautiful maidens and has built a high golden fence to imprison them and to protect a magic fruit tree that bears golden apples that attract the Firebird. Still unwittingly in the enchanted forest, in wonder at his encounter with the Firebird, Ivan encounters some captive maidens. The loveliest princess warns him that the evil sorcerer traps innocent wanderers and turns them to stone. Ivan and the princess fall in love, but at dusk the princess and the other maidens leave in fear, while Ivan remains bewildered in the forest. Suddenly the evil Kaschei enters with his monster-slaves and attacks Ivan to kill him. Remembering the Firebird, Ivan waves her feather in the air and provokes the monsters to madness. The Firebird leaps into the forest, spinning so fast that chaos results. As she dances away, the Firebird gives Ivan a golden sword, with which he kills Kaschei. Ivan finds the princess, and the couple bow in thanks to the beautiful Firebird who has saved their lives. The Firebird, dancing gracefully alone, consigns the rest of the monsters to an endless sleep, restores peace and serenity over all, then flies away. The ballet ends with a song of thanksgiving to the Firebird as Prince Ivan weds the lovely princess in a beautiful ceremony of rejoicing.

These ancient stories remind us of the necessity to begin our own spiritual quest. They stress the impossibility of ever capturing the human spirit and the dire consequences of attempting to limit it by forcing it into a man-made cage, whether that cage be a political system, a patriarchal culture, a rigid view of human existence, or simply our individual presuppositions about ourselves and others. However, there is a side of all of us that wants security and that tries to possess things, tries to make rules that prescribe rigid and conformist behavior rather than allow life and natural energies to flow freely. This dominant tendency is particularly evident in a patriarchal culture based on acquisition and control, based on the building of cages.

THE BOREDOM OF MRS. BRIDGE

Usually docile on the surface, a woman who is a Caged Bird may be boiling underneath with resentment, furious at being owned, possessed, controlled, or dominated. She does not express herself or develop her talents, and she suffers overtly or secretly from lack of confidence and low self-esteem. Failing to assert herself, she lives another's life, concealing her problems and using subterfuge to get what she wants or needs. If she does assert herself and do what she wants, she feels guilty. The Caged Bird's facades of timid pleaser or martyred caretaker are familiar to many codependents, who live in an imprisoning cage of addiction. Below these flat exteriors, however, the Madwoman rages, relegated to the shadows, ready to burst out. A young woman's despair as she struggles to fly out of her cage door is expressed in the following poem:

Trapped

Trapped in darkness, within the heart of me,
A captive bird struggles to be free.
Wings beating madly, risking mutilation,
She fights against the fear of silent suffocation.

Seeking unknown freedom and passions unrestrained,
Becoming bruised and battered, feathers brightly
    stained.
Bleeding, struggling blindly, crashing against her
    cage
Propelled by old desires and unacknowledged rage.

Oblivious to the cruelty of illusion's impenetrable walls,
She flies against the painted bars, crumbles back, and falls.
And as she shudders, dying, upon the sharply splintered floor,
She suffers, still unseeing, beneath her ever-open prison door.

In our time, the Caged Bird is more likely to be conscious of her condition, but many women remain unaware that they are trapped, and they never integrate their experiences of the Madwoman energy. Consider the example of India Bridge in the film *Mr. and Mrs. Bridge*. Mrs. Bridge, a fiftyish, midwestern, sweet, suburban housewife, has been married all her adult life to Mr. Bridge, a lawyer who comes from a family of men who were judges and military officers. Identifying with men who are stronghearted fighters, he cannot, or will not, express his tender feelings. Honorable and upright, he decides everything for his wife and protects her, even from the knowledge of his own ailing heart condition. Brought up to believe that a good wife should stay with her husband at all costs, she always follows his directions, votes the way he tells her to, and is glad to have a man around to take charge.

Mrs. Bridge loves her adolescent children, but she cannot understand them because she is bound to the Victorian conventions of her own generation. She is prudish and upset by the different sexual values of her children and shocked by their rebellion. Unable to understand their painful or angry feelings, she hides her confusion with clichéd maxims about life that she learned as a girl. Mrs. Bridge cannot tolerate being "different." Keeping up a good appearance is her main concern. She judges people by their cleanliness, their manners at the table, even the condition of their shoes. On the surface she is always polite, even if offended when others disagree. Accustomed to cover up any awkward moment, she tries to prevent silence in a conversation.

Despite her ease of life, Mrs. Bridge, like many of her women friends, is bored. She plays cards to pass the time, and she tries to lose herself through shopping and light conversation. But underneath the surface, ominous emptiness is making itself known to Mrs. Bridge. While most of the women in her circle try to ignore such anxious moments, her best friend, Grace, begins to question her life: "Do we believe the right things?"[7] Grace asks, knowing that she has experienced very little of life. This questioning disturbs Mrs. Bridge.

As her children become more independent and start to leave home for college, and as her husband continues to put all his energy into work, Mrs. Bridge finds herself at loose ends. Since the maid does all the housework, she has little now to do. She becomes restless; the days seem interminable. Never sure what she wanted from life or what life wanted from her, Mrs. Bridge feels as though she were waiting, but she doesn't know what she is waiting for or why. Often she finds herself staring into space, oppressed by a foreboding that what she values will be destroyed. But she tries to shake from her mind these nagging doubts about her life. "Could she explain how the leisure of her life—that exquisite idleness he had created by giving her everything—was driving her insane?''[8]

While Mrs. Bridge is largely content to remain in her life of conventionality, part of her wants to break out. Yet she cannot understand how to respond to her art teacher's suggestion that she let herself go in her painting. At the suggestion of a friend, she begins to read Veblen's *Theory of the Leisure Class.* In an attempt to discuss it with Mr. Bridge, she is upset when he dismisses it as socialist trash. She cries about her husband's lack of feeling and mentions divorce, but Mr. Bridge is able to push her feelings aside by giving her a sip of beer and holding her on his lap.

However, Mrs. Bridge is confronted with moments of truth. While she is shopping, an elevator cage crashes only ten steps away from her. Shocked, she sees the trapped people looking out of the cage in a daze—a mirror of her own confused entrapment. One night before bedtime, absentmindedly putting cold cream on her face and wondering how she can occupy the next day, she is shocked by the cold cream to look more closely in the mirror. Who is the woman staring at her? Why is she alive? Beneath her mask, she realizes she is not smiling; she has been covering a silent scream.

Depressed, Mrs. Bridge feels she needs help and decides to tell her husband that she wants to go into psychoanalysis. Her friend, Mabel, already in analysis, has said it is a voyage of self-discovery. It takes her weeks to gather courage and wait until Mr. Bridge is in a good mood, yet when she blurts out her despair—and her hope that analysis might help her—Mr. Bridge continues to read his newspaper and ignores her. "Analysis is no better than fortune telling," he says, offering to buy her a new car, as if that would solve the problem. Mrs. Bridge refuses the offer and drops the subject.

When Grace confesses that she feels like she is losing her mind, Mrs. Bridge tries to cover up the crisis, which becomes a lost opportunity for the two women to connect with each other and to break out of their psychological and physical cages. In tears, Grace asks, "What is it all for?" pleading with Mrs. Bridge to drop her false gaiety and listen to her feelings. But Mrs. Bridge can only pat her hand and offer comforting clichés, so Grace withdraws, cutting off the relationship. Mrs. Bridge does not want to acknowledge that Grace, in her crisis, is experiencing what she herself has been feeling, too—an inner emptiness and a "malignancy in the universe"

that leaves a sour taste in her mouth but also "a wild, wild desire."[9]
Mrs. Bridge knows that Grace is no different from herself and the
other women in their circle, except that she has allowed herself to
feel and articulate the emptiness in the hollow life they share.

In the middle of the night, Mrs. Bridge awakens, feeling something is wrong. In the morning, she learns that Grace is dead. Covering up, she attempts to suppress the facts, telling most people it was
a case of ptomaine poisoning. Only to her closest friends and husband is she frank: Grace has overdosed on sleeping pills. In grief,
she turns to Mr. Bridge, who can only blame Grace, saying that she
should pity the husband who had given his wife everything a woman
should want.

Attempting to resume her ordinary life, Mrs. Bridge becomes
lost in confusion. She feels the shadow of World War II and cannot
understand its useless slaughter. Feeling a sense of unreality with
which she cannot cope, she increasingly dreams of the staring eyes
of the hungry, homeless street people. She begins to lose faith in
the future. Like Grace, Mrs. Bridge is reeling, but she tries to avoid
these feelings by thinking back to happier times.

Then comes the final blow. Mr. Bridge collapses at the office one
day and dies as a result of his ailing heart. Mrs. Bridge is left alone.
Trying to escape into forgetfulness, Mrs. Bridge sleeps more and
more. She sees old age approaching and starts to move more slowly.
Living in the past, she stays at home, waits for the mail or for someone to telephone, and looks at her picture album, trying to recapture the past. One cold and snowy day, Mrs. Bridge goes out to do
some shopping. Her car stalls and gets stuck between the garage
doors. The car is dead; its doors won't open wide enough to let her
out. Stuck, she tries to attract attention. She calls out: "Hello? Hello
out there?"[10] But no one sees or hears her. Mrs. Bridge is trapped
in the freezing cold. All she can do is wait helplessly in the cold—a
stark metaphor for the way she has been living her life. Passive and
dependent, she has been caught in a cold cage of frozen emotion.

In the novel, Mrs. Bridge waits in the cold but no one hears her.
Drifting into unconsciousness, she will freeze to death. In the film
version, Mr. Bridge, still alive, has tried to telephone his wife that
day. When she doesn't answer, he thinks she just went shopping. On
the way home, he impulsively buys her roses and drives home singing his favorite song, "Where are the men who are stout hearted
men?" Arriving in the driveway, he sees his wife's stuck car and

rescues her at the last moment, although he forgets to give her the roses. The film suggests that Mr. and Mrs. Bridge continue to live their lives as always, without change.

Mrs. Bridge may seem a relic from another generation, but many women today are like Mrs. Bridge, suffering in stultifying lives of drudgery, routine, or poverty. Hollywood chose to change the ending, enabling Mr. Bridge to rescue his wife, but covering up—as we all do every day—the inevitable and real tragedy. The fear of ending up like Mrs. Bridge is a current one and is based on actual possibilities. No one is exempt from Mrs. Bridge's tendency to try to preserve the status quo, to hide uncomfortable feelings, and to avoid change in order to be safe, secure, and protected. Mrs. Bridge's experience is the fate described by Charlotte Perkins Gilman in the previous century—the meaninglessness of a life without purpose and without contribution, which a woman totally protected and dominated by her husband and culture will feel and which can lead to the cold madness of passivity. Gilman depicted this tragedy in her story, *The Yellow Wallpaper*.

DESCENDING INTO MADNESS: *THE YELLOW WALLPAPER*

The Yellow Wallpaper is a short story of a creative woman who is trapped in a conventional life of unrelieved boredom. It was written at the end of the nineteenth century by Charlotte Perkins Gilman, who fought a nervous affliction similar to her protagonist's by writing out this story. Having dealt with her own inner barriers to her mental freedom, Charlotte Gilman became an early feminist who struggled to show the ways in which women were deprived of their freedom. Nearly a century later, *The Yellow Wallpaper* reminds women living today how a woman who suppresses her talents can make herself a victim and prisoner of her own creative urges. If she denies this creative energy, it can turn into a self-destructive rage. This self-destruction can take the form of addiction, depression, phobias, and anxiety reactions; sometimes it can end in suicide.

Significantly, the protagonist of *The Yellow Wallpaper* does not have a name. Her identity to others is only the wife, obedient to her paternalistic husband. Although she wants to be a writer, her husband and her brother, both physicians, tell her that work of any kind will worsen her nervous condition. Writing, especially, is dangerous, they say, for it can lead to fantasies that would feed a woman's excitable imagination and disturb her rest. They tell her that any show of feeling would be bad for her. Whenever she feels angry, they exhort her to subdue her rage, which she does, even though she knows this suppression exhausts her. She remains silent, conceals her feelings and conflicts, and hides her talents because her husband is loving and protective. Directing all her activities and scheduling every hour for her, her husband calls her his "blessed little goose" and tells her she is his only comfort, all he has in this world.

Her husband objects to her choice of a room she wants to have for herself—a ground-floor room that opens out onto the garden to inspire her writing—and he chooses instead an upstairs room for her, a former nursery with barred windows (and space to put his bed so he can be with her at night). This room bothers her because the wallpaper, faded and peeling, is a horrid yellow color. It even smells yellow, exuding a revolting odor. Its aging pattern seems to move in convoluted shapes, making her dizzy. The yellow wallpaper confuses her, chaotically intruding upon her mind and her vision.

Writing is her only relief from the invading wallpaper and the strange ideas pressing in upon her, for writing helps her deal with the wallpaper's crazy patterns. Because her husband and his sister, the housekeeper, agree that writing makes her sick, however, she has to sneak her writing time as an alcoholic hides bottles. She longs for friends with whom she could share her writing, but she has no one with whom she can be intimate.

As she stays in the room, she notices two absurd eyes that crawl around and stare at her from different spots behind the peeling paper. This makes her feel nervous and fretful much of the time, but she hides the fact that she cries about it from others. In time, the wallpaper fascinates her. Beneath the distracting designs that plunge in all directions on the surface, a vague and formless figure peeks through. Each day she notices that this figure looks more and more like a stooping woman crawling around, trying to get out.

One moonlit night, she becomes afraid of the moving figure and tries to tell her husband that she is getting sick by staying in this room. He reminds her that he is a doctor and knows she is getting better. He later encourages her to sleep in the daytime after every meal, a habit that she hates. But she decides it is better to deceive him, for now she fears him and wonders about his own sanity because of his determination to control her every moment.

She becomes determined to be alone and master the erratic pattern of the yellow wallpaper. In the daytime, as soon as she thinks she has tracked it, it turns tortuously on her like an optical nightmare and changes with every shift of light. At night, when the moon shines in, she sees in the pattern a woman behind bars struggling to get out. The crawling woman is the raging Madwoman in herself, imprisoned by the male certainty and judgments imposed upon her by her husband and the patriarchal culture. The drama of the wallpaper occupies her, like unraveling the plot of a detective story. She discovers that the pattern moves when the woman behind it shakes it as she crawls. Sometimes she sees many women shaking the yellow bars. One day, after the woman creeps out from behind the yellow wallpaper, she begins to creep herself, locking the door so her husband and his sister can't see her. She wants to help the imprisoned woman shake free from the yellow wallpaper. Together they strip off yards of paper from the walls. Creeping around the room with the crazy woman, now she can come in and out of the wallpaper too. But at other times, she fears to be like the crawling Madwoman and ties herself to the bed to protect herself from going outside to be discovered. Her husband breaks into the room and sees her on the floor, the yellow wallpaper stripped away. In shock, he asks her what she is doing. "I've got out at last . . . in spite of you . . . And I've pulled off most of the paper, so you can't put me back," she replies in defiance.[11] The story ends as her husband faints in her path, while she creeps over him again and again.

BREAKING THE BARS THROUGH WRITING: CHARLOTTE PERKINS GILMAN

Although the heroine of *The Yellow Wallpaper* succumbed to madness, her creator, Charlotte Perkins Gilman, survived by writing. Gilman, like the protagonist in her story, was told by her physician to devote herself to the conventional role of wife and mother and "never touch pen, brush, or pencil as long as you live."[12]

Married young to an artist who was a talented, idealistic, and lonely person like herself, Charlotte described him as tender, sexually attractive, and a help with housework. But liberal as he seemed, he believed that a free-spirited woman like Charlotte would be happy to return to the safety and love that marriage offered, after the world had tossed her around in her attempts to find free expression. Early in the marriage, Charlotte suffered extreme periods of depression, as though "a sort of gray fog drifted across my mind, a cloud that grew and darkened."[13] Insomnia, weariness, and an incapacity to work made her feel miserable. In this period she gave birth to a daughter for whom she was too sick to give proper care.

Following her physician's advice almost cost her her sanity, Gilman recorded in her autobiography, causing her so much anxiety that she would hide under beds and in closets, as though she could escape the distress of this diagnosis. She took a trip to California and found that away from her husband she felt much healthier. Upon returning to family life, however, she became fatigued and depressed once more. After four years of marriage, she and her husband agreed to divorce, deciding it was best for her daughter to be in the care of her husband and her best friend, his new wife. If she had to choose between creative life and the passive role assigned to women in conventional marriage, Charlotte could choose only the former, for she remembered her childhood experiences of her mother's painful and tormented life.

Charlotte's mother had given birth to three children in three years and neither gave nor received physical love. Her father abandoned the family soon after Charlotte was born, in 1850 in New England. Charlotte grew up without receiving tenderness from her cold, rejecting Ice Queen mother who was herself a Caged Bird. To survive, Charlotte developed determination, willpower, and a passion for knowledge and perfection. She inherited a Puritan sense of duty and responsibility and was intensely devoted to her work. As early as her late teens, Charlotte had become aware from her great aunt, Harriet Beecher Stowe, that women suffered under an unjust society. Wanting to change this unjust world through writing and lecturing, Charlotte wanted all her life "to find out what ailed society, and how most easily and naturally to improve it."[14]

In 1890 she moved to California, where she lectured on women's rights, taught school, edited newspapers, and wrote *The Yellow Wallpaper*. These years between 1890 and 1894 were the most difficult of her life, and she had to fight constantly against lethargy, depression, and fatigue, as well as face the hostility of public opinion. *The Yellow Wallpaper* was rejected for publication by the editor of *The Atlantic*

Monthly. Later, when it was published in 1892, it received mixed reviews. It was preserved for literature when William Dean Howells, who admired it, included it in the 1920 edition of *Great Modern American Stories*.

By writing out the story of the Madwoman in *The Yellow Wallpaper*, Charlotte Perkins Gilman transformed the Madwoman in herself. Overcoming her debilitating fear of being caged, she became famous as a feminist writer and lecturer at home and abroad, publishing poems, short stories, utopian novels, and nonfiction books in which she criticized the economic and social systems that kept women hostage, articulating many of the characteristics of family life that we now recognize as dysfunctional. Prime among these is the dominant behavior of a father/husband who "owns" and subordinates his wife and keeps her subservient and dependent. In an attempt to free women from this yoke so they could find self-respect and meaning in their lives, she advocated community child-care centers, communal kitchens, and respect for women's work, whatever it is they choose to do, along with equal rights in the workplace.

During the initial years of her professional life, Charlotte led a nomadic life, lecturing throughout the United States and Europe, researching and writing. Whenever she could, she tried to spend time with her daughter, Katherine. During this period, community was important for Charlotte. Invited by Jane Addams, she stayed at Hull House in Chicago, which offered her rest, regeneration, and communal life among intellectual and social reformers of the day such as John Dewey and Robert Ely. Most important was the opportunity this gave her to be with an extraordinary group of brilliant women.

While her professional life flourished, her personal life lacked the intimacy of daily relationships. Periodic depressions still left her exhausted, and she still feared being imprisoned by a primary relationship, conflicted by the either/or choice of love or work. Her writing helped her to integrate her feelings and experiences and to note, record and understand that her depressions were due to internal as well as external causes. Although her depressions kept recurring, she no longer feared them, seeing that they did not destroy her, she accepted their cyclical nature, and she viewed herself as a survivor. She worked "to live as I would wish my daughter—as I would wish all women to live"—with confidence, self-love, and self-esteem.[15] She struggled to reconcile the many conflicts in her life—

her public persona and her private self, her need for independence and her need for an intimate relationship, love and work.

In her late thirties she reencountered her cousin, George Hampton Gilman, a lawyer seven years younger than she, who was gentle, kind, nurturing, and her cultural and intellectual equal. They maintained a three-year-long courtship, during which they had an intense correspondence. Charlotte revealed to him her fear of abandonment, her recurrent depressions, and the conflicts she felt. As the possibility of the happiness of marriage drew nearer, she fell into a severe depression. But although she was afraid, she did not withdraw in terror from Gilman or their life together. Having written out her worst fear—that of the Madwoman in *The Yellow Wallpaper*—and in subsequent years having worked to improve the conditions of women in society, she now felt strong enough at forty to envision the integration of a loving relationship. Because the couple's love was based on friendship rather than impulsive passion, and because her new husband put his energy more into marriage and family than into career, Charlotte was able to trust and feel safe with him. Their marriage lasted more than thirty years, until his death, providing a stable atmosphere in which Charlotte was able to do some of her most creative work.

In 1898, she published *Women and Economics*. The book was an immediate success, and she became known internationally through its many translations. The book criticized the patriarchal systems that made women dependent. In it and other works, she argued that the way we earn a living is the major influence in our lives. Thus, if a woman is economically dependent upon a man, her "economic profit" depends on her powers of sexual attraction and on her role as servant. This way of "profitting" produces a stifling dependence that narrows women's lives, as well as the lives of their husbands and children, who are negatively affected because women's subservient role contributes to selfish behavior by both sexes. For example, Charlotte observed that men who are considerate in their work lives can be tyrannical and brutish at home, while their wives become greedy and demanding. Instead of a center of peace, which a genuine home could provide, "a workshop of discontent" results in which everyone is hurt. The patriarchal system, Charlotte stated, breeds women for sexual activity and housework, just as a domestic cow is artificially adapted to produce extra milk. When a woman is bred to be a sexual object she loses her direct relationship to nature, her strength, and her independence. She contrasted this "walking milk-machine," the domesticated cow, with the wild cow, which is maternal but also "a light, strong, swift, sinewy creature able to run, jump and fight if necessary."[16] For women to become independent, she argued, they must be allowed to develop naturally, which requires that they earn their own living. The emancipation of women from their artificially restricted role will result in emancipation for all, she predicted, depicting healthier societies in her utopian novels, *Moving the Mountain* (1911), *Herland* (1915), and *With Her in Ourland* (1916). In Charlotte's vision, when a woman could become a "world servant" rather than a "house servant," she would make the world a better home for her children and all humanity.

In later works, Charlotte wrote that the human world is made of interdependent social processes, so that individualism actually obstructs our achievement of happiness. She argued that we actually find our greatest pleasure when we work for the good of the human community. Working for humanity is as natural as breathing, since we are created to do meaningful work that unites us.

Charlotte also challenged the notions of property rights and personal ownership and demonstrated how these lead to the imagined right of men to dominate women. She maintained that competition and reward, encouraged by male-dominated literature that emphasizes the themes of desire and war, is not conducive to genuine learning and results in masculine standards as the criteria of excellence. She believed that women writers open up new creative realms, since "the basic female impulse is to gather, to put together, to construct." She concluded that the feminine values of endurance and cooperative service augment human life and argued that religion was dominated by the patriarchal system's emphasis on possession and on blaming women (Eve) for sin and humanity's fallen state. In contrast to the masculine obsession with death and happiness in the afterlife, she noted, women emphasize birth, growth, nurturance, forming, and building, so they focus on creating a better future on earth for coming generations. These feminine values provide a basis for religion as an energy for the good of the whole. "Women have always tried to heal, teach, and help," she said. Understanding "God" to be the life within us rather than the patriarchal Judge projected by many organized religions, Charlotte Perkins Gilman proposed that a birth-based feminine religion would be a force in the world for growth rather than combat. Even at the beginning of this century, as a result of breaking out of the cage of mental, physical, and societal strictures, she saw the flight of feminine spirit that was possible by returning to a feminine-based religion and embodying a feminine creative wisdom on this earth. Today these feminine "goddess" religions are growing as women return to women's ways of knowing, to Wicca, and to other spiritual practices in accord with Nature and her seasonal cycles. The following story shows this process in the dreams and development of a contemporary woman.

FREEING THE CAGED BIRD: THE STORY OF CONSTANCE

Constance lived part of her life as a Caged Bird. While she was going through a midlife crisis, Constance dreamed of a Madwoman. Struggling with this figure in her dreams, consciously doing active imagination, and identifying and changing a debilitating pattern of codependency, Constance was able to free herself and transform the imprisoned, mad energies into her own positive way of living and self-expression. Like all in-depth transformations, Constance's journey to find her creative self was a gradual process—it happened "one step at a time" and with daily commitment, she later said.

Constance came into psychotherapy because she felt trapped in her marriage and unable to find and express her own creative energies. Happy to be a mother, she loved and enjoyed her children, but she was afraid she might stifle them if she didn't find other outlets for herself. Her own mother had experienced enormous mood swings and had been both possessive and rejecting of Constance, needing Constance to mirror her, to be like her, and to provide her with self-affirmation. Constance did not want to repeat this pattern with her own children.

As a child growing up in Alaska, Constance had felt trapped. Like many adult children from dysfunctional families, Constance had a traumatic childhood. She was abandoned by her father, an alcoholic who died in his twenties when she was seven years old. Because he was unknown to her, in her imagination he became an exciting but unattainable figure. This formed the basis for her later attraction to men who were "ghostly lovers," romantic but unavailable. After her father had turned out to be unreliable and because her mother was still a young teenager, her grandparents took Constance to live with them. But when Constance was only two, her mother stole into her parents' house in the middle of the night and took her back to live with her and her new husband, a violent man who was abusive to his stepdaughter and beat up her father whenever he tried to see her.

Home was always chaotic. An only child, Constance feared her stepfather's anger and her mother's unpredictable feelings and crazy rages. Either her mother was in a manic state, spending money and dressing to the hilt, or she lay in bed, depressed and inert. Her mother's emotions dominated the house, leaving no space for Constance to have her own feelings or develop a sense of her own identity. She felt like a "lost child."

When Constance began to go out socially as an adolescent, her mother became jealous of all her friends and screamed at her to stay home. Comparing herself with her attractive daughter, her mother felt inferior, then criticized Constance, making her feel guilty. Unconsciously, the mother wanted her daughter to be a caretaker—to share her misery in their common cage. Throughout her teenage years, Constance's mother accused her of being selfish, saying, "You only think of yourself." One night, in a rage, she made Constance leave the house forever. Somehow Constance survived this rejection, but she suffered psychologically and physically. Her menstrual periods stopped for a year. She had difficulty talking in social and academic settings; she gained a lot of weight; and she began to have thoughts of suicide.

In college, Constance fell in love with men who were exciting but immature, like her father. In the end they left her for drink and drugs. Because she was bright and a good student, she was able to finish school. Longing for economic security and a home free of conflict, she chose to marry a fine but passive man whom she could control and who would provide her with financial security and a more stable life. In this way she avoided being abandoned or harmed. For a while, her cage felt like a haven, providing the needed stability she had not received in childhood.

On the conscious level, Constance wanted life to be predictable; she wanted to be in control. But unconsciously she yearned for drama and romance. She was still secretly in love with a romantic outlaw whom she had dated in her adolescence, and she spent most of her time fantasizing about him. At home, she felt trapped and would find herself shouting irrationally at her husband and her

children. This disturbed her, for she loved them and she did not
want to become like her mother. These conflicts brought her into
therapy.

Early in therapy, the Madwoman emerged in her dreams:

> I am with some ruffians, outside the shabby house of an older
> woman in her sixties. Suddenly the woman comes outside,
> holding two cats that look like mine. To our shock, the older
> woman viciously bites off the heads and the limbs of the cats,
> who are afraid and don't defend themselves. We stand
> paralyzed and do not know how to respond to this hideous
> violence. I awake in horror.

The cats symbolized to Constance the natural, instinctive side of
her feminine self. Their lack of defense against this Madwoman
reminded her of her inability to defend herself against her mother.
The Madwoman of Constance's dream resembled the Maenads of
Greek legend, discussed earlier, who could destroy by tearing off the
heads and limbs of babies and animals (as in the dream) or nurture
wild animals at their breasts. The Maenads also symbolized the wild
energy to rip the cage apart.

While this dream disturbed Constance, it also announced the
presence of a character inside herself—an inner Madwoman who
could destroy or create and who could help Constance to break out
of the cage. She could see how this mad, feminine figure had been
internalized as a mirror image of her Mad Mother. But blaming her
mother for her own troubled life would not solve her problems. The
Maenads showed the two directions—destruction and creation.
Somehow Constance had to face the interior Madwoman, work
through her rage, and redirect that energy into a positive force.

Once when Constance was using spontaneous active imagination, an image of a female alligator appeared. The alligator grabbed
Constance in its huge jaws, holding her in a fetal position. Afraid
and immobilized, she asked the alligator, which she saw as an animal image of the Madwoman, what it wanted. The alligator replied,
"Your energy," and spewed Constance out of its mouth. Through
this imaginal process, she clearly experienced and felt, on the conscious level, the way in which the Madwoman was eating up her
energy, just as her mother had devoured her as a child. Constance
also saw that the alligator could symbolize the capacity to protect

her creative energy, for the alligator mother can also symbolize the protective aspect of the Mad Mother who waits for her offspring's maturity, their readiness to be on their own. It will hold its hatchlings in its mouth until they are ready for the world and will attack anyone—particularly the father alligator, which often eats its own progeny. Again, Constance was reminded of the wild and primitive female energy within herself, needing to be transformed.

The dream, together with active imagination and much conscious work on her inner fears, showed Constance how to go out into the world and develop herself—something her mother had never done. In the beginning she had been unconscious of being caged, but during the therapeutic process she became conscious of the limitations she was making for herself, and she felt the pain of being trapped. By going through the suffering involved in her descent into the chaos of her unconscious, she realized how important freedom was to her and how much she wanted to develop herself professionally. The combination of working internally via therapy and externally by developing her career in the world helped her define her self-identity, who she was, and what she needed, which had been left unformed as a result of her chaotic childhood.

This new identity required Constance to continue to work consciously to differentiate herself from her mother as well. Like many daughters, Constance had an unconscious connection with her mother. When her mother was angry with her, even though they were separated by thousands of miles, Constance would feel her mother's rage in her own body. Like her mother, Constance was subject to frequent spells of sickness and depression, which was connected in some ways to the chaos of her mother's life. So long as Constance was trapped in this symbiosis with her mother, she was not her own person. Her existence seemed like a living death. She felt bad much of the time, and when she didn't feel bad, she seemed cut off from her feelings. To change this pattern, she knew she had to cut the symbiotic cord—and that she needed her own Madwoman energy to do this.

Constance began to take responsibility for her own life and actions. By sorting out what she didn't want in her life, she was able to determine what she did want. She was able to give up the illusion that she needed others to define her own character. She learned what was acceptable to her in her relationship with her mother, and what was not. Constance became firm and drew limits and boundaries with her mother. She refused to assume the guilt that her mother tried to foist on her and to expose herself to unnecessary criticism. She was no longer afraid of her mother and her emotional extremes, for she had identified, acknowledged, and integrated her own mad energy.

In her marriage Constance also felt less trapped, less unhealthily and inextricably entwined with her husband and her children. She saw she had many potential energies in herself to develop. A dream confirmed this feeling of promise of her developing self: In the dream, diamonds came out of her mouth. When she awoke, she realized that she could let go of her previous insecurities about her ability to talk and communicate, a recurrent fear that dated back to her late teens, when her mother had thrown her out of the house. At work she found that not only could she express herself easily, she could write excellent reports. Now able to formulate and embody her ideas, she was also able to envision being a writer once again, something she had dreamed of as a child.

During her therapy, Constance had many "house" dreams. For her, the symbol of the house was rich with meanings, including the body, the self, and the inner home. It also signified the cage in which, as a child, she had felt trapped in a dysfunctional family and later, as an adult, bored and stifled in her marriage. In the beginning of her therapy, Constance often dreamed of shacks and ill-kept houses like the ones in which the old Madwoman who dismembered the cats had lived. Often, perverted old men who lurked around these shabby houses tried to attack and abuse her. These shabby and threatening houses symbolized aspects of the cage in which she felt trapped. As her therapy progressed, Constance began to dream of newer homes, some of which were unique and quite fantastic in design. Once she dreamed of two massive cathedrals sitting above the small cagelike house where she lived. Enormous refurbishing was already in progress in one of the cathedrals. This dream confirmed not only the changes that Constance was undergoing but promised an even greater spiritual attainment and dimension of being and expanded her awareness of who she could become. Her former caged-in, low self-esteem was being replaced with an appreciation of who she really was and the new woman she was becoming.

Toward the end of her work in therapy, Constance had a healing dream that filled her with wonder and joy. Another house dream, it showed the healing and metamorphosis of the Madwoman and the

Caged Bird aspects of her life into a woman in touch with her inner-most nature.

> I am walking in nature, and I see a wooden cottage at the
> edge of the wilderness. The house is open so I enter. Inside
> the house are beautiful rugs woven in earthtone colors—
> brown, orange, and green. A woman in the house offers me
> tea in lovely porcelain cups. Older than I, she is serene and
> nurturing, as are her surroundings. I feel I belong here and
> am peaceful in this woman's presence and in the warm
> atmosphere of the house. As I look out of the many cottage
> windows that open onto the wilderness, I delight in seeing so
> many different animals—deer, cats, and all kinds of birds. The
> wild animals are friendly and look into the home unafraid.
> The deer are alert; the birds chirp and fly; wise owls look in
> too. I feel a mystical communion with the wild animals that
> want to join us in this home. The older woman of the cottage
> is whole, sensual, and earthy. I am glad she has no false
> persona or plastic flashiness about her. Her life feels
> congruent to me, reflected by the natural and colorful
> warmth of her home, which is open to Nature outside.

For Constance, this woman, living in her element, symbolized the transformation of the interior Madwoman into a serene, mature woman, at home in the wild and before the hearth, open and free, at one with herself.

OPENING THE CAGE

How can women open the cage door to free their feminine spirit for full flight? The first step in this transformation is to identify the particular cage in which we are trapped and acknowledge being in it. Through images, dreams can help us discover the outlines and dimensions of the cage in which we are caught, the way in which we are trapped, and sometimes even the way to freedom. For example, one woman, Carla, dreamed that friends gave her a yellow bird in a cage for her wedding anniversary. She wondered why the bird never sang. Then one day she heard a small peep. When she listened more closely, the bird was saying, "I'm unhappy, I'm an addict," over and over again. Upon awakening, Carla was confused. What did the dream mean? She herself was not addicted to alcohol. She eventually realized that her addiction was codependency and that the dream was pointing to the fact that she felt trapped in her marriage. By working with the dream, she began to free herself from her dependent behaviors and create a better relationship with her husband.

Another woman, Jill, was trying to decide whether to get a divorce. Her husband was a wonderful man, but she felt stifled in their marriage. For excitement, Jill became involved in an affair, then felt trapped by the need to choose between the two men. She started having recurrent dreams about a bird trapped in a cage. Sometimes in her dream she left the cage door open so the bird could fly around the house. She was afraid she'd forget to shut the windows and the bird would fly away altogether and get hurt. She was also afraid that with the cage door open, a cat would creep in and kill the bird. Of course, Jill was the dream bird in the cage who desperately wanted to be free but was afraid to fly on her own. The dreams continued until Jill developed enough confidence to trust that the bird would be safe and that she could leave the cage door open. She decided to leave both the marriage and the affair, which had become a substitute for developing herself.

Sometimes the cage in a dream symbolizes the attachment to a parent. A single woman, Renée, desperately wanted to get married and had a dream that she was a little girl captive in a huge cage with big black bars. She called for help and saw her father riding a horse freely in a green pasture nearby, but he did not seem to hear her. Renée struggled, trying to get out of the cage, but the cage toppled over; she was still trapped inside. Through working on the dream, Renée realized that the cage in which she was trapped was her longing for the father, who had abandoned her, and that she feared being abandoned by every man she loved. Her fears kept her from allowing intimacy to develop. Thus, she was caught in a self-fulfilling prophecy; her relationships with men never materialized. The dream "caught" Renée's attention, and she tried to understand how these dynamics worked within herself so she could transform them and free herself from the "cage" of her fears.

Dreams can also help parents see how they are caged and in turn encage their children. A mother named Margaret, who was caught by the Ice Queen pattern, dreamed that she was trapped in a huge drainpipe. When she tried to get out, she found that the ends were frozen over with ice that she could not crack. Upon awakening, Margaret realized that she had not been able to cry about a depression from which one of her daughters had been suffering, a situation that was draining her energy. She realized that her feelings were frozen, just as her own mother's had been. Margaret decided to enter joint counseling with her daughter. Suddenly in one session she cried, and her tears melted the "ice" between them. Both mother and daughter were able to hug each other for the first time in months. After they cried, the "frozen bars" melted, and the daughter's depression started to lift.

A bird in the cage can also be a dream motif for men. One jealous man, Bob, tried to keep his wife caged. But this woman was independent and demanded her freedom, talking of divorce. One night Bob dreamed that she had died and lay in a coffin shaped just like a cage. A voice told him that if he would open the cage doors, she would be able to fly freely and return to life. At first, he was afraid to open the cage door, but then he realized that if she were free to fly out, she would also be free to return of her own accord. In the dream Bob opened the cage door; in his marriage he began to do the same. He recognized that his own jealousy was behind the desire to keep her locked in the cage. By digging deeper within himself, he saw that his own behavior had been shaped by his father's jealousy of the close relationship Bob had with his mother. Bob was repeating his father's pattern—wanting to be the center of his wife's life and resenting anyone who claimed her attention. He also wanted to hold on to the tight bond he had with his own mother. By putting his wife in a cage, he had been seeking unconsciously the all-encompassing love of a mother. As he began to relax his demands on his wife, she felt freer and their marriage began to improve.

Dreams can also reflect the process of breaking out of a Caged Bird pattern of behavior. One woman had recurring dreams that she was a bird trapped in a cage. But as she began to see and understand herself more clearly, she had dreams in which the cage became more spacious and she had more room to fly around. Eventually, she dreamed that the cage door opened and the bird was able to fly safely around the outer edges of the cage. To her, this symbolized the gradually increasing freedom that she was struggling to gain for herself.

Opening the cage door requires breaking through our denial that we are trapped. To do this, we must recognize what we gain from remaining caged. For some women, living out the Caged Bird syndrome may allow them to indulge themselves as victims. In this way, they justify their own passivity and avoid facing the challenge of change. While their cages most likely were constructed in the past, by their parents or their culture, staying in the cage is, in most cases, their choice. Opening the cage door takes courage and commitment. It requires the death of an old identity, an old addiction, or old securities, and a rebirth with the decision to fly adventurously into the unknown.

Sometimes the cage door has to be forced open. Here especially, the Madwoman's power comes into play. Often it takes rage to shatter the barrier. We may need to tap into our anger at the external forces that have held us imprisoned, but we also need to acknowledge our own anger toward ourselves for having remained victimized. Therapy can help us deal with the fear of our own anger by providing a safe haven for confronting our anger. In therapy, we can metaphorically construct a safe temporary room that connects to our anger with a door that can be opened under supervised, controlled conditions to help a woman become accustomed to her anger and learn how to handle it. Different kinds of therapy can also help us identify the exact nature of the cage that imprisons us. For example, in art therapy addicts often picture themselves in cages surrounded by fire, symbolizing the addictive process that consumes its victim.

Abused women must acknowledge that they are abused and have the courage to open the door and leave. Until they are able to admit their own rage, however, they will remain victims of the abuser. Many need to recognize that their fear of their own anger often keeps them from leaving. Yet even after making the decision to leave, women are unprotected by the legal system and often are further threatened, beaten, or even killed by abusive men. We all need to help women find agencies that can help them and continue to work to try to improve social conditions. By working against such abuses, both in ourselves and in the social system, we work on opening the cage door.

After anger has been acknowledged and expressed, we need to transform it before it hardens into resentment, depression, illness, or anxiety, which can become another cage with even bigger bars.

One of the Caged Bird's penchants is concealment. Remember Mrs. Bridge and how she hid her anger, even from herself. By hiding her own frustration, she failed her friend Grace, thus missing an opportunity to heal herself. When a woman shares her story with other women, acknowledging the pain and suffering but envisioning a different ending, she creates a new story through which she can change and grow, thus helping herself as well as others.

The Caged Bird experience can teach a woman many secret strengths, such as patience and endurance, qualities essential to all creative growth, as well as diplomacy, vulnerability, and gentleness. The sense of stability, limits, and order that the Caged Bird gains is another positive and necessary tool for growth. Learning the appropriate times to express and to contain feelings is essential to a mature and healthy life. If the cage can be transformed into an open and healthy home that offers balance and stability, it can become a nurturing nest.

The following fairy tale, by a modern woman, is a touching expression of one way the Caged Bird is likely to develop and then break free from the cage to build her own nest.

There once was a little bird
who lived with a King.
The King gave her mother a wide gold band
her mother stayed with him forever.

The little bird charmed the old King
because she learned so fast
and because she flew in perfect circles.
However, she would lose herself
in thrilling reveries
and exultation around sunbeams.
Thus she would fly in erratic, erotic,
imperfect (semi-)circles.

The King would anger
and smack her on her back—
on the right side—just where her wing attached.
He loved her tender, peachy, underdown,
which shone as she dove and spun . . .
but he broke her wing with his disappointment.

One day a distant young King approached.
He took her away, to his own cagedom,
banding her with heavy gold.
There she healed.
He adored her flights of fancy
and gazed in splendored admiration
at her peachy underfeathers.
He let the cage door open
and she flew all around—
building nests in apricot and crabapple and under juniper.
Each nest so . . . splendidly, aromatically different.
The young King would have to reach for the little bird
each time she ventured out.
And since a wicked mother
had placed a thorn within his heart—
it pained his heart with each reach.
It infuriated his Kingliness so much
that he began hitting on her mended wing.
She—of course—would fly off to one of her nests to recoup.
He—of course—would suffer in bringing her back,
and punish her once again.

Finally, she took one trip too many,
and the King slammed the cage door
on her (little) back.

He found other little birds
who would not fly off to private nests
who would choose to stay caged and entertain him.

Our Bird—
with the rebroken wing—
flew off
to build her very own mud nest.
She lined this nest
with the peachy down shed beneath her feathers.
She began to mend . . . and to spin . . .
once again.
This time . . .
with no one to please,

no one to bring her home,
and no one to punish her
but her self.

The Long Way Home

One of the most extraordinary examples of integrating the Mad-woman's spiritual strength with the transformation of the Caged Bird was shown in the film *The Long Way Home.* Here we see the plight of two caged women—one a wealthy white suburban house-wife, the other her black maid. Set in the South, it illustrates the struggle of blacks against the cage of segregation. Protesting segre-gation on the buses, the blacks decide to boycott the bus system. They choose the harder way—to walk instead. The black maid (played by Whoopi Goldberg) walks every day the long way to work, even when she is exhausted and her feet are blistered. Neither martyred nor complaining, she simply adds her individual strength to the cause. She is an earthy, stable woman, nurturing to her family and to her employer's little girl. But she is caught, by being black, in the cage of prejudice.

Her white employer (played by Sissy Spacek) learns to admire her maid's strength and simple commitment. Remembering the love and devotion of her own black nanny who had nurtured her as a child, she secretly empathizes with the maid's struggle. At first the white woman tries to help the maid for her own convenience; some days she drives the black woman to work so she can be on time. Caged in her own marriage and suburban consciousness, leading a stifled life dominated by her ambitious husband, initially she hides the fact that she is helping her black maid.

White retaliation against the blacks mounts in the community, and when her husband discovers what the white Caged Bird has been doing, he shouts and criticizes her for being weak and foolish. But then she begins to think for herself. When she learns there is a carpool system to help the blacks, she asks her maid about it. Wisely, the maid gives her the facts, neither encouraging her nor asking her to help. The maid calmly voices her conviction that in time the blacks, through their spiritual commitment, will win equality step by step. She tells the white woman the difficulties and ostracism she would face as such a volunteer.

Now conscious of the constricted life she has been living, the white woman decides to confront her husband. Furious, he threatens to leave her if she continues to drive the black maid back and forth to work. Despite his threat, she breaks out of his restrictions and acts as her inner feelings and values dictate, deciding to do the carpool work as well.

Meanwhile, the white men of the town band together to threaten the blacks in their fight for rights. One night an angry mob of men with weapons approach the black women waiting at the carpool parking lot for their rides. Seeing the white woman who is there to help the blacks, they threaten her and demolish her car. Then they beat up a black man standing nearby. Tension mounts as the hostile white men move toward the black women.

For a moment the two groups—the white men and the black women—stare at each other in silence. Then the black maid moves forward slowly, standing her ground before the threatening mob of men. The menace of imminent violence mounts. From the group of women behind her, she is joined by a black sister, who has a crazy look in her eyes. The mad-eyed black woman holds the courageous maid's hand, as though it were an anchor, and the two start singing a spiritual. Astounded, the men look in fear and amazement, seeing the mad, determined look in the women's eyes. As the men hesitate, the other black women sing with their sisters, joining to face the menacing men. In tears, the white woman joins her black sisters in the line of singing women. Singing together, all the women, black and white, stand their ground as the white men back off in disbelief, afraid of this manifestation of strong feminine spiritual energy. When integrated with a grounded feminine spirit, the Madwoman's energy can overcome the most powerful enemy.

As human beings, we live in the paradox of our need for freedom and independence and our desire for security and safety. We need to accept certain limitations, but learn not to live inside a cage of stifling conventions. We all have imprisoned parts of ourselves. We are all Caged Birds to some degree. We must adopt different roles, wear different clothes for different occasions to live in society effectively. Jung calls this necessary ego adaptation the *persona* or mask that we wear to face the outer world. We need to learn to don the mask that reflects most truly who we are, rather than those that someone else wants or expects us to wear. Even if we love our work, whether it is at home with children or in the outer world, parts of us that are not as clearly developed want and need to be expressed. If we reduce ourselves to one role or identity, rather than try to integrate the many sides of ourselves into a whole and healthy human life, we become our own jailors. This is when the Madwoman is likely to emerge within.

While I was writing about Mrs. Bridge, I myself felt anxious. Why, I wondered, would I become anxious, since my life as an independent professional woman is so different from Mrs. Bridge's life? What part of me was caged? Then I realized that beneath Mrs. Bridge's tranquil exterior, beneath the boredom and anxiety she tries so desperately to suppress, rages the Madwoman's prophetic concern about the modern condition of human existence. The shadow of war and destruction that she felt fifty years ago has not disappeared. Rather, it exists more starkly for us today in the image of worldwide environmental devastation. We are all Caged Birds in our finitude and our mortality on earth. Only if we admit to ourselves and each other that we are selfishly obsessed with security, material comfort, victory, and control, to the exclusion of the rights of other living things and our own humanity, can we actively try to stop destroying the planet. If we can open our cages of self-justification, we can allow the spirit within us to fly free.

4

THE MUSE

*In a way, her strangeness, her naiveté,
her craving for the other half of her
equation was the consequence of an
idle imagination. Had she paints, or
clay, or knew the discipline of the
dance, or strings; had she anything to
engage her tremendous curiosity and
her gift for metaphor, she might have
exchanged the restlessness and
preoccupation with whim for an
activity that provided her with all she
yearned for. And like any artist with
no art form, she became dangerous.*

—TONI MORRISON, *Sula*

IN MY YOUNGER DAYS, I HAD FANTASIES OF BEING A MUSE. I
had heard of Madame de Staël and Alma Mahler,
whose creative salons attracted geniuses from all
over Europe. More to my own liking was Lou
Andreas-Salomé, who inspired the poet Rilke and
the philosopher Nietzsche, but who also wrote herself and later trained with Freud to be a lay analyst.
How wonderful it would be, I reflected, to inspire a
great poet or artist to create a work of beauty and
spiritual meaning and in that way to contribute to
the world!

Being a Muse is appealing because it has been an
acceptable role and a feminine ideal for women in
our culture throughout the ages. At the archetypal
level, as the "eternal feminine," the Muse inspires
the spirit and leads the soul on its creative journey,

as Beatrice did for Dante. To inspire means to breathe life into, to ignite the creative fire.

Women in touch with Muse energy tend to be mysterious and spiritual; their inspiration comes from love. They enjoy others' creativity and genuinely encourage it. Generous, they tend to give without expecting in return. Often they are trusting, fresh, receptive, and caring, and their simplicity opens the way for new images and ideas to develop. They value beauty and can create an emotional atmosphere through a special shower of love that allows imaginative life to flourish. The difficulty for these women is that often they inspire others at their own expense. When a man wants a woman to inspire him but not to create herself, he can make her mad. Living the role of a Muse or *femme inspiratrice* can be difficult and frustrating or a way to remain passive.

According to Jung, women who are Muses have a special capacity to reflect the "anima" or the feminine spirit or soul of the man. Like chameleons, they change and blend into the backdrop on which the man wants them to be seen instead of being themselves. They become mere reflections, mirror images of another's wishes and desires. Such a woman does not know who she is because she has not developed a relationship to her feminine center.

THE INNER MUSE

Who were the muses originally? What is the purpose and underlying quality of the muse energy? In Greek mythology, the muses were honored for their ability to create beautiful songs and poems. The muses were the daughters of Zeus and Mnemosyne, the goddess of memory, who knew all that had happened since the beginning of time and told it in stories. The muses took Mnemosyne's tales of creation and the trials and tribulations of heroines and heroes and transmuted them into verse and lyrics so humans would not forget them. Each of the nine daughters had a unique gift of turning her mother's memories into a different form. Terpsichore was the muse of dance and song; Calliope of epic poetry; Erato of lyric poetry and hymns; Clio of history; Urania of astronomy; Euterpe of the flute; Polyhymnia of the mimic art; Melpomene of tragedy; and Thalia of comedy. The muses could sing in chorus so harmoniously that the birds were said to remain silent in awe to hear them. They could inspire kings and entertain the immortals. They were patrons of the creative and intellectual arts. And they knew how to lessen human anguish. The mortal poet Orpheus, who sang and played the lyre so beautifully that he could enchant even the rulers of the underworld, was the son of Calliope, the muse of epic poetry.

Both male and female poets—for example, Yeats and Rilke, May Sarton and Anna Akhmatova—acknowledge the Muse as an interior, feminine source of creativity. Artists of all kinds understand that the Muse symbolizes a transcendent energy that cannot be controlled. They treasure the energy and give thanks when they have it and lament when they lose it.

Actual women who have invoked the muse energy, inspiring others and creating as well, include Lou Andreas-Salomé; Maud Gonne who inspired Yeats yet worked for Ireland's political freedom; Anais Nin, who inspired Henry Miller yet wrote novels and validated the genre of journal writing from the source of feminine feeling and intuition; Simone de Beauvoir, who inspired the philosopher Sartre and wrote a ground-breaking feminist analysis of women's condition as well as many novels and journals. In the film *Casablanca,* Ingrid Bergman portrayed the loving Muse who inspires a man to change his life and work for good. Bergman also inspired filmgoers all over the world who admired and adored her, yet in the 1950s, when she followed her heart to live with the Italian film director Roberto Rossellini, whom she had also inspired, the puritanical American audience was aghast and chastised her. For years she was ostracized by Hollywood. Toward the end of her life she inspired filmgoers again through her personal courage and integrity and by showing in her portrayal of Golda Meir in *Golda* how Muse energy can be integrated with that of the Revolutionary to work for social justice.

THE MISUSE OF THE MUSE

The inspirational role of the Muse can also be misused for destructive purposes, however. The celebrated image of the beautiful Helen of Troy, whose face launched a thousand ships, is an example of the Muse misappropriated for war. The propaganda of warring nations often features images and songs of women idealized to provoke patriotic feelings. Rainer Werner Fassbinder's film *Lili Marleen* dramatizes the tragic fate of a beautiful and loving singer who was used in this way. In a commercial society ruled by greed for money, fame, success, and power, the Muse can be reduced to an external means for gain and thus abused, as in the misrepresentations of the Muse as a glamour or sex object in advertisements, on billboards, and by television and Hollywood. The inner inspirational energy of the Muse becomes externalized and debased into a one-sided image for women to emulate and for men to possess—an image that fits the male fantasy and that many women try to achieve, to the detriment of their physical and mental health.

The misuse of the Muse can feed the destructive side of the Madwoman: Women hungry for love literally starve themselves to be the thin, glamorous model that feeds male fantasies, often suffering from anorexia and bulimia—prevalent and dangerous diseases for women in our time. Some undergo psychological and physical tortures—face-lifts, liposuction, even the remodeling of their very bones. Psychologically, they sell their soul to their loves in their desire to *be* the Muse. They sacrifice their own creative lives to support a man's efforts to attain fame and fortune, or to inspire his artistic work, as Picasso's lovers did, or to feed his narcissism. Consider the woman who neglects her own creativity to encourage her husband's projects or to provide him with the good feelings and the home life he idealizes.

Resenting such sacrifices, usually unconsciously, some women turn their anger inward in the form of various addictions such as shopping, sex, alcohol, food, and codependent behavior. Others rebel against the ideal of the beautiful but passive women whose life revolves around attracting and inspiring a man. Instead, they actively seek power over others. These women often repress or suppress their own inner Muse. For them, the Muse remains a shadow figure, and they may resent that quality in women who embody it. Often they live out the patterns of the cold Ice Queen and the fire-breathing Dragon Lady, who manipulate and abuse both men and Muse-type women as well as their own potential for creativity. The siren who seduces men, then coldly destroys them, is a shadowy Muse who combines characteristics of the Ice Queen and the Dragon Lady. Films such as *Jules and Jim* and the German classic *The Blue Angel* show this mad manifestation of the Muse energy turned destructive.

ON THE PEDESTAL: THE MADWOMAN AS MUSE

The Muse can also be seen in any woman who tries to embody her lover's idealized fantasies of women instead of developing herself. She may accept her husband's or boyfriend's vision of what their relationship is without ever asserting her own needs or nature. She may also be a Caged Bird, caught in society's and her family's views of how a good wife or nice girl or good mother should behave. To the external eye, these women may seem happy in their secure roles; confident, socially successful, adored, and even idolized by their husbands, friends, and lovers. However, Muses are also often the object of envy, sometimes even hated by their "less fortunate" sisters. Although they may receive lavish attention and luxurious presents from the men they entice and may even be supported financially by their husbands or lovers, their inner self-esteem and dignity is frequently shaky. For they usually realize, if unconsciously, that their worth in the role they have chosen depends entirely on the projections of their men or the culture or the vision someone else has of them rather than on their own nature or independently formed identity.

A traditional Muse, whether she is a mistress, wife, lover, or mother, lives her life around another and reflects his ideals and aspirations, his wishes and desires, and sometimes even his dark and dangerous passions. A Muse may be a slave to a man's madness— and can be driven into a complex, frustrated, mad state of mind. A Muse may be charismatic to one person, to a few people, or even to an entire culture. Whether she is the golden goddess or the darker femme fatale, whether she is a cultural icon or an ordinary housewife, her life is created in another's dreams, not her own. She belongs to the person or culture she has captivated and who has put her on the pedestal.

Modern-day manifestations of the Muse include the roles of actress, singer, cheerleader, beauty queen, model, and the superstar who becomes a cultural icon. Teachers and therapists in the healing arts, as well as intuitive facilitators of the creative arts, often act as Muses too. The mistress or wife who fosters her lover's creativity at the expense of her own can be seen as an evocation of the Muse, as can the student who inspires her professor, the young secretary of a corporate executive, the wife who believes in the genius of a young graduate student and sometimes supports him through school, and the society wife of a wealthy man who takes care of his feelings and whose life is lived wholly in his schedules. Although I am describing the external manifestations of the Muse as a woman living out her life for a man, the same pattern can occur in homosexual relationships, both gay and lesbian, as well as in heterosexual relationships in which the man serves as Muse for his wife, lover, or mother.

Men are often Muses for their mothers. Sometimes they try to live out their mothers' unexpressed creativity. One man, Charles, attempted to please his mother this way and found that no matter what he produced in his work and life, his mother criticized his creations. Soon Charles found himself blocked creatively. His dreams frightened him when the Madwoman started to appear in them and attack him. The Madwoman in the dreams helped Charles realize that he needed to get in touch with his own anger at the way he had become his mother's Muse, internalized her criticisms, and interfered with his own creativity. Another man, Alan, who had been a Muse for his mother, grew up in the Morman Church. When Alan discovered he was gay, the role of Muse was shattered; his sexuality did not fit with the Church's or his mother's ideals. By getting in touch with the rage of his inner Madwoman, Alan was able to shake off the golden expectations of his Church and family. Although he was regarded as "mad" by the Church collective, relating to the interior Madwoman helped Alan to keep his core identity and separateness. He took strength from the Madwoman and began to distinguish the spiritual feminine for himself rather than merely keeping society's ideas of an appropriate spontaneity.

Men often give themselves away to a Muse whom they marry instead of forging their own creative identity, perhaps believing that women are by nature more able to define their lives for them by nurturing them, or that women are inherently more artistic than men. Michael's first two wives were Muses for him. He encouraged their creativity but did not commit to his own art. He thought that each of these women was more finely attuned to spirit and beauty and to aesthetic and moral values. In each relationship he was the practical partner, supporting the woman financially while he neglected his own creative work. At the same time, he tried to put each wife in a cage, for he wanted to obtain social prestige from her talent and beauty. He wrote poems to his first wife, who inspired him and was his private audience. Basking in her private admiration, he did not do the work of refining his poems so they could be published. He supported the musical talent of his second wife, but he wanted her to sing in their home like a Caged Bird. Both wives remained Muses but failed to commit themselves fully to their respective arts. They lived off Michael's adoration and practical support. Neither of his wives committed fully to her own creativity. Both marriages ended in divorce. After much self-analysis, Michael realized he had developed a great deal of residual anger toward his wives, for he felt his support had been devalued by them. His anger toward his Muses revealed the face of an inner Madwoman in himself who was angry that he was not committing to his own creative work. Michael began to withdraw his projections onto beautiful inspiring women and develop his own art. He joined a poetry-writing group, established his own writing schedule, and sent out his poems, which received public recognition. Relating now to his own inner Muse and creating for her, he was able to remarry and be true to his own aesthetic and spiritual values.

A nun who left her role of Muse in the papal patriarchy by accepting the power of her inner Madwoman expressed her transformation as follows:

I have given my life to ministry in the Catholic Church,
working under a priest, in a patriarchal system. I have been a
nun for thirty-four years. The man in my life has been the
patriarchal Church. The religious order I belonged to was the
patriarchal church in my home, in my personal life. The male
pastor has needed my gifts to succeed—and I have served
him, letting go of my own leadership gifts up front to support
his leadership. In my midlife transition I have left institutional
church ministry. I will now minister in my own *center*, without
male domination.

Outwardly, the Muse may be beautiful and brilliant, charming and gracious, bewitching and beguiling, sweet and demure. Despite her alluring mystique, the rage of the Madwoman simmers within, fed by her divorce from her personal energies and desires. She feels outraged and ashamed because she has betrayed herself. In *The Second Sex,* Simone de Beauvoir pointed out the seduction and bad faith to which a woman is subject when she submits to being an admired object. In a bad-faith relationship, the Muse who lives an inauthentic life can be a slave. She becomes codependent, addicted to a dysfunctional existence in which she is cut off from her own center of creativity.

Sometimes these women are victims, pawns in the man's plans for himself and his life. Sometimes they manipulate others powerfully through their ability to mirror and charm, used by men but using them too. Sometimes a Muse takes a certain amount of control over her life. She may take a series of lovers. If she feels a man's adoration waning or coming down to human proportions, she may leave him for someone who will put her back on the pedestal. Some Muses use men to avoid being alone. If they have not developed themselves into anything but a prop or function, they feel panicked at the void they have become. A Muse may use others for whatever she wants, to gain success in her career, or she may move on to another person or place.

The bait that lures the Muse into this pattern of behavior is the sense of self-importance that she enjoys. She is idealized, seen as a living goddess or perfect wife. Living above the human dimension, in a perfect fantasy, it is hard for her to come down to earth. As Muse she is allowed—or condemned—to remain in the realm of the ideal, always in potential, rarely having to deal with the human struggle to understand. While she often has a fear of actualizing herself, of developing her innate talents and capabilities, secretlv she may hate herself for not embodying her being.

Often the Muse is a secret artist who values creativity and beauty. But to be an artist requires being an active agent of one's own life. It also requires devotion and commitment to one's art, discipline, and the struggle of hard work. If a woman remains passive and fails to develop her own artistic gifts, she may also, consciously or unconsciously, hate the lovers who keep her in this role by projecting their idealizations upon her.

Zelda Fitzgerald is a famous literary and real-life Muse. Her own literary talents were considered less important than those of her husband, F. Scott Fitzgerald, even though today certain writers believe she wrote sections of Fitzgerald's works. Scott also idealized her and used her as inspiration for many of his most memorable female characters. Zelda suffered nervous breakdowns and hospitalization as she struggled between her role as Muse and writer. Her biographer, Nancy Milford, described Zelda's madness as trying to live out the "American dream," a cultural projection that has led us and the world into mad consumerism and frenzied role-playing.

At its extreme, the Muse's inflated existence can conceal terrible feelings of inadequacy and dehumanization. In touch with this awful feeling, she sometimes dehumanizes others. Think of the numerous biographies of famous actresses that reveal their terrible tempers and their mistreatment of their children, especially their daughters. And think of our own eagerness to know the Madwomen who hide beneath those perfect figures. We are attracted by the Madwoman, drawn to her in all her forms. We seek to know her because she is so much a part of us, lurking below our surface. We see her in our most exalted cultural icons, our dark goddesses. We fear her energy because we deny her presence in ourselves. Even as we devour the stories of screen goddesses and their tantrums, however, we don't acknowledge those forces in ourselves.

The Madwoman is a rampant energy that can rage through the Muse's being—frightening her in dreams at night, intimidating her in the daytime world in the form of angry women whom she fears and who harass her, or terrifying others if she acts out the Madwoman by drunken escapades, suicidal impulses, or murderous, raging attacks on the feelings of others. Because the Madwoman draws attention to every Muse's inner conflict about being a passive mirror, many women work harder to suppress that energy. The Madwoman energy pushes for transformation; it tries to force change into stagnating circumstances, to shake us up and out of routine, unconscious behavior. And many Muses, their lives built on being at the center of others' lives, cannot face change in themselves or in their external situations.

Greta, a contemporary woman artist had the following dream, which shows the ambivalence many women feel about the emergence of the Madwoman energy.

I am in a large dining room and pull out the business card of a man I will be dating for the first time. Before leaving for the date, I look in a mirror and see red spots on my right cheek. At first I think this is an allergic reaction, but then I look at my hairline and see red crystal beads on the top of my forehead. The beads get bigger and bigger, and they are bloodred crystals. My date is outside waiting, and I wonder how I will get these off. Finally, I try to cover them. When I meet my date, I hug him, hoping he won't look at my face and notice the bloodred crystals. I awake afraid they will be seen.

Greta associated the bloodred crystals with the creative energy of spirit embodied in matter. In the dream, she was afraid they would be seen as signs of madness. She had been attending a conference on creativity in which many women had expressed their rage, particularly some older women who were feeling the loss of love and bodily touch from men. Some had been Muses in their youth, but in their current life stage they demanded something else. For women entering middle or old age, untransformed rage and grief at the loss of youth and beauty often stands in the way of their passing into fullness, into an appreciation of themselves as mature, wise women. Greta was afraid that the red crystals on her forehead would destroy her attractiveness in the eyes of men, especially if the man felt she was angry. Yet the bloodred crystals also symbolized what Greta was learning from the pain of living—a wisdom she could express in her artwork. For she was learning to contain the pain of not being seen or understood by men for who she was. Rather than acting out sexually, as she had done in the past, Greta was trying to hold her rage and grief and transform it into art. To her, the bloodred crystals symbolized her own potential to contain the passion of the Visionary Madwoman and use it as a prophetic power in her art.

Like Greta, some Muses struggle consciously in the conflict between their desire for relationships and their need for independence and their own growth. This struggle can result in personal development and individuation. But those who become trapped in the Muse role, to the detriment of their own creativity, often become frustrated and bitter. Consider the story of Alma Mahler, a beautiful and talented woman who lived in the early twentieth century, a time when women had even less opportunity than today to develop their innate gifts.

THE GOLDEN GODDESS: ALMA MAHLER

Alma Mahler was a Muse for many men. The artist Oskar Kokoschka created for her some of the most beautiful love letters in history, a series of handpainted fans that are now museum pieces.

She also inspired and was married to the composer Gustav Mahler, to the Bauhaus architect Walter Gropius, and to the poet and novelist Franz Werfel. Other men, all geniuses of their time in many different fields, fell in love with her as well. Capitalizing on her beauty and allure, Alma Mahler lived her life as a Muse. Like most Muses, she genuinely valued creativity, but she sacrificed her own to others'. Alma had wanted to compose songs, but she lived at a time when women composers had little chance to be acknowledged. Even for someone as brilliant and talented as she, Alma's beauty and charm were her main assets because she was a woman. Eventually, her inner Madwoman made herself known in Alma's psychology and behavior. Even though Alma married two Jewish men (Werfel and Mahler), she prized her Christian "Aryan" heritage and was inclined toward the extremes of fascism and anti-Semitism. Her life unfolded as though her unconscious Madwoman wanted to destroy the very men who adored her. This internal and external conflict tore at her; she became bitter about the sacrifices she had made, drank to excess, and mourned her lost beauty.

Like many Muses, Alma had been adored by her father, Emil Jakob Schindler, the most celebrated landscape painter in late nineteenth-century Austria. Alma was her father's princess, and he showered both fantasy and love upon his eldest daughter, nourishing her imagination by telling her wonderful stories. The magical house at the edge of the Vienna Woods where she grew up fed her taste for luxury and beautiful objects. "Play to allure the gods," Alma remembered her father telling her once while they were at the edge of the ocean, watching the drama of the sea's white-capped waves—from which the goddess Aphrodite is said to have arisen.[1] When she was twelve, her father died, but her robust and practical mother always nurtured her.

When her mother remarried an art dealer, Alma was thrust into Vienna's social circle of artists, many of whom courted her, including her music teacher, Alexander von Zemlinsky, and Gustav Klimt, the famous painter. Often called "the most beautiful girl in Vienna," Alma had a magical charm and was usually the center of attention at social affairs. To compensate for a hearing problem that she tried to hide, she would listen raptly to others, directing her big blue eyes on one person, who would feel enormously flattered. Alma thus developed the art of nurturing and soothing the male ego.

At twenty-two, she met Gustav Mahler. Twenty years her senior and debt-ridden, the famous composer had converted to Christianity to preserve his career. Despite these differences, Alma was drawn to Mahler. She was talented musically and had written many songs by this time. Enchanted by Alma's youth, beauty, and intelligence, Mahler proposed to her, but on the condition that she be his wife, not his colleague. Mahler had no interest in her songs. In a love letter, he wrote her: "You must give yourself to me *unconditionally,* shape your future life, in every detail, entirely in accordance with my needs and desire nothing in return save my *love.* . . ." [2] Despite her intense desire to be a composer, Alma decided to marry Mahler, adapting her life to his strict composing routine, protecting him from interruptions, arranging finances, and copying his compositions.

Although Gustav was pleased, Alma felt deprived. In her diary she called him egocentric and confessed her suffering—that she loved her own art and wanted to resume it. Like the Caged Bird, Alma felt imprisoned by home, children, and her role as practical partner. She resented being treated like a servant and child by Mahler, yet she continued to be his Muse, nurturing his creative career and giving birth to two daughters. After their oldest daughter died at five, however, Alma became ill and depressed. Mahler's health also suffered. Worrying whether she was still attractive to men, she wrote of her need for love and life. Panic attacks, melancholy, and a series of nervous breakdowns began to plague her. Life with Mahler taxed her nerves, and the doctor ordered a long rest cure at a spa. Dependent on Alma, Mahler feared he might not be able to endure the separation.

At the spa, she became fascinated by a handsome young architect, Walter Gropius, who fell madly in love with her. Gropius even proposed to her in a letter to Mahler, as though Alma were his daughter. Alma remained loyal, but Gustav was jealous, fearing he would lose her. When he consulted Sigmund Freud, the psychoanalyst told him that Alma had loved her father so much that she could love only another father-figure like Gustav. Freud added that Mahler unconsciously sought in Alma, who was often ill, his own adored but ailing and careworn mother. When, at Freud's suggestion, Mahler attended more to Alma, even listening to her songs and insisting she start composing, she said it was too late to commit herself seriously to her music.

Mahler died in 1911, after ten years of marriage, leaving his thirty-one-year-old widow financially secure. Soon many admirers appeared, including the promising artist Oskar Kokoschka. Seven years younger than Alma, Kokoschka idealized women and would fall hopelessly in love with them. He was fascinated with the young widow, who seemed lonely and beautiful in the tragedy of her mourning, and he seemed to hear her sing Isolde's *"Liebestod"* for him alone.

A passionate tryst began between Alma the Muse and Kokoschka the genius. In their fantasy, she was the woman who would save Kokoschka, as in Wagner's opera *The Flying Dutchman*. Wanting to merge with Alma and be her one and only, Oskar was jealous of any potential lover and even of any friend to whom Alma gave time and energy. He even signed his letters with both their names as one— Alma Oskar Kokoschka.[3] Her very aura gave him his being.

After she told him she would not marry him until he had painted a masterpiece, Kokoschka painted love-letter fans for her. Alma was the beautiful muse in many of his paintings, including the famous masterwork *Die Windsbraut (The Bride of the Wind),* a painting of two lovers who lie on a bed of swirling colors. The woman (Alma) is much larger than her lover and is asleep on his shoulder, while the man (Kokoschka) lies anxiously awake. Oskar once wrote to Alma: "My Alma, I love you more than I love myself. . . . I must have you for my wife soon, or else my great talent will perish miserably. You must revive me at night like a magic potion. . . . You are the Woman and I am the Artist. . . . I have seen how strong you can make me and what I'll amount to when this force is constantly active. You revive useless people, and I, the one you are destined for, should I go wanting?"[4] About this time, Oskar painted a mural of himself surrounded by serpents in Hell, while Alma rose in flames to Heaven. In letters he wrote of hopelessness and death, implying that the responsibility for his life was in Alma's hands.

Alma wrote in her diary that she knew each person had to find his or her own strength, acknowledging that the unconscious desires that had fired her life and led her to Gustav could lead her back to music now. But her energies still went to her romance with Oskar. She became pregnant with his child, but when Oskar could not tolerate Gustav's death mask in the home, Alma arranged for an abortion.

Although Alma was fascinated with Oskar all her life, she could not bear his dependence on her, after having lived with Mahler's. She wanted freedom, but she was still ambivalent and uncomfortable about being alone. The two traveled and met in romantic places all over Europe for many years. Continually vacillating between her role as Oskar's fascinating Muse and her wish to focus on her own development and music, Alma located Walter Gropius, the young architect who had proposed to her. She convinced him that she loved him, and he fell in love with her again. The unhappy Oskar joined the military and departed for war. Caught between her attractions to Kokoschka and Gropius, Alma chose to marry the latter, whose talent and handsome "Aryan" appearance won her. With him, she hoped to find herself again. For a while, she was happy and bore him a daughter, Manon.

Alma initiated a series of Sunday social gatherings, salons to which brilliant people were invited. Through these salons, she created an inspiring atmosphere for gifted people, but they were also another opportunity for men to admire her. At one of these salons, Alma met her next love, the poet and novelist Franz Werfel. Although Alma disliked Werfel's Jewishness and his revolutionary politics as a Social Democrat, she loved his poems and his sensitivity to music. She played music while he sang. With Werfel, she felt a soul connection that she did not have with the rigid and serious Gropius. Another passionate love affair began. Alma became pregnant; she was not sure whether the father was Gropius or Werfel. Even though Gropius was away on the front lines of war most of this time, she believed he was the father of her son, who nearly died in premature birth. Alma felt caught between the two men. In pain herself, she had great trouble asserting herself and her own feelings, afraid to hurt the feelings of others.

When her son's health weakened and she realized he would die, Alma felt guilty and considered suicide, but she lacked courage. Facing forty, fraught with conflicts, feeling that her passionate life was over, Alma decided to put on her Sunday salons again. There, dressed in a golden gown in the red music room, she wished she could forget the conflict between being Gropius's wife and Werfel's mistress. Alma finally divorced Gropius and married Werfel, even though she did not want to be the wife of another Jew. But she loved, nurtured, and provided stability for the sensitive poet. She also kept custody of Manon.

Nearly fifty, Alma was approaching menopause, worrying about

her beauty and her desirability. Her older daughter was about to
marry, but Alma was uninterested. Being a potential grandmother
did not fit her self-image. Drawn to fascism during this period, Alma
became friends with Mussolini's mistress and came under Hitler's
spell. Although the signs of danger to the Jews (and, therefore, to
Werfel) were increasing—it was 1932—she saw no reason to leave
Europe. Instead, she became entranced with a Roman Catholic
priest, who she felt was destined to be the next Cardinal of Vienna
and who saw Hitler's role as like that of Luther. The priest told her
she was the first woman to whom he had been attracted and that she
would be the last. In turn, she worshiped him and echoed his admiration for Hitler, as she had echoed the thoughts of other men.
When proscriptions against Jews were enacted and Werfel's books
were burned and Mahler's music taken, Alma kept quiet at the
priest's advice.

Then, in the late 1930s, political reality descended upon the
Werfels. If they did not go into exile, extermination threatened
them—he as a Jew, she as his wife. Alma and Franz left Vienna and
tried to settle in various places in Europe. But the Nazis kept encroaching. Bitter, Alma felt homeless, condemned to wander with
the Jews. As an "Aryan," she felt this fate was unjust and suffered a
nervous breakdown. When war erupted in France in 1940, they
joined the long lines of refugees to get visas so they could emigrate.
Luckily, although they endured months of hardship and Alma lost
most of her possessions, they were able to emigrate and begin a new
life in America.

Starting over was difficult for Alma, who was becoming increasingly rigid, bitter, and dogmatic. Her daughter Manon had died,
and Alma was becoming more and more cynical. She felt that God
must be evil. So many close to her had been taken early: her father,
Gustav, two of her three daughters, her son, and many friends and
lovers. She began to dress in black, but ever glamorous, she still
wore silk and brocade jackets, stockings, and jewels. Alma returned
to drinking Benedictine daily, a habit she had given up much earlier
at Mahler's request but that she now continued until her death at
eighty-five. Meanwhile, the flexible Werfel continued writing and
became successful. Nominated for a Nobel Prize, one of his novels,
Song of Bernadette, was made into a successful film. The couple
moved to Los Angeles. Envious of her husband's success, Alma felt

she had accomplished little. Feeling bored and hopeless, she wrote, "Nature is empty and monotonous."[5]

Franz's health became poor, and Alma, depressed and drinking daily, felt she could not live without him. But she resented nursing him and dealing with his incontinence, of which he was ashamed. In her diary she wrote, "Marriage is really like an egg, in which two people are surrounded and separated from the world."[6] After Franz died in 1945, she became distraught and anxious, taking sedatives and sleeping in the hospital bed used by Franz in his last days.

Suffering intensely from loneliness, worrying about financial security, and approaching seventy years of age, she returned to Vienna to retrieve her belongings. There she found that her stepfather, to whom she had given power of attorney, had sold her artwork and her houses. She was met with anti-Semitism by Viennese officials for having married two Jews. Bitter and alone, a widow blamed for the "sins" of the two men she had married, she was no longer the celebrated Muse.

Alma returned to Beverly Hills, where occasionally she was honored when Mahler's symphonies were played. She collected gifts and letters from her lovers, giving Kokoschka's special attention, though she always burned the ones she had written, a practice she had started years earlier. On her seventieth birthday in 1945, she was uplifted when Kokoschka sent her greetings, calling her a "wild brat" and saying that their passionate love would always be "on the stage of life" and go down through history.[7] When her daughter Anna came to California to live near her, Alma dominated her, demanding Anna's constant time and attention. In Dragon Lady style, Alma tried unsuccessfully to destroy her daughter's love relationship with horrid gossip. Then Alma moved to New York City.

Her parlor was filled with books and paintings, mostly Kokoschka's, including a favorite portrait of her. Her bedroom contained a piano, Gustav's portrait, music, and some paintings by her father. Her former housekeeper in Vienna came to America to take care of her. Alma socialized, inviting her guests to tea—that is to say, cocktails. Various works, musical and literary, were dedicated to her. She still had famous friends—Bruno Walter, Erich Maria Remarque, and Thornton Wilder among them. But when Kokoschka came to New York and asked to see her, she refused. She wanted him to remember her youth and beauty, not her aged, feeble appearance. Knowingly, Kokoschka sent her a telegram proclaiming: "Dear Alma, in my *Windsbraut* in Basel we are eternally united."[8]

By 1946, Alma's health and mind were failing. Even so, she dressed and made herself up carefully every morning. Under the illusion that she was still a beautiful young Muse at age eighty-five, believing that the Crown Prince of Austria had met her on a mountaintop and wanted her to have his child, she died.

Alma Mahler's life exemplifies the demise of the woman who remains trapped by the golden girl image. Underneath her light and shining surface brews her anger at the sacrifice of her own talents. This hot resentment at her lovers and at younger women who take her place burns through to color her personality as she ages. Bitterness and a personal, inner ugliness are the fate of many a "darling doll" who remain idle, relying on youth, charm, and beauty, failing to develop their talents and to embody their *inner* beauty.

DARK MUSES

While we often envision Muses as angelic, as inspiring golden girls, some Muses have a dark, passionate, tragic nature. The tragic Muse attracts others through her immersion in the unconscious and her creative intensity. Often the man who is inspired by this dark Muse has not acknowledged or integrated his own wild side and unknowingly seeks, through contact with this dark, mad feminine energy, to gain access to his own creativity, to the shadowy recesses of his own unconscious. The naive man projects all his own darkness onto this Muse and lives vicariously through her. Sometimes he watches her destroy herself; sometimes he allows himself to be destroyed in the process. The conflict can resonate with overtones of the Madwoman and the Judge.

The film *The Blue Angel* is a classic example of a seductive siren who manipulates an inexperienced man. In the film, an aging German professor with no life experience goes to a cabaret, where he becomes fascinated by a singer (played by Marlene Dietrich). He is seduced and gives up his profession to marry her. At first she is amused by him, but as he comes under her power, she begins to humiliate him. At her direction, he performs on the stage as a clown. Losing his mind, he crows like a rooster when he sees her kiss another man. Totally debased, he goes mad and finally dies in the classroom he abandoned.

The femme fatale of *The Blue Angel* is consciously manipulative, luring men into her seductive net and then destroying them, like the sirens of Greek mythology who lured sailors through their singing into dangerous waters and to their deaths on the rocks. But more often such a woman is trapped by a man's projection of his own dark passions onto her. She may act out a role that he designs for her, frequently bringing on her own self-destruction. Or she may be vulnerable, due to her own dark, romantic fascination with love and death, and he may unconsciously manipulate her and hurt her. The relationship of the Mexican painter Frida Kahlo to the artist Diego Rivera, had many of these tragic aspects. Imaginative women who fail to free themselves from their role as Muse may become addicted to alcohol, sex, romance, danger, or drugs. Some fall into madness.

The dark or tragic Muse is the woman who lives out a man's dark romantic side and is often used by the artist as the model of mad forces. Zelda Fitzgerald, as portrayed by her husband, Scott, in *Tender Is the Night,* is an example from our century, as are many of Picasso's models and lovers. May Morris, the model for the Pre-Raphaelite painter Dante Gabriel Rossetti, is another example. Morris, who married Rossetti and modeled for his painting of Persephone, queen of the underworld, died early as a result of her addiction to laudanum, a drug frequently prescribed by physicians of her time for wounded women suffering from emotional pain.

The dark Muse shares and shows her vulnerability, her suffering and emotional pain and her experience with depression, mental disintegration, alcoholism, or frustrated obsessive romantic and sexual longing. Often she serves as a sacrificial guide in our own descent into our dark, mad side—an inner journey that we must make for the purpose of our psychological integration, maturation, and growth. Having gone through hell herself, the dark Muse can bring the fascinated observer close to that frightening but necessary process of self-discovery and change. Marilyn Monroe, for instance, has served as a tragic Muse for our entire culture. Her vulnerability and low self-esteem, the tragedy of her insatiable longing for love, and her descent into addiction and suicide were immortalized by Arthur

Miller in *After the Fall.* Toni Wolff is another dark Muse; she was an analysand of Jung's and inspired his own descent into the unconscious, from which he returned to describe it and the process for the benefit of others. She became Jung's lover as well as one of the first women analysts to write about feminine forms of the psyche, although she wrote little and her work was tied to Jung's theories. In later life, she was left alone, the fate of many mistresses. Freud's theories were inextricably entwined with his troubled, dark Muse patients, and even today women patients fascinate their usually male therapists in Muse-like ways.

Popular singers frequently serve as dark Muses to the culture, expressing people's longings and fears, their deepest feelings. Take, for instance, Edith Piaf, Judy Garland, and Billie Holiday. These women were creative geniuses in their own right, but they all died early and tragic deaths—Garland and Piaf in the course of addiction. Billie Holiday died of a drug overdose, unattended at a hospital, rejected as an anonymous black woman. Indeed, a whole race can be used by part of society as a tragic Muse. For example, Native American Indians inspire us with their spiritual relationship to all living things. Their traditional wisdom, grounded in Nature, may ultimately help us save the earth from our destructive misuse. Yet their abuse and mistreatment is well known, most recently shown in the films *Dances with Wolves* and *Thunderheart.* Toni Morrison, in *Playing in the Dark: Whiteness and the Literary Imagination,* has pointed out how white writers and readers can use the black Africanist character as a way to think about themselves, to keep their own darkness at a distance or even to deny it altogether in themselves, another pattern of behavior that participates in the psychology of the dark Muse.

THE TRAGIC MUSE: CAMILLE CLAUDEL

The passion and intensity of the dark, tragic Muse is central to creativity, but it can also lead to isolation, despair, and paranoia, which can escalate into real madness. This is particularly likely to occur when a creative woman betrays herself and her own talents by becoming identified as a Muse for a talented man. Then her inner Madwoman, who might have led her to understand, express, and assert her creativity in the outer world, turns against her instead.

The story of the French sculptress Camille Claudel, who was a dark Muse for the sculptor Auguste Rodin, shows this process.

Born December 8, 1864, in a small village in the Champagne district of France, Camille was encouraged by her father to develop her artistic gifts. Although he was authoritarian and often ill-tempered, he valued the creative talents of his three children. He provided them all with a first-class education in Paris, even though he had to work hard and be apart from them to do so. Camille's mother, in contrast, was rigid, bourgeois, and bound to the conventions of duty. She opposed Camille's creativity at every turn. She never loved nor understood her high-spirited, temperamental oldest daughter and was blind to her art and offended by her eccentric behavior. Camille's Ice Queen mother rejected her with the coldness of a martyr.

Although her parents' continual fighting and different expectations of her made her childhood difficult, Camille thrived on her mystical love for art and Nature. She was a Muse to her younger brother Paul, who became one of France's greatest writers, influencing him powerfully in his early years. They loved to walk in the eerie moorland, awed by its strange, gigantic rocks. Only their younger sister, Louise, failed to develop her musical talents, remaining at home, subservient to their domineering mother.

As a young girl, Camille worked with clay, insisting that every member of the family pose for her. The film biography of her life shows her going out at night to dig clay in order to sculpt. Unafraid of the dark, Camille was ready to dig into the depths of her own nature to follow her creative destiny. By the age of fifteen, she had created three notable pieces, and her talent came to the attention of the sculptor Alfred Boucher, who influenced her career, educating her particularly in Florentine art.

Camille first met Rodin when Boucher recommended her to him as his most promising student. At the time Rodin, at forty, was widely discussed but not yet famous. Camille was Rodin's first female student and was regarded by many as the most creative of all his assistants. Working silently and diligently on his sculptures, she soon became his collaborator. She posed for and helped sculpt his great works, including *The Gate of Hell,* modeled for many of his sculptures, and inspired his more lyrical style when he was in a dry period. Critics say that after *Balzac,* most of Rodin's works were variations of themes from *The Gate of Hell*—the masterpiece on which he and Camille had worked together. Meanwhile, Camille was developing her own style, surpassing Rodin in her ability to cut marble.

After Rodin and Camille became lovers, Rodin rented an idyllic and romantic studio for her—an old classic building almost in ruins in the midst of a wild garden. There they met for seven years, from 1887 to 1894. They took summer trips away from Paris to spend more time with each other. All this time, Rodin also lived with a common-law wife, Rose Bauret.

Rodin genuinely cared for Camille but was unable to abandon Rose, his longtime companion, in order to marry her. Even when Camille became pregnant, Rodin was unable to leave Rose, and Camille is said to have had an abortion.[9] Camille was angry at being in this compromising position. At the turn of the century, it was scandalous to be a woman artist living alone. Financially, she was dependent upon her parents, who disapproved of the illicit liaison. Her mother and sister especially condemned Camille for her disgraceful relationship with Rodin, treating her as if she were a prostitute and accusing her of having a low moral character.

Despite all these difficulties, the relationship between Camille Claudel and Rodin lasted fifteen years. By 1893, Camille had separated her work and living accommodations from Rodin and moved to another studio, but she continued to see him, to join him on holidays and seek his advice. In 1894 she wrote a note congratulating him on his statue of Balzac. Shortly afterward, Camille stopped the correspondence, as her love for Rodin was turning to hatred. In his own way, Rodin continued to love Camille and support her in her artistry, while despairing over their separation and her increasing enmity toward him.

In addition to being a Muse for her brother and Rodin, Camille was also a Muse for the composer Claude Debussy, who fell in love with her. Camille was too attached to Rodin to reciprocate Debussy's love. Harsh words from Camille ended the relationship, which Debussy lamented in a letter: "I weep for the disappearance of the Dream of this Dream."[10] Until he died, Debussy kept her sculpture *The Waltz* on the mantelpiece of his studio. By thirty, however, Camille's romantic life had ended. Her youth, she felt, was spent. Later, she wrote to her art dealer, Eugene Blot, about the loss of her romantic youth, describing it as an epic like the *Iliad* or the *Odyssey:*

"It would require a Homer to tell it. I won't attempt to do so today and I don't want to sadden you. I have fallen into a void. I live in a world that is so curious, so strange. Of the dream that was my life, this is the nightmare."[11]

When Camille Claudel first left Rodin, she lived in her studio on the Boulevard d'Italie and decided to break with Rodin's style of art. She wanted her own art to express the ordinary world, the people she saw passing by, the street scenes of daily life, as in her sculptures *The Gossipers* and *The Old Blind Singer*. She sketched, took notes, and tried to capture psychological moods and the dress of her figures. She also painted many portraits. She worked intently, avoided social life, and refused Rodin's invitations to receptions.

At this time, Camille was living in semipoverty. Her studio was reputed to be a mess, and she had become a recluse. She begged for money to pay her rent and for the costly materials with which to sculpt. Accumulating debts for the Italian marble she needed, she was hounded by creditors. Her father and brother gave her money during this period, although they hid their aid from her mother and sister. Her sculpture was exhibited; critics wrote about her work, and collectors were interested in her art. But she refused to commercialize her art, as she felt Rodin was doing. Instead, she continued to experiment in new directions. She compared herself to Cinderella, "condemned to stay by the ashes of the chimney without the hope of ever seeing the Fairy Godmother or Prince Charming arrive to turn my rags into fashionable dresses."[12] She regarded Rodin with scorn as she saw him glorying in all his success and fame.

Her finances grew worse, and she moved to a small, dreary apartment on the Île-St. Louis, where she stayed until 1913. The once slender, beautiful Camille let herself grow heavy and disheveled. She drank and began to look much older than her age. Despite the uniqueness of her style, most of the art world and the critics still considered her merely a pupil of Rodin—a slap in the face to Camille, who was intent on differentiating herself from him. But her resentment about this was not directed at the critics. Instead, she suspected that Rodin was behind this conspiracy, and in her mind, he became her persecutor. She began to believe he was stealing her ideas, hiring people to ruin her work, and even influencing and corrupting the minds of her workmen, her models, her casters, and her friends. She began to blame Rodin, too, for using her family to persecute her. Her suspicion may have been a psychological metaphor for how she had given away her creativity, her own genius, to Rodin.

Love can turn into hatred when a person is so linked to another that she cannot separate and be herself. A part of Camille, the part that was a successful artist, was attached to the unavailable lover, Rodin. By leaving Rodin, Camille tried to extricate herself outwardly, but she was unable to separate from him internally. Most likely, many elements combined to account for her dilemma: jealousy, poverty, her addiction to alcohol, the abuse from her mother, her victimized position in society, and her lack of rightful recognition. To help herself separate from him, she substituted hatred for love.

Even though she was creating original, unique pieces, Camille became deluded that Rodin was stealing her ideas and even her actual sculptures, one by one. She accused a friend of Rodin's of breaking into her studio and stealing a sculpted figure of a woman in yellow that Camille kept there. Another time, she said a cleaning woman had slipped a narcotic into her coffee to put her to sleep in order to take a piece called *The Woman with the Cross*. Camille refused offers to exhibit in Prague and other places, fearing her work would be placed next to Rodin's and that he would get the credit. Soon her obsession that her works were being copied and that Rodin was persecuting her everywhere began to drain her creative energy.

From 1905 on, Camille's condition deteriorated. She could no longer remember which works she had done with Rodin, and she accused him of ordering two of his models to break into her house and kill her. She began to destroy most of the work she had created. Her studio was full of the debris of broken sculptures, which she ordered buried. During this period, according to a letter of one of her few remaining friends, Camille was drinking heavily and inviting many strangers to her house to stay the night and party.[13]

In a letter Camille revealed some of the reasons she had mutilated her work: She could not bear disappointments and frustrations, and she destroyed her own creations in retaliation. After a friend died, she wrote to his wife: "When I received your announcement, I was in such a fury that I took all my wax models and threw them into the fire, they made a huge blaze and I warmed my feet by the light of the fire, that's what I do when something unpleasant happens to me, I take my hammer and I crush a figure. The death of Henri cost a lot! more than 10,000 francs. The big statue was quick to follow the fate of its little wax sisters for the death of Henri was followed a few days later with more bad news: without any warning, they all of a sudden stopped giving me any money, I find myself from one day to the next, without any resources, it is Rodin's band that has worked on Mother's head to obtain this result. And a lot of other capital executions took place right away afterwards, a pile of plaster rubbish is accumulating in the middle of my studio, it's a veritable human sacrifice."[14]

In the film version of Camille's life, based on the biography by Reine-Marie Paris, Camille appears at the opening of her own art exhibition, dressed garishly in red, her lips and cheeks painted in that same bright color, symbolizing both her passion and her rage. A drunken Madwoman, Camille shocks everyone. Humiliated, even her brother abandons her in shame. Later, she is shown smashing the sculpted head of an innocent young girl, thus symbolically destroying hope.

In 1913, when her father died and was buried, Camille was not notified and so was unable to attend the services. A few days later, at the age of forty-nine, she was forcibly incarcerated in an asylum, after a joint decision by her brother and mother. Conscious of her situation, she considered it a terrible martyrdom and continually wrote letters to relatives and friends imploring them to help her get out. All this time she continued to believe that Rodin was responsible for her imprisonment, when in fact her family had agreed to the internment. After Rodin died, she began to see her mother as the enemy. Camille spent the rest of her life (some thirty years) in the madhouse and could not bring herself ever to sculpt again. She died in 1943 in misery, an old and unknown Madwoman.

Camille Claudel was a creative genius and a great sculptress. Today her remaining works, representing less than half of her creations, are housed mainly in museums. Critics agree that the essence of her art is earthy, yet glows with an inner light. Her sculptures, always inspired by her sense of touch and by the earth, which was her own Muse, are introspective self-portraits, expressing intensity and tenderness, sadness, and a sense of emptiness. To view Camille's work, radiating as it does with fragile luminescence, is to experience the expression of feminine vulnerability and intimacy, and the inner tragedy of her own soul.

ACTUALIZING THE INNER MUSE: CELESTE'S STORY

The story of Celeste, a contemporary woman, shows the dynamics of many women who become Muses for men at the expense of their own self-actualization. But because Celeste was always struggling to grow and develop, her story also reveals some of the transformative possibilities for the mad Muse.

Celeste, the second of three daughters, was gifted with unusual beauty, a sweet and loving disposition, high intelligence, and artistic talent. Paradoxically, she was both a pleaser and a rebel. Her father, an officer in the military, dominated his family with a rigid authoritarian manner and changing moods due to a debilitating disease. Although he loved his family, he constantly judged his children, particularly Celeste, whose artistic and mystical temperament did not fit his conventional view of how women should behave. She was never encouraged by her parents to pursue her artistic and intellectual gifts. Her mother was a sweet and nurturing woman who served her husband and her family but catered to her husband's whims so much that she never lived her own life. Her mother's inner Madwoman was so suppressed that her anger negatively affected her health. Celeste's first model of feminine nature was thus a loving but codependent mother who served Celeste's authoritarian, perfectionistic, and unpredictable father.

Because she had an unusual sensitivity to feelings and instinctively empathized with others, Celeste became the family mediator in an effort to create constant harmony. She repeated this role with her friends and lovers. In her desire to please and nurture others, she forgot about her own needs and talents.

Without direction and always intent on pleasing others, Celeste got good grades but drifted through high school. Her beauty enticed many admirers, but she always chose charming, exciting boyfriends who drank and took drugs. Rebelling against her father's authority while attempting to please her boyfriends, Celeste spent her last high school years drinking, drugging, and taking a lot of LSD trips. Later, she would see this destructive behavior as an early manifestation of the inner Madwoman trying to engage her hidden anger but succeeding only in self-destructive ways. Luckily she survived this period, graduated from high school, and went to college.

In college, she majored in theater. She still lacked focus and got mediocre grades. She felt alienated in her large, anonymous university. At this time, she was consciously searching for meaning and purpose in life, while her fellow students wanted to play and have a good time. Having survived her earlier dangerous flirtation with drugs, her peers' interest in sororities and football seemed superficial, but she could not find her own way in the impersonal academic maze. Depressed, she dropped out of school and worked as a waitress.

In high school, Celeste had been inspired by a teacher who introduced her to the psychology of Jung. Jung's symbolic approach to understanding the meaning of human existence appealed to her intuitive temperament. Her encounter with this teacher and with Jung's work had actually helped her grow beyond the high school drug scene. When Celeste dropped out of school, she reconnected with the teacher and began reading Jung again. The two women became close friends, and Celeste became a young Muse devoted to this older teacher, who replaced her father's authority. Although there were many positive features of this creative friendship for Celeste, eventually she felt dominated and judged by the older woman. Again, she was pleasing someone else and felt she was under her friend's power.

Still out of touch with her inner anger at her own passivity, Celeste began to project the negativity of the Madwoman onto her friend instead. At about this time she went into Jungian analysis and learned some of the psychodynamics behind her tendency to be the eternal girl, the charming *puella* who could dance with beautiful possibilities but had difficulty in choosing one way in which to concentrate and actualize her potential. She had many dreams about sick, mad men trying to kill her, symbolizing a dependence on male authority that was strangling her creative life. Eventually, as she became more conscious and self-confident, she was able to value her own decision-making process and become more independent. This freed her from the authoritarian influence of both her father and her friend. Returning to college, she majored in psychology and graduated with straight As.

At the end of her senior year she fell in love with one of her professors. After she graduated, they married. Celeste spent the next ten years in a relatively harmonious and compatible marriage, but she remained a beautiful, eternal girl. The marriage took a traditional form; Celeste enjoyed the domestic role of the beautiful hostess and nurturing housewife and occasionally helped her husband by doing secretarial work. But despite the couple's compatibility, something seemed to be missing in Celeste's life. Constantly torn over her lack of professional direction, she could choose to actualize neither her artistic talents nor her desire to be a psychotherapist. So she remained in limbo. Inwardly, she agonized over her passivity, while outwardly she basked in her husband's adoration. She felt at times as if she were living in a fascinating fantasy.

In her thirties, the fantasy began to fade as an early midlife crisis descended upon her in full force. At this time she decided to pursue her dramatic inclinations more actively and to this end went on several trips to study acting. But her attraction to men and romance was more powerful than her plans to study, and she became embroiled in a torrid love affair that eventually contributed to the disintegration of her marriage and interfered with her new career plans. When the love affair ended, she was left with nothing.

Celeste had always enjoyed the delicious euphoria that alcohol gave her, and from time to time she would binge. During her married years, her drinking had been relatively controlled, but now, in her new loneliness, she began to drink more heavily. She moved to Los Angeles to fulfill her dream of becoming an actress, got a job, and studied acting. Inwardly, she was still lonely and living in despair. Then she met a handsome actor, newly divorced and of some reputation. They fell in love, and Celeste's life became a whirlwind of celebrity parties, champagne balls, and exciting trips to Europe and the Orient. Her lover adored her and gave her exquisite gifts. She, in turn, worshiped him. The two wined, dined, and danced together at the top of the world, and finally they decided to live together and become engaged. Celeste let go of her plan to be an actress. She had become once again a man's fantasy figure, the beautiful princess who inspired and nurtured her lover's creativity.

Soon the practicalities of life descended upon her, as well as the consequences of her drinking. Her hangovers became worse and worse, and her blackouts increased; humiliating incidents in social situations became more frequent. As Celeste's drinking increased, so did her suicidal fantasies. Once, raving in a drunken monologue, angry at her fiancé and fearing he no longer really loved her, she almost threw herself down a long escalator that descended into a

subway. The Madwoman was emerging from the depths with a vengeance.

In daily life Celeste began to feel like a Caged Bird, reliving her
mother's life of constantly acquiescing to her father. No matter how
much Celeste tried to please her lover, she never felt it was enough.
She became so obsessed with pleasing him that he felt trapped too.
He defended himself by becoming as critical of Celeste as her father
had been. The couple became caught in the psychological war between the Madwoman and the Judge.

Initially, Celeste blamed her lover for her depression and dependency. But underneath she was enraged at her own weakness. Her
suicidal impulses came out of her desire to kill off her own dependency and self-betrayal. She felt she had no say in their relationship
and that her lover was using her beauty for his own power needs and
ego-aggrandizement. In her former marriage some of these feelings
had also surfaced, though she had tried to put them out of her
mind. Now, ten years later, they resurfaced with a force so powerful,
she could not ignore them. She realized that she had trapped herself by revolving her life so much around another person that she
had lost her own center. She was infuriated at her captor. She knew
that destroying herself would hurt him, but she also wanted to live.

Celeste's situation became intolerable. Fears of becoming a "bag
lady" frightened her. What would happen when her beauty faded
with age? How would she support herself if she were alone? Her
drinking increased. Then she read some books about addiction. She
began to see that she was addicted not only to alcohol but to
codependency. In fact, these two were interacting in a vicious cycle
in her life. She fought the realization and acceptance of her own
addictions for a long time. How could the beautiful white swan in
one of her favorite ballets, *Swan Lake,* also be the destructively bewitching black swan? How could the Muse be an alcoholic? It didn't
fit the picture that she or others had of her. Yet every time she
drank, the excruciating pain and horror increased.

Depression, anxiety, and suicidal impulses frightened Celeste
into entering an inpatient recovery program. She also started going
to twelve-step meetings. This was a very difficult period; she had
terrible cravings for alcohol and even more terrible cravings for the
romance and glamour that drinking once had given her. But she
persisted in her recovery because she knew that if she didn't, she

would destroy herself and her relationship. At the same time, Celeste began to reconnect with her spiritual side. After a year or so in recovery, she became clearer about herself and her life. She realized that, along with her addiction to alcohol, she had been "addicted" to being a dark Muse, serving a man as the very image of his soul. She saw that by living out the dreams of others, she had lost access to her own.

Celeste began to surrender her attachment to being the Muse for others and began to be her own Muse. During her early recovery, Celeste had seen the film *Camille Claudel,* and she identified with the artist on many levels—especially with Camille's desire to be Rodin's Muse, which conflicted with her own creativity, her pain and rage, and the descent into drinking and madness that finally destroyed her life. Celeste opted for the transformation of her own mad Muse. She shifted her focus from her fiancé's creative career to her own. She decided that her major energy for work was in the healing professions; she researched various programs in psychology and applied to graduate school. To her delight, her fiancé supported her in this venture. Celeste found that if she was clear about what she wanted for herself, if she set limits and assertively asked for what she needed, her fiancé and other people accepted and honored her requests.

At the beginning, her metamorphosis was not easy. Celeste had been dependent on alcohol and being the Muse for men for twenty-four years. Going to graduate school was so terrifying that she had a strong urge to drink and undo all her progress. But then she had a dream that confirmed her new path and showed her how she could transform her self-destructive Madwoman energy into a creative expression. Celeste actually had prayed for a dream, for she felt she had lost contact with her spiritual side. The dream countered her terror and fear of failure and gave her the courage to pursue the original vision that she had had at twenty, to be a Jungian analyst.

In the dream, she was interviewing for admission to graduate school. Her fiancé was also there and was called separately for his own interview. Then an older woman called Celeste to her interview in a large room. This teacher read poetic images to Celeste while projecting visual images and symbols onto the wall. The visual images were primitive—the jungle and the earth, as well as human life. The poetry described the pain of consciousness as well as a significant mystical experience. Celeste was touched, for she felt the wonder of the images. When Celeste interpreted these primitive, earthy, and mystical images as revealing the birth of the heroine, the woman interviewer, astounded at the depth of her understanding, checked Celeste's academic record and said, "You'll be an asset to our school," and admitted Celeste into training.

For Celeste, the dream showed her transformation from an anima woman and Muse into a self-actualizing woman who used her intuitive gifts for creative healing through her understanding of the inner life. Celeste's native mystical temperament, which had been so criticized by her father and even regarded as a sign of weakness, was affirmed by the woman in the dream. For years, Celeste's visionary side, her longing for spirituality, had been her most valuable resource, even though her visions had often been demeaned by others and supplanted by her own romantic worship of men. Her drinking had taken her fantasies and visions to the point of madness. Now Celeste could see that she had misused the Madwoman energy through drinking and concentrating on attracting men's adoration, thereby neglecting her own creative inspiration. In this dream, which signified the painful birth and maturation of consciousness, she herself was the creative heroine, not the men to whom she usually assigned this role. The older woman mentor was a transformed, wiser side of Celeste and initiated her into the recognition and appreciation of her own creativity. Celeste wondered whether this dark-haired woman initiator was a positive form of her own inner Madwoman.

Celeste always had been afraid of the Madwoman in herself and had feared this energy in others too. Sometimes she nurtured others and was nicer than necessary because she feared the consequences of rejecting them or setting up boundaries with them. Now she realized that breaking through the fear was part of the transformation of the Madwoman. She had needed to integrate the Madwoman energy in order to feel the power and authority of the dark feminine side of herself, who possessed the energy that she could use in her future work in the healing professions and in her artistic endeavors. Celeste now had the courage to invoke the Muse for her own creative life.

TRANSFORMING THE MUSE

How can a woman who is trapped in the role of Muse transform herself into a woman of her own, particularly when the secondary gains of the Muse role are so enticing—the romance, the adoration, and the glamour? How can she grow beyond a culture that glorifies beauty and youth?

Once a woman has experienced the thrill of creating from her own center, despite all the hard work this entails, she will not want to be *only* a Muse to anyone. She begins to sense the artificial quality inherent in the adoration of mere beauty or charm. Living up to others' idealizations sucks the life and inspiration from a woman. Like vampires, idealizations drain their beautiful victims' blood. Alma Mahler sensed this many times in her life. She resented becoming an object for her various husbands and her other smitten suitors. More than once, she felt the need to make a choice and commit to her own life. But the power she held over so many creative men pulled her away from her struggle to be herself, perhaps because it was the only power she knew as a woman in a patriarchal culture. Caught in this ambivalence, she became armored against her own desires and lost herself.

The Muse who has begun the process of change knows what it feels like to be her own person rather than another's fantasy object. Initially, the experience can be thrilling and euphoric. The attention gives a "high" feeling. But as in every addiction, there is eventually a fall. As she grows older, the Muse feels her beauty fading. She no longer can live on the gratuity of loveliness and youth, and she experiences men's eyes looking elsewhere and passing her by. To avoid the pain of aging, some women become like papier-mâché dolls and paint themselves with powder, makeup, and eyebrow pencil, trying to add color to their lives by putting on extra rouge and eye shadow. Their face-lifts frequently erase the lines that show the women's wisdom they might have shared. Others hide themselves from view and retreat from life. Here, in a rage over their wasted life, the Madwoman often enters. In the film *Sunset Boulevard*, Norma Desmond, an aging actress, kills a reporter who has come to her home to see what became of her. She can't bear to be seen as an "old has-been."

Like all women, the Muse has to endure life's suffering. She must descend into darkness, into fears she has not faced, in order to integrate the pain with the pleasure that life brings. The golden girl Muse, like Alma Mahler, may think she is above the travail of ordinary life. When she suffers anyway, she is likely to fall into resentment that culminates in bitterness about her life, trapping her in the end into the destructive aspect of the Madwoman. In contrast, the dark Muse, like Camille Claudel, is more likely to romanticize darkness and act out the role of the tragic heroine. By remaining the tragic Muse, she too falls victim to the Madwoman.

When pain and suffering are not acknowledged or consciously faced, the destructive aspect of the Madwoman takes over. Celeste faced her darkness and acknowledged the pain and anguish of her addiction and her unlived life. She realized she had to work to get herself out of her dead end; she dared to commit herself voluntarily to hard work, took responsibility for herself, and started to make a difference in the world.

It is possible to be a Muse in a healthy way if one does not fall victim to the desire for adoration. For example, the writer Lou Andreas-Salomé was a Muse for the philosopher Nietzsche and the poet Rilke, as well as many others. But she insisted on being a creative woman in her own right as well. She used the Madwoman's energy when she told Rilke, who idolized her, to go his own way. She knew they both needed to follow their own creative calls. Consciously relinquishing the roles of Muse and lover, she remained his friend while creating on her own, and she wrote many books herself. Anais Nin is another example of a Muse who created in her own way. Remaining true to her own vision, she created from her own center of feeling and intuition. She wrote many novels and brought the journal form into popularity.

Other women are able to use their muse quality to host others' creativity without giving up themselves. For example, Gertrude Stein held salons in Europe that helped inspire new writers like Ernest Hemingway. But she led the way and never ceased writing herself, even developing a new genre of literature.

By integrating the darkness of the Madwoman, the Muse may transform herself, turning to her own inner beauty. Her strength is a creative relationship to soul that need not be misused. If she lets go of the romantic ideals that keep her trapped, she can refuse to relinquish her humanity, and she can sacrifice the false validation she has received as an adored idol. She can honor Nature by surrendering to the body's process of aging. With the discipline of active work, she can learn to transform the chaos deep inside, which the Madwoman brings, into creations of her own. She can become a Muse for herself.

Many of us may not be as outwardly beautiful and charming as Alma Mahler or as gifted as Camille Claudel, but all of us inwardly have our own unique mystery. The power to fascinate and inspire others can be used creatively. It is destructive only if it shrinks our own souls. Ultimately, we can use our Muse energy to create and make the world a more beautiful place. We can be Muses for the earth.

5

THE REJECTED

LOVER

*She laughed and said she was taking
up arms against God Himself. Lucifer
had tried and failed, but he was male.
She thought she might do better, being
female.*

—FAY WELDON,
The Life and Loves of a She-Devil

A WOMAN I KNOW LAMENTED THAT SHE WAS HAVING RECUR-rent dreams of abandonment by former lovers. Even though she thought she had worked through the feelings of rejection that she had experienced in each relationship, her general feeling of rejection and despair at being abandoned persisted. More than anything, she wanted to be in a conscious relationship in which each partner encouraged the other to develop and mature. Her recurring dream kept reminding her of the pain of romantic rejection and emphasizing how important a real meaningful relationship could be.

Romantic rejection is a universal human experience. Its tragic aspects are most celebrated in American culture with sensational accounts of lovers' revenge recounted in the press and recreated in movies, and in the tragic love songs of rock, blues, and country western music.

A Rejected Lover is easily trapped in negative behavior and psychological patterns of victimization, where she can believe herself to be a tragic heroine. But underneath that dark, romantic, often depressed image, rejection tends to release rage in its victims, rage at being betrayed, for betrayal is one of the greatest of women's fears. When it occurs, the Madwoman can burst through the Rejected Lover's surface, in spite of her attempts to cover up her pain and pretense of coping, disrupting life and work and soul. Brokenhearted, consumed with rage and tears so great that the soul and body can hardly bear it, some maddened Rejected Lovers experience homicidal impulses toward their betrayer, as in the film *Fatal Attraction,* or the urge to kill themselves, as in countless other tales, having reduced their lives to the one function of lover-in-relationship. Other Rejected Lovers cling to the relationship when it is over, living in delusion. Possessed by their own fantasy, they simply cannot believe it when their lover says, "No, it's over." Consumed in the fires of resentment and martyrdom, many rejected women burn out creatively and professionally. Still others compensate for their rejection through obsessive workaholic patterns, or by compulsive eating or self-denial, as in anorexia, or by drinking, drugging, shopping, and other addictive behaviors. Fearing rejection, some women act crazily as soon as they enter a new relationship. Panicking when they are faced with intimacy, such women enact the Rejected Lover by pushing the partner away and rejecting him or her before she has a chance to be rejected herself.

Women who have suffered as Caged Birds in tightly controlled marriages may be rejected later in life by their husbands. This betrayal often happens at menopause, when, emotionally and hormonally stressed, a woman can already feel crazy and confused about her feminine identity, which she must rethink and change as she enters a new stage of life. A Muse can become a Rejected Lover at an even earlier age in the life cycle, as did Camille Claudel.

Denial that the relationship is over and revenge-seeking behavior are dominant features of the Rejected Lover syndrome. Indeed, the passion the woman feels for her beloved often is fanned by the rejection. If she believes her very life depends upon the other's love, she will not be able to accept or believe in the termination of the relationship. Thinking she can change her lover's decree, she holds on to her delusion. Caught in this state, she feels victimized. She may become ill and use pity to try to hold on to the lover. She may drift into dreamy madness, like Elvira, the protagonist of the opera *I Puritani,* or she may threaten or actually commit suicide like Anna Karenina. Others become consumed in crazy pursuit of their fantasy, as in the film *The Story of Adele H.*

In a maddened moment, Adele H., daughter of the Romantic novelist Victor Hugo, tells her rejecting lover: "I am not me without you." She has followed the fiancé who abandoned her from France to the wilds of Nova Scotia, where he is an officer in the military. Writing letters, stalking him in the streets, so obsessed with him that she can think of nothing else, her life is reduced to haunting him. Convinced that he really does love her, she believes she can win him back. When he tells her clearly that the relationship is over, she cannot hear him. She writes to her father and tells him they will be married. The engagement notice is published in the French papers, and the young officer reads it. Upset, he confronts Adele again, but she is lost in clinging memories of their past. Pathetically, she continues to follow him from place to place, unable to believe he no longer loves her. Lacking the reality of the relationship, her fantasies take her over. In the end, it is not the real lover she seeks anymore but a fictional figure in her imagination. Finally, when she passes the actual man in the street one day, she doesn't even recognize him.

We all tend to have ideas and expectations of the ideal lover that we project onto the actual person with whom we fall in love. Sometimes these wishes are developed from our early experiences with our fathers. If a girl's father is absent through death or sickness or is distant or too idealized, if she has minimal contact with real men, more fantasies are likely to arise in her as a woman. She may imagine a Ghostly Lover, an ideal man who exists only in her imagination.[1] The task of a healthy psyche in a healthy relationship is to break through these fantasies and projections to true intimacy and real relationships, something the Madwoman—if her energy is used correctly—can help us to do.

Men's fears of the unpredictable explosions of the Madwoman who is rejected in love, and their impotence in the face of her rage, have been dramatized in many modern films. The protagonist of

Woman on the Verge of a Nervous Breakdown burns her bed in rage when her lover betrays her. In *Fatal Attraction,* a crazed mistress embarrasses, frightens, and threatens the family of the man who leaves her after a brief affair. In dealing with her escalating rage and madness, he ends up killing her. In *Presumed Innocent,* a betrayed wife cleverly kills her husband's lover, a famous prosecuting attorney. These cinematic Madwomen frighten us because they portray the formidable force that exists within the psyche of both men and women "in love," the lust for control and revenge.

REVENGE OF THE SHE-DEVILS

Even the most contained, proper, and mature woman can turn crazy when she is betrayed. Lesley, a very controlled Englishwoman, always the dutiful daughter and wife, followed her husband into a pub after she learned he was having an affair. She went over to the table where he sat with his date for the night. He told her to leave and stop ruining his fun, and she broke down. Her Madwoman emerged, and screaming, she threw a Bloody Mary in his face, including the glass, which broke and cut him. Two huge bouncers came and pinned her to the floor, then forcibly dragged her outside, leaving her crying in rage to the full moon. Today she can laugh at this incident; she knows that her mad reaction to it helped her break through her denial about her husband's cruelty and the marriage's downward trend, so that eventually she freed herself from it.

The ways Rejected Lovers have sought revenge are legion. They have madly spent all the funds of the unfaithful husband's credit cards, read his private journals and correspondence, and slashed the tires of his car (a car often embodies a man's freedom, masculine power, and control). They have run naked into the bedroom of the new lovers, thrown into his face once-lovely wedding pictures cut into grotesque pieces, and followed the new couple. Howling insults, they have made threatening phone calls to the new woman, harassed the man at work, and turned his children against him.

In *She-Devil,* a film based on the novel *The Life and Loves of a She-Devil* by Fay Weldon, revenge fantasies are taken to the extreme. When she learns her husband is going to move out to continue having an affair with Mary Fisher, a pretty, petite, sentimental writer of best-selling romantic novels, Ruth—a gangling unattractive woman whose mother had rejected her because of her ugliness—snaps. In cold rage, Ruth plots the demise of her husband and the woman who has taken her place. She craftily sets fire to the gas stove, exploding her suburban house and setting herself up to be a pitiful victim. Now homeless, Ruth takes her children to the High Tower, a fairy-tale-like house on a cliff above the sea where her husband now lives with Mary Fisher. Ruth leaves the children there, knowing that the unruly, demanding children will interrupt the lovers' tryst in the High Tower. Ruth also plots to send Mary Fisher's crazy old mother, who is now at a nursing home, back to live with her daughter as well.

In her marriage, Ruth had tried to be a "good wife," pretending to be happy when she was miserable, never complaining, proving her gratefulness for food and shelter by cleaning and taking care of everyone's needs. She had remained faithful when her husband praised younger women in public; she had pumped up his sexual vanity; and she had pretended to be his inferior. Now spurned, she despises her former dependence and decides to become powerful and rich. Ruth sneaks into her husband's files, alters his accounting books, and makes it appear as if he were embezzling money. Meanwhile, she puts the money in a secret Swiss bank account for herself. Starting an employment agency for women, she helps many women tap their energies to leave their Caged Bird existence and enter the exciting world of business and power. Then Ruth enlists the help of some of these grateful women in her plans of revenge. She sets up her husband to be arrested, convicted, and sent to jail.

Meanwhile, in the High Tower, Mary Fisher is losing both her looks and her money. The stress caused by the unruly children, her aged mother, and her lover's financial needs to get out of prison—all new, practical concerns—interfere with the romantic formulas of her best sellers. Her new books fail; her royalties are confiscated; her hair thins; her complexion dulls, aging. She is diagnosed with cancer, caused by the stress of her practical life, and she dies. During this same time, Ruth improves her looks. She loses weight and goes to a plastic surgeon and a team of doctors for a total body makeover. The pain and the extremes of self-mutilation she undergoes exemplify the mad things many women do to change their bodies and their looks, symptomatic of women's collective body-loathing. She has her face redone, her legs cut down, and her nose and jaw remodeled; she gets a new set of teeth. She gives the surgeons a picture of the woman she wants to look like, and she comes out an exact replica of Mary Fisher, the image of all pretty women.

Now rich and beautiful, she has the money to get her husband out of jail and even to buy the High Tower. She remakes the wild and natural place to her taste, ruining Nature with artificial grass and plastic statues—a sign of her control. In the end, she takes in her husband, a confused and beaten man. Once her master, he is now her servant; he suffers while she sleeps with other men. She treats him badly, causing him the misery he once caused her. Proud to be a mad multimillionairess, now all she-devil, she has eradicated the woman in her. Her new credo is:

> I do not put my trust in fate, nor my faith in God. I will be
> what I want, not what He ordained. I will mold a new image
> for myself out of the earth of my creation. I will defy my
> Maker and remake myself. I cast off the chains that bound me
> down, of habit, custom, and sexual aspiration; home, family,
> friends—all the objects of natural affection. . . . A she-devil is
> supremely happy; she is inoculated against the pain of
> memory. At the moment of her transfiguration, from woman
> to nonwoman, she performs the act herself. She thrusts the
> long, sharp needle of recollection through the living flesh into
> the heart, burning it out. The pain is wild and fierce for a
> time, but presently there's none. I sing a hymn to the death
> of love and the end of pain.[2]

Weldon's *The Life and Loves of a She-Devil* may be a fantasy of what many Rejected Lovers would like to do to their husbands. In reality, they engage in less protracted and less effective acts of revenge, or they simply become paralyzed and turn to stone in their lives, consumed by their revenge fantasies. Identifying with the madness of being a Rejected Lover is ultimately self-destructive. Later in this chapter we will look at ways women have worked through this energy so that they do not become stuck in it and remain victims.

MEDEA

In contrast to the cold, calculating she-devil, who participates in an Ice Queen kind of mentality, the story of Medea reveals the Madwoman in one of her rawest, most primitive forms: the vengeful Dragon Lady. Medea, a barbarian sorceress, is the only surviving daughter of King Aeetes of Colchis. She falls in love with Jason, who has come to her father's island with the Argonauts to retrieve the Golden Fleece in order to claim his inheritance of Thessaly's throne. Medea's father sets Jason some seemingly impossible tasks before he can have the Fleece: among them, Jason must master and yoke fire-breathing bulls and sow an acre with the teeth of a dragon that guards the Golden Fleece and never sleeps. Medea helps Jason with her magic to perform the tasks, even slaying the dragon herself. She betrays her father for Jason, who pledges his eternal love and loyalty to her. She also sacrifices her brother so she and Jason can escape with the prized Fleece. When the couple arrives in Thessaly, Medea tricks the king's daughters into killing their father and cutting him into bits. When the murder of the king is discovered, Medea and Jason must flee Thessaly for Greece. There, in exile in Corinth, Medea gives birth to two sons.

There Jason betrays Medea, who has sacrificed everything for him, by asking Creon, the King of Corinth, for his daughter's hand in marriage. Jason tries to justify his betrayal by telling Medea that he wants to protect their children, who as bastards have no civil rights. (Nor did women or aliens in Greece at the time.)

In despair at Jason's betrayal, at first Medea cannot eat; she can only weep. Her melancholy and rage mount, however, until all she can think of is revenge. She will destroy the whole household for this injustice. Her life has lost its meaning; she prefers death. She says to herself: "Woman in most respects is a timid creature, with no heart for strife and aghast at the sight of steel; but wronged in love, there is no heart more murderous than hers."[3]

Hearing of her curses and fearing Medea's sorcery, King Creon decrees that she and her children be exiled from the land. But Medea begs the king to let her stay one last day to prepare for her departure, and he relents. This gives Medea time to execute her revenge. Medea plans to send her own children with gifts for the new bride—a robe and a golden headpiece, infused with poison. When the princess dons these gifts, she will die, as will anyone who touches her. After that, Medea determines to hurt Jason the most by murdering their children. To effect this plan, Medea tricks Jason into thinking that her fits of temper were only temporary by apologizing to him; she asks him to intercede and to beg Creon to let the children stay and have a home. She promises to send them with special presents for his new bride. Jason, thinking Medea has come to her senses, agrees.

Medea agonizes over her plan. She knows her revenge will shame her and that she will be condemned to wander homeless, never finding peace. Deprived of her children, her life will mean nothing. In her mind's eye, she sees their sweet smiles and relents for a time; she will take them with her in exile; she cannot hurt them. But when she sees how much her sons resemble Jason, the sting of insult returns. Medea knows the horror of her intended crime, but her passion outweighs her reason. Possessed with madness, she invokes the Black Furies to destroy the love and pity in her heart, and she carries out her plan. When she hears that the princess, disfigured from the poison, has died violently and that her father the king, who touched the corpse, has died in agony as well, Medea triumphs. Dedicating herself to the dark goddess of hatred, she slays her children as she curses Jason, saying, "Yes, it was your father who killed you!"

Jason asks the gods to punish Medea. Riding in a chariot that is pulled through the air by winged dragons with the bodies of her dead children, Medea shouts to Jason that *his* lust and new marriage, *his* betrayal, is to blame for these murders. Justifying her actions, she says she killed the children to punish him.

Like Medea, some women rejected in love hurt their own children in revenge, displacing their anger at their ex-husbands onto them. "Murdering one's children" can take many forms. It may be enacted by gross physical child abuse, or by soul murder, by killing the child's sensitivity, gifts, and talents. This is most likely to happen if the children of a rejected mother are different from the mother, especially if they look or act like their father. A child who does not live according to a mother's expectations is also likely to suffer from her revenge. A mother might also kill off the child in her sons and daughters by making them overly responsible beyond their age. Some rejected mothers who have attempted to avenge themselves against their husbands ultimately feel guilty and sacrifice their children by giving up their custody rights to their ex-husbands. Still other women murder the child in themselves, martyring themselves, becoming joyless and rigid. They may murder their inner creative impulses, ceasing to create or destroying their existing work, as Camille Claudel did after she felt rejected by Rodin. In modern times, we can look at the life of Maria Callas, the great dramatic artist and passionate Greek soprano, who also sacrificed her creativity after she was rejected in love.

THE TRAGEDY OF MARIA CALLAS

Maria Callas was famous for her portrayals in many operas of women who are betrayed. She expressed the raw and primitive emotion of the Madwoman in all its darkness. Through her daring interpretations of these famous women in opera, "the Tigress," as Callas was sometimes called by her public, opened up the realm of the dark side of feminine nature. She sang Bellini's fragile Elvira, the abandoned bride in *I Puritani* who drifts madly into dreams of the past after she mistakenly thinks her fiancé has betrayed her; and Donizetti's *Lucia,* who goes mad when forced to marry a man she does not love. She portrayed the ambitious *Lady Macbeth,* obsessed by guilt after she has her husband kill the king; and *Anna Bolena,* the queen who furiously accuses the court judges after she has been betrayed. Many times she sang *Tosca,* who commits suicide after her lover is killed by a fiend who seduces and betrays her. Consciously identifying with the betrayed Norma, the druid priestess who kills herself after breaking her holy oath in sexual passion, Callas sang her dark agonies to the world. In *Medea,* the opera she made famous, Callas expressed the murderous fury and vengeance that the Rejected Lover feels. In 1961, when she herself was betrayed by her lover, she said before her final performance of *Medea,* "The way I saw Medea was the way I feel it: fiery, apparently calm, but very intense. The happy time with Jason is past; now she is devoured by misery and fury."[4]

As a young girl, Maria Callas seemed unlikely to become one of the most haunting, beautiful, and commanding prima donnas ever to grace the opera stage. She was the second daughter of a Greek immigrant couple who had hoped for a boy to save their marriage and to take the place of their son, who had died at age three. Maria's mother is said to have turned her eyes from the baby girl when she was first put in her arms, looking instead toward the icy hospital window and asking the nurses to take the baby away. A snowstorm raged outside, and Maria's mother lived her life as an Ice Queen, bitter about the death of her son and her unhappy marriage. Maria's mother had abandoned her desire to be an actress for a traditional marriage to a successful pharmacist, but she longed for the glamorous life that her father, a military officer and singer, led. After moving unwillingly to America, Maria's mother consigned herself to martyrdom, secretly projecting her hopes for fame onto her daughters.

Maria showed vocal talent early and began to take music lessons at seven. Her father opposed this frivolous expense, but her mother insisted upon it. Music became Maria's life. Disciplining herself to practice, pushed by her mother into talent contests, she won many prizes. In 1937, Maria's mother moved back to Greece so Maria could have the proper training for her singing career. Although her mother praised her achievements, Maria felt deprived of her mother's love, which was lavished on her pretty, graceful, and socially charming older sister, Jackie. In contrast, Maria felt she was the ugly duckling, clumsy, shy, and heavy. To compensate for her lack of love, Maria overate. An outsider at school, she did not develop close friendships, nor did she date. She suppressed her adolescent urges and desires and worked. Years later, complaining about the loss of her childhood, she said: "I work; therefore I am."[5] She was determined to win love by becoming a famous singer. All her life, Maria would resent her mother's rejection, feeling that her older sister received unconditional love while she had to work for it. Maria put the energy from her anger at her mother into her singing. This consuming trauma of rejection became a fiery alchemical source for her immediate, instinctive ability to express the raging passions of the brokenhearted and betrayed lovers whose sufferings she sang on the stage.

According to her biographer, Arianna Stassinopoulos, Maria Callas always needed someone to sustain her and to believe in her talent and greatness, first her mother, and then her first music teacher, Maria Trivella, who encouraged her talent and nurtured her as well. Next, Elvira de Hidalgo, the great Spanish music teacher, trained Maria, gave her motherly love, showed her the arts of feminine dress and movement, and introduced her to the great tragic heroines of opera. With de Hidalgo's devotion and belief in her destiny to be a great singer, Maria blossomed. She was devoted to her mentor, a magical "good mother," while she saw her natal mother as the "bad mother" who never understood her emotional needs.

At seventeen, Maria sang professionally for the Athens opera, electrifying audiences with her passion. Offstage she became known for her irrational outbursts. In 1945, when her contract was not renewed by the Athens opera, Maria decided to go to America. There she hoped to reunite with her father, separate from her mother, and become famous and free.

In New York, her father was caring but did not share her love of opera. The New York opera world, unimpressed with her Athens success, rejected her. Hurt, she withdrew from the opera scene. For a while, she enjoyed eating in New York restaurants, decorating her apartment, and cooking for her father. Her weight soared to 180 pounds. Then the Metropolitan Opera offered her a debut to sing the leading roles of Leonora and Madame Butterfly. She rejected these offers, saying that her intuitive "voices" had advised her against accepting. Although she was actually intuitive by nature and believed in her own instincts, Maria also felt unfit for the part of the fragile Madame Butterfly because she was overweight. She felt her decision not to perform was right, but when other opera companies subsequently rejected her, she began to doubt herself, fearing that her previous success had depended on her mother's presence. So Maria asked her mother to join her in New York. Playing the martyr, her mother came. Maria was caught between her aversion to her bitter, rejecting mother and her dependence on her mother's ambitious belief in her success. Blaming her disappointments in life and love on her mother, whose views of men were pessimistic, Maria fought and used her mother as an enemy who energized her fighting spirit in her career.

When Maria was asked to sing for the Verona opera, she met the first romantic figure in her life, Giovanni Battista Meneghini, a businessman who loved both opera and women and who had been assigned by the Verona festival to be Maria's official escort. In his early fifties, Meneghini was stable and influential, and he devoted himself to the rising young opera star. He courted her, admired her genius, and appreciated the woman in her. He also nurtured, encouraged, and supported her, gave her gentle and constructive criticism, protected her, and listened to her fears and worries. Maria also met conductor Tullio Serafim, who saw her genius and fed it with his faith. With the love and attention of these two men, Maria felt happy. She astounded Italian opera lovers with her dramatic voice and her unique interpretations of their beloved tragic heroines. In January 1949, Maria did the impossible in one week: She sang both the high coloratura role of Bellini's Elvira and Wagner's deep and mighty Brünnehilde—an operatic feat, since these two roles are so vocally and dramatically different. This was a turning point in her career, and Maria was celebrated and invited to make recordings and international tours. She married Meneghini—then, a few days later, left for South America alone. Maria put her work and singing and her public before everything—even her new marriage and her private life.

On her Mexican tour in 1950, Maria invited her mother to join her, allowing her to triumph in her fame. But emotionally Maria remained distant. Only once did she show any vulnerability in front of her mother, confessing in tears that she wanted children and would like her mother to help bring them up. But the next day, when her mother tried to show affection, Maria exploded, screaming that she was no longer a child. Revealing her vulnerability to her mother had been too threatening to Maria. She gave her mother a symbolic parting gift—a fur coat to protect her against the cold. Maria never saw her mother again. When her mother wrote reproachful and accusatory letters, sensing Maria's desertion as well as her replacement by Meneghini, Maria withdrew even more. Rejecting the mother who had rejected her, Maria now feared being used and devoured by her. When her mother requested money to help her sister and herself, Maria refused.

While she was onstage singing, Maria was happiest and most at ease. Before a performance she panicked; afterward, she often suffered severe headaches. Social gatherings after the opera were always a trial, for she lacked confidence about her dress and social skills. A driven woman, Maria was often irritable and moody. She frequently became sick and had to cancel performances. She seemed unable to enjoy life, to rest, and simply to be herself. Despite her successes, she worried about past mistakes and feared for the future. Her own worst critic, she demanded perfection. If an entire performance wasn't perfect, she was unrelenting with herself and others. Increasingly, Maria fought with opera directors who had difficulty controlling her and dealing with her temper. Her husband always supported her in these conflicts, often feeding her anger. Like her mother, he identified with Maria's fame and wanted to direct her life and her feelings.

By 1952, Maria, not yet thirty, was at the top of her career, despite her personal difficulties. Revered when she sang *Norma* in London, she suffered when reporters made snide remarks about her size. Once when she sang *Aïda,* a critic wrote that her legs were the size of the elephants in the performance. This cruel comment haunted Maria to the end of her life. Determined to lose weight, she suffered the rigors of a severe diet in addition to her demanding work schedule. She wanted to diet both for appearance and for health, for she attributed her headaches and dizzy spells to her excessive weight. She aimed to become as thin as Audrey Hepburn, which meant losing more than sixty pounds. This goal took her almost two years to accomplish. But most of all, Maria wanted to express the roles she sang as fully as she could, and she felt that a heavy singer should not perform a young and beautiful heroine. In particular, she wanted to portray Medea, the murderess, whose chin needed to be sharp and tense with the fury she bore at the rejection of her love.

When in 1953 Maria first sang Cherubini's *Medea,* which was then a relatively obscure opera, she made it a huge success. Her Medea was so powerful that audiences demanded to hear it at La Scala. Directed there by Leonard Bernstein, he said of her performance, "The place was out of its mind. Callas? She was pure electricity."[6] In a bloodred cloak, Maria sang the raw damnation of her fury to an audience that was forced to face the full primitive forces of jealousy and revenge in the human psyche.

Sixty-two pounds lighter, Maria was tall, thin, and very beautiful. She had large, dark, striking eyes, and the magic power—even genius—to become whichever character she acted. World-renowned, she had influenced opera by her emphasis on drama. Her sense of dramatic truth would not allow her to sing in contrast to the part, regardless of criticism. She introduced directors whose hearts were in theater to the opera world—Luchino Visconti, Alexis Minotis, and Franco Zeffirelli. Maria fell in love with Visconti, who admired her intensity and artistic genius but was homosexual. She flew into jealous rages over the men to whom she imagined he was attracted, including her beloved Leonard Bernstein.

Success brought her notoriety. The press published her rejecting letters to her mother and the envious comments of her colleagues. The fickle, idolizing public became hostile. At La Scala she became the target of scandal. She also became embroiled in several lawsuits. Underneath her tough exterior, Maria was very sensitive, even girlish and naive, and she was hurt by this hostility. But when betrayed, her tendency was to retaliate.

Singing at the Met in 1956, she encountered the cold criticism of New York columnist Elsa Maxwell, a grande dame of international café society. Maria decided to charm her, and Maxwell became enamored of Maria. This began a new "mother-daughter" relationship, and Maxwell initiated Maria into an intriguing new world. Maria reneged on a performance in Edinburgh in order to attend one of Maxwell's parties in Venice, and the British press criticized her, calling it "another Callas walkout." Even though her doctor had advised her to cancel the performance and rest due to her overworked state, to Maria, party life was new and exciting, not exhausting like a performance, and the ball in Venice was being held in her honor. At the ball, Maria met Aristotle Socrates Onassis, who began to court her even though they were both married.

During the late 1950s, Maria began for the first time to put her personal life before her art. The critics did not like it. When Maria canceled part of an engagement with the San Francisco Opera due to ill health, the director, Kurt Adler, was furious and canceled the rest of her appearances. He reported her to the American Guild of Musical Artists, who later reprimanded her at a court hearing. They denounced her for not meeting her professional obligations and for betraying art due to self-indulgence. It was as though she was enacting the dilemma of Norma, the high priestess, who falls into conflict between her holy oaths and her passion for love.

Fame and adulation dimmed in Maria's eyes. "We pay for these evenings," she said. "I can ignore it. But my subconscious can't. And that's worse. I confess there are times when part of me is flattered by the high emotional climate, but generally I don't like any moment of it. You start to feel condemned. . . . The more fame you have, the more responsibility is yours and the smaller and more defenseless you feel."[7] Maria continued to sing, sometimes to hostile crowds that she then enchanted with her magical performances, but the cold atmosphere continued at La Scala, causing her to leave this home. Other public squabbles with directors left Maria with an empty schedule.

Onassis had meanwhile begun to court Maria in grand style. Although he detested opera, he and his wife gave a gala party in Maria's honor before a performance of *Medea* in London. He invited Maria and her husband for a three-week Aegean cruise on his yacht where Maria fell passionately in love with Onassis. It was the first time she had ever totally surrendered to anyone. She found Onassis expansive, passionate, extravagant, fun, vigorous, impetuous, tender, and a playmate. Like Maria, he was also a fighter and a winner—and he was a multimillionaire. After the cruise he came to the Meneghini home and serenaded Maria under her window. That night Maria left her husband for Onassis. Scandal ensued; the press printed criticism from her mother and bitter comments from her husband, who said he had molded Maria from a fat, clumsy gypsy into a star.

But Maria was deeply in love. It was the first time she had ever been able to be happy in the moment. The couple left for a two-week cruise. On Onassis's yacht Maria could relax, merging with the one she loved. In her marriage and work, Maria had been a Caged Bird. "I had the feeling of being kept in a cage for so long," she said, "that when I met Aristo, so full of life, I became a different woman."[8] She became able to make friends. Lighter and softer, she tried to reconcile with directors at the Met and La Scala. Maria accepted La Scala's invitation, but in the next years she sang fewer operas at fewer places, increasingly plagued by anxiety about her performances. Most of her energy went toward her great love. The director Zeffirelli said, "All she wanted was to be with Onassis, to be his wife, his woman, his mistress. If he had not pushed her to go on singing, as a kind of showcase for himself, she would have probably stopped altogether."[9] Maria had told Zeffirelli, "You cannot serve two masters," after she missed the high E-flat notes in *Lucia,* one of his productions. Her "voice" seemed to be deserting Maria.

Maria wanted to devote herself to marriage: "I don't want to sing anymore. I want to live just like a normal woman, with children, a home, a dog," she said.[10] But Onassis, a restless man, suddenly started to disappear from the relationship. As soon as he returned, Maria would be at his disposal. Onassis did not want a divorce, but when his wife did divorce him, he did not marry Maria. He was the center of Maria's life, but she was not the center of his. Adapting to *his* routines and wishes, she was at his side at nightclubs, card games, and superficial gatherings, even though she did not enjoy them.

Maria was growing older. She practiced less, and her soprano voice was no longer able to hit high notes consistently, though she still had a strong mezzo-soprano voice. Longing to be free of the nervous tension resulting from overwork that had paralyzed her life, she took on no new operatic challenges. She still hoped Onassis would marry her, but she was not to have the "normal" life of marriage and children for which she had hoped.

Instead, she was besieged by her ex-husband Meneghini, who made nasty comments in the press, and by her mother who, using a Dragon Lady tactic, wrote a scathing book about her daughter. She also received negative reviews for her few performances. She still had successes—a triumphant *Tosca* in London and New York. But in Paris her voice broke while singing *Norma*. In 1965 she sang her last opera.

Having said good-bye to opera, all that was left for her was Onassis. But he began to treat her abusively. He ridiculed opera in front of her, yelled at her, and belittled her in front of his children, treating her according to his moods. He sabotaged a creative project—a film of *Tosca* planned by Zeffirelli for Maria to star in. By giving herself over to Onassis, Maria had put herself at his mercy. Then, at forty-three, Maria got pregnant. Onassis told her if that she kept the child, it would end their relationship. All her life she had wanted a child, but Maria betrayed herself and chose Onassis. Although she still hoped for marriage, the relationship was coming to an end. She was willing to do anything to keep him and aborted both her child and her creativity. Their quarrels got worse. She intuited that another woman was replacing her as the center of his life. Maria had accepted that Onassis had affairs; she had an old-fashioned view that a woman should serve the man she loved. But to be replaced as the central woman in his life was torture. The new woman was Jacqueline Kennedy, whom Onassis had been courting for some time and whom he married in 1968.

From this time on, Maria lived in anguish. She sought sleep as an escape, using tranquilizers and pills. She felt at home nowhere.

Naively, she couldn't understand how anyone could be so cruel. After nine years with him, all she had was humiliation, rage, and tears. In agony, Maria accepted an offer to play Medea in a film by Pier Paolo Pasolini. Inwardly, she knew she was living out the myth of Medea. By turning her confusion and rage into art, she could dramatize her own torment and fury in this ancient story of the Rejected Lover. Pasolini had seen Medea's universal story in Maria's personal life, saying, "Here is a woman, in one sense the most modern of women, but there lives in her an ancient woman—strange, mysterious, magical, with terrible inner conflicts."[11] In his *Medea*, Pasolini recreated a ritualistic world in which natural and supernatural intermingle, in which mystery penetrates the ordinary in a strange and uncanny way.

By dramatizing this myth, Maria hoped she could reexperience her own feelings and transform her bitterness and rage, her "nine years of meaningless sacrifice," into a new life. Identifying with Medea, she said, "She was a semigoddess who put all her beliefs in a man. At the same time she is a woman with all the experiences of a woman, only bigger—bigger sacrifices, bigger hurts. She went through all these trying to survive. You can't put these things into words—I began to look into the depths of the soul of Medea."[12]

During the filming, which took place in the wild surreal landscape of Turkey and in other places where myth and reality seem to merge, Maria was so involved with the film that she once fainted on the set while running barefoot on the arid land. She insisted on acting in the dangerous fire scene, refusing a stand-in performer. Maria lived totally with Medea during the months of filming, and afterward she felt she had retrieved some meaning from her experience with Onassis—that there was a greater meaning to life than any individual experience. She also developed a brotherly friendship with the sensitive Pasolini. His *Medea* was a great work of art, although it was not a commercial success. The elite were not seized by the great archetypal beauty and drama of the film at its premiere in Paris. Although Onassis had reserved a special box for the gala event, he was not present.

Onassis started pursuing Maria again, despite his marriage to Jackie. He telephoned, sent flowers, and finally whistled under her window. Cautious at first, Maria gave in and saw him. Then a letter was published that Jackie had written to a former suitor while she was on his yacht. Insulted, Onassis spent four nights with Maria, whose hopes were raised. But when Jackie wanted him back, Onassis returned to her. In a daze, Maria took too many tranquilizers and ended up in the hospital.

Despite everything, Maria realized that Onassis was important to her, and she called him her closest friend. Onassis also realized that Maria had loved him for himself, since she later stayed by him during a series of tragedies: the marriage of his former wife to his greatest rival; the death of his son in a plane crash; business losses; and poor health. When he died in 1975, Maria was devastated and lived through a haze of tranquilizers.

Meanwhile, she became more passive in her own life. She drifted into a relationship with the great tenor Giuseppe Di Stefano, whose voice, like her own, was fading. The two made recordings together; they went on a world tour; they were asked to codirect an opera. None of these attempts to recapture old glory were artistically successful. At home, Maria lived more and more in the past, listening to tapes of old concerts, looking at old photographs. Perhaps her most successful effort at this time was to teach master classes at Juilliard. On her fiftieth birthday, during their world tour, Di Stefano sang "Happy Birthday" to her as a surprise. The audience was delighted and showed their love to her. But her artistic career was over, and the critics knew it. One night, after she heard of impresario Sol Hurok's death, she nearly had a breakdown onstage. She saw his death as an omen of bad luck, for he had organized her American tours. Onstage at Carnegie Hall, she attacked the way opera houses were managed, particularly the Met. The audience was shocked and embarrassed as she rambled on incoherently, but when she threw roses to them, they leaped to get one. Earlier in her professional career, Maria had sung the Madwoman onstage. Now she was acting it out in her personal life.

After Aristotle Onassis died, Maria lost many of her friends. Visconti died, and Pasolini was murdered; she said she felt like a widow. In poor health, she isolated herself, canceling meetings with friends on the spur of the moment. She ended her affair with Di Stefano, then lamented her lack of strong, intelligent men, saying, "I would love to find such a man. That would be the solution to my psychological problems."[13] She complained, too, about the fate of women who were trapped by society, unable to go out alone at night. In her last days, she watched television, went to movies, regained the weight that she had spent twenty years fighting, walked her dogs, and practiced singing. Alone most of the time, she took pills so she could pass the time in sleep. Shortly before she died of a heart attack in 1977, at the age of fifty-three, she said, "I have nothing. What am I going to do?"[14]

Like many women who are conditioned to expect to find the answer to their life when they find a man, Maria Callas sought the answer to her problems outside of herself. She did not really look within. Sometimes she questioned herself; once she even said she needed to take an inventory of her subconscious. But she never did the inner work, except through her art. She always remained the victim, trapped by resentment and self-pity, the Rejected Lover and the Rejected Child. Trapped as well in her role as high priestess of opera, the legendary figure to whom she and others referred as La Callas, who tried to keep up the public front of dignity, she suppressed her vulnerability, which might have opened her to more intimate relationships with others. Always affected by the rituals of the Greek Orthodox Church, she once lamented her lack of religious commitment. If Maria could have surrendered to a higher spiritual energy, she might have been able to redirect her great passion and longing for love, as once she had done in her art, to something transcendent that could have sustained her. The public had called her La Divina. Her story ends tragically because she could not reap the benefits of the divine inspiration and elation she could give to others.

FROM VICTIM TO THE FEMININE SPIRIT: BARBARA'S STORY

The following story of a contemporary woman, Barbara, who identified with the Rejected Lover patterns shows some ways in which we can break out of the victimized mindset and into a healthier relationship with ourselves. Like Maria Callas's and Camille Claudel's stories, Barbara's reveals that rejection by an Ice Queen mother is often at the core of this debilitating manifestation of the Madwoman.

For many years, Barbara had had a series of short-term affairs, although she had not fallen in love. She customarily became involved with unavailable men. One day at a professional conference, her eyes met those of a man, Mark, to whom she was immediately attracted. He told her he was married, but he spoke of wanting a friendship with Barbara. She felt grounded enough to enter into a friendship with Mark. She liked his playfulness and depth, and that he shared the same profession as she. In their first meetings, they explored each other's feelings, discovering they had the same values and hopes for the future. This closeness enhanced their growing attraction to each other, and, after two months of getting to know each other, they made love.

Barbara's feminine nature bloomed. When she was with Mark, she felt wonderful. But in the long spaces between their meetings, Barbara's doubts and frustrations surfaced. During the Christmas holiday season, Mark told her he needed time by himself to sort things out. She began to get confused and frustrated about their relationship. Right before Christmas, they had a wonderful day together. Then she had a series of dreams that revealed her inner Madwoman raging about her greatest fear—betrayal.

On Christmas night, she dreamed she was in bed with him. But they were not alone. A beautiful blond woman joined them and moved her naked body over Barbara's face to wrestle with the man. The scene switched; Barbara and Mark had planned to go to a wedding. But he disappeared. Then she saw him coming back from a dance in the hotel where they were staying. Her face was red and swollen from tears she had shed in fear and jealousy. She tried to hide her face, which showed emotional pain and her poisoned feelings, afraid that seeing this would drive him away. He asked her what was wrong with her face and then went on to say, without regard for her answer, that he wanted to give up the wedding and stay there and dance with the people. Then he walked away. Barbara associated the red swollen face with her inner Madwoman, who was enraged due to the accumulated, unreleased anger and jealousy that poisons over time. Barbara didn't know what to do with all those bitter, frightening feelings. Later, she reflected that the blond-haired woman on the bed who was taunting her so crudely was the cultural stereotype of man's desire, the Playboy bunny, whom Barbara did not respect but who still held power over her. That her lover chose to dance rather than go to the wedding signaled that the bridegroom for both the inner and the outer wedding preferred casual fun to commitment to the sacredness of marriage.

The next night, Barbara had another significant dream. She was holding a baby girl a few days old, but the baby wasn't breathing right, as though she had no will to live. Soon the baby died. The parents, who were her lover and his wife, stood on either side, powerless to help this baby. After this dream Barbara had a second dream about a baby dying in her arms. She later associated the baby's death with the death of the relationship and also with the death of her awakening femininity. Barbara awoke from both dreams sick with fear.

When Barbara and Mark met after the holidays, it was clear that he felt torn between his feelings for Barbara and those for his wife. They agreed they would not see each other until he knew what he wanted. Crying together, they shared the pain of the situation. As they walked around a small lake, Barbara saw mothers strolling with their babies, a scene that stung her to the quick. She wanted desperately to give birth to a baby. The world seemed huge and empty. Was she to be alone again?

Barbara waited for Mark to write, the one form of communication upon which they had agreed. For her, this was a time of holding the relationship and hope in the midst of a great unknown. But after six weeks, when no letter came, she felt swollen with the poisonous feelings that her dream had imaged. She suspected he was breaking his promise to her that the December parting would not be the final contact, that no matter what choice he made, he would be there to help her through the process. One night, unable to contain herself any longer, the Madwoman took over. Barbara was not a big drinker, but this night she drank herself into oblivion. She called a friend and drunkenly blurted repeatedly: "I'm broken, I'm broken." Then she threw up and passed out in the bed, lying in her vomit. What had broken was her ability to wait and "hold" the relationship. She had been keeping the sacred space they had agreed upon without knowing where he was in his process. Unfortunately, she had not set a time limit upon the waiting period. Retrospectively, she felt she experienced a turning point that night.

Two nights later, after the hangover passed, she knew she had to make contact with him. She called him but reached only his answering machine. Driven now to break the silence, she called every twenty minutes for hours until finally his wife answered and Barbara relayed a message for him to call her. No call came, and she fell asleep, waking at four o'clock, the hour of the wolf. Unable to wait a moment longer, she dressed and drove to his office in the city. She felt possessed. When he arrived, after she made a call to him, she felt strung out and furious. He seemed cool and distant. He told her that his dog, who was the child in their marriage, had been killed and he was grieving the death. Then they shared their feelings about the separation, and in the warm glow that enveloped them, Barbara's anger disappeared. She felt he still loved her and was relieved that their love hadn't been a lie.

But another dream intruded upon her sense of relief. In this dream she was lying on her stomach in a boat when she heard gunshots. Looking up, she saw men shooting at her. To save herself, she had to either jump off the boat or hang from it. When she awoke, she thought that if she didn't act, she'd be killed.

The dangerous boat ride symbolized the "night sea journey," the dark transformational path that this experience was providing her. After two weeks with no word from him, her rage returned; she felt it coming like a tornado. But when she had gotten drunk before and unconsciously acted out the fury, it had felt like a breakdown, since underneath the anger was helplessness. And she had learned little about where the relationship was going. Now she felt that the rage could provide a release if she could remain conscious of it. She telephoned him; he was distant. She tried to hold her anger to find out why he wasn't calling as he had promised. But his distance and lack of communication enraged her, and she exploded on the phone. He hung up on her. Later, when they talked again, he admitted that he didn't think their relationship could work, saying he didn't want to be a caretaker for her "crisis." He felt unable to deal with her emotional outbursts, which from her point of view were caused by his distance and the "not knowing." He told her that he and his wife were in couples' counseling trying to see if their relationship could work.

Barbara felt betrayed; he had told her that he loved her, but his actions revealed that to be a lie. Instead of informing her of his decision to commit to his marriage, he had left her hanging. This time Barbara confronted him directly. Part of what had made her feel crazy was this deception, especially because he had affirmed repeatedly that the foundation of their relationship was friendship. For her, this confrontation was transformational. Usually she took all the responsibility for a relationship, trying to hold in her negative feelings. This was a pattern she had developed in childhood, when she had learned that expressing her feelings and desires elicited her mother's icy rejection. The connection between her mother's rejection of her and the betrayal in this recent relationship had been captured in her dreams.

During this waiting period, Barbara had several dreams in which she was back in her parents' house. In one, she was sleeping on a couch in the living room when her parents intruded upon her. In the dream she did not have a room of her own. Old feelings about the rejection she had felt as a child, particularly from her mother, flooded her. Whenever she had been emotional, she had been punished by her mother, just as she now felt punished by her lover when he hung up after she exploded on the phone. Her father, whom she had experienced as indifferent, showed embarrassment whenever she expressed her feelings, but her mother had harshly judged any display of feelings and was contemptuous of her vulnerability or feminine sensitivity.

An armored amazon, her mother was bitter about sex and felt martyred by her husband's lack of affection. Ignoring her daughter's needs, Barbara's mother lived through her sons and was interested only in money and power. Her values were rigid and male-dominated. A veritable Ice Queen, Barbara's mother gave money instead of love but provoked guilt in her daughter whenever she accepted it. In this atmosphere of rejection and criticism, Barbara struggled with low self-esteem.

Even at forty, Barbara was still trying to get little morsels of love from her cold mother, but she always paid a price for them. Her mother had offered Barbara, who was finishing graduate school, money to visit home for a family reunion, then criticized her for being unable to pay her own way. Instead of getting really angry and confronting her mother, Barbara guiltily defended herself. But after she hung up, she felt bitter and fell into a pit of hopelessness about ever having real intimate contact with her mother. The innocent childlike side of her still wanted her mother to see her and accept her for herself. In reality, Barbara was a creative and courageous woman on a quest for higher feminine consciousness and transformation. The very qualities that made her mature—her sensitivity to others, empathy, introspection, capacity for intimacy—were threatening to her mother, who did not want to change. In her relationships with both her mother and Mark, Barbara had to learn to let go of her projections onto them to give her the intimacy she wanted and move on to situations where she could develop a true relationship. She had to transform the cold internalized mother and confirm the power of her own choices.

When she saw the Camille Claudel film, Barbara identified with the heroine—both in her blossoming femininity that opened through Rodin's love and in the imprisoning isolation that closed in upon her and darkened her life when Rodin rejected her. Like Camille Claudel's mother, Barbara's mother was an Ice Queen. Barbara experienced this coldness in emotionally withdrawn men, and she had to meet it with the energy of her own inner Madwoman. Barbara had to release her emotions rather than smolder in powerless revenge fantasies. Barbara's mother, too, had been caught in the wounds of rejection and revenge by the iciness of her own mother but chose to remain unconscious of it.

In contrast to her mother, when Barbara felt the Madwoman raging inside her, she confronted it—both in herself and in the relationship. At first she had acted it out the night she got drunk, but she knew acting out was not ultimately transformative and would only keep her victimized. Barbara knew she needed to release the poison inside her. She did this later, when she confronted her lover about concealing from her the decisions he was making about their relationship, thereby keeping her in a powerless position of waiting. She also told him clearly that he had ignored her authentic feelings, treating her as an hysterical woman and rejecting her for being mad, breaking his promise of friendship. It took the Madwoman energy to confront him, since she was so conditioned to hiding her feelings and taking responsibility for everything in a relationship.

To help herself process the dark and painful feelings, she wrote in her journal twice as much as she usually did. She worked consciously on accepting the fact of her lover's betrayal. She became able to forgive herself for entering a relationship with a married, unavailable man and, after many months, was able to forgive Mark. She accepted the grieving process and allowed herself to cry as much as she needed. She also spent a lot of time alone; she needed solitude for regeneration. She simplified her life, and she put new energy into her graduate school studies, working on the professional side of her life. To be certain she had cleared out any residual resentment, she met with her former lover four months after their last call. When they parted, she felt free. It was late spring, and she felt the hope of new life inside herself as well.

Because she wanted to change, Barbara transformed her rage at being the Rejected Lover. She recognized the repetitive pattern of being hooked by unavailable men, and she changed this syndrome when she realized it left her feeling inadequate and lonely. She also learned that what she really wanted in a relationship was not just the thrill of romance but the sacredness of the divine wedding. Never again, she promised herself, would she break into the sacredness of another marriage. An affair, she thought, helped married men move either toward divorce or back into the safe container of marriage.

Barbara reaffirmed that the center of her life had to be her own spiritual development and not the longing for love. She consciously used the Madwoman's energy to transform the low self-esteem she had inherited from her mother. In learning the necessity of letting go of the relationship with her lover, Barbara could see that it was necessary to let go of her intense need for intimate contact with her mother, who would not or could not give it to her. Later, she was even able to communicate better with her mother, on more equal terms. She learned to recognize and draw her own limits and to say a fierce no when necessary. She learned that saying no did not preclude saying yes. With these insights and actions, she was becoming free to be her authentic self.

TRANSFORMING THE REJECTED LOVER

What does the Rejected Lover need to do to understand and integrate the pattern that is controlling her life? Trapped by her obsession with the person she cannot possess, she needs to be able to surrender to the reality that she cannot control and to let go of the illusion behind her obsession. Most often, when we cling to someone who is rejecting us, we are really trying desperately to hold on to a projection upon them of a quality within ourselves, something we long, often secretly, to be. It may be any quality—independence, creativity, success, detachment—something that will help or enliven us. But it might also be that we're attracted to something harmful, a shadowy aspect of ourselves that needs to be acknowledged and integrated in some other way. The Rejected Lover needs to look within and break down into components of her projections onto the one who has abandoned her. By identifying the source of attraction, the qualities she has admired and pursued in the loved one and those she feared to see or has tried to ignore, she can begin to understand them in herself and start to develop or work with them.

For example, one woman fell in love with a series of rejecting men—all writers. Secretly, she had always wanted to write herself, but her father had discouraged her. He looked down on writers and artists. Instead, he said he would pay for her education if she pursued a practical occupation suited to women, so she became a social worker. But her unlived creative energy was eating away at her. Underneath her erotic attraction to writers was her own suppressed desire to be a writer and the unconscious resentment and envy that attended it. The subterranean anger that she felt as her lovers succeeded at what she wished to do herself drove her to criticize them, particularly around the home. She also became jealous of her lovers' friends. Finally, through a lot of work in therapy, she was able to recognize this projection. She ultimately enrolled in a creative writing program, began to write, and felt as if a burden had been lifted off her mind and heart.

Transforming the Rejected Lover requires a lot of inner work. We have to face the rage that comes from rejection in order to understand why it is so strong, what its origins are, and why we can't accept that the other has moved on, so that we can. We have to ask the Madwoman what she really wants from us, what we really want, and turn her energy into a creative process. Working with dreams and active imagination can be helpful in this process. The following dream provides a haunting image of the Madwoman's relation to rejection. Working with the dream image helped Claudette, the dreamer, identify her own rage and free herself from its toxic effects.

A giant pink insect with many sections to her body is dragging its huge body behind it through a house. The pink insect is a mother, and her body is inflated and filled with poisonous fluid. I know she wants to eat me up. In horror, I try to escape this poisonous pink bug. But on awakening, I knew I should have tried to puncture the insect to kill it or to let the poisonous fluid out.

At the time Claudette was being rejected by her husband as well as by another man whom she had loved. The giant pink poisonous bug was a grotesque image of the Madwoman's rage that the Rejected Lover feels. Claudette had felt this mad rage from her mother's jealousy of her and also from other women as she was growing up, but it was looming in herself now as well. While Claudette recognized that she was angry, she knew her anger could become poisonous if it were inflated and held in resentment. The dream of the poisonous pink bug was helpful to her to use as an image, and she worked with the toxic feelings unleashed by the rejection she'd experienced in order to transform them and free herself for her creative work as artist and mother.

Women can be rejected by other women as well as by men. The sad early experience of a daughter being rejected by her mother can reinforce the expectation of rejection in all her later relationships and cause her to act in ways that set up repeated abandonments. Rejected daughters often do seek positive mothering from older feminine models such as teachers or therapists and can thereby heal the early psychological wound and move on to healthy relationships. The Rejected Lover-Daughter can herself choose to reject the humiliation she once felt from her mother's icy or toxic rejection and heal herself within.

Another woman, Carol, who was caught in the Rejected Lover pattern was able to see that her madness was, at bottom, part of a codependency pattern in which she would obsess over a relationship, think she could control it, get angry when she couldn't, and feel crazy in the process. As soon as Carol identified the codependent, addictive aspect of this pattern, she was able to start working on the steps of recovery from any addictive pattern. As part of her transformative process, whenever Carol caught herself obsessing about a man, she prayed for the dissolution of both the obsessive fantasies and the clinging to her expectations and projections of what a perfect outcome in her mind would be. This mental exercise enabled her eventually to free herself from the need to stay connected to the man.

The Rejected Lover pattern is frequently entangled with the addictive process, as in Carol's case. The steps for recovery from addiction can work for transforming the Rejected Lover as well. First comes the step of surrender—accepting one's powerlessness over the addiction to the rejecting lover, accepting that the relationship is over, and accepting that clinging to it has made life unmanageable and crazy. Then comes the leap of faith and surrender to the greater powers within that can free a woman to live out of her creative center and be open to a genuine relationship. Following that, it takes a lot of work to sift and sort the rage and resentment about being rejected and to let go of the fears of being alone again. Anxiety, depression, loss, anger, fear of the unknown, grief—all need to be felt by the Rejected Lover and processed consciously before they can be released. Otherwise they will remain unconscious and fester into resentment and revenge. Addictive love relationships have a "vampire" quality. The Rejected Lover often feels like one of the "living dead."[15] It is essential to let go of these vampirelike resentments and desires for revenge upon the lover, for they can keep one hostage to the old relationship. But in order to let go, the Rejected Lover has to see how and where they have been operating in her life and take responsibility for her part in the untenable relationship.

Once the Rejected Lover has freed herself from her particular obsession, she will be free to sacrifice her role as victim in order to gain access to her own power to determine what she will do with her life. Forgiveness is essential to this process. The Rejected Lover has to forgive herself for falling into such an untenable relationship and for being so blindly driven by it and her expectations. Also, she has to forgive the other in order to be free, even if he consciously played on her fears and insecurities, and even if he was cruel to her. This entails seeing the real limitations of the other person, that is, accepting the fact that he can't commit or can't be faithful or can't return her love or devotion. She has to see willingly the reality of the situation instead of clinging to her dreams, wishes, projections, and expectations. Once released from the craziness of her self-generated fantasies, a woman will find enormous energies within herself. She will be able to see her own needs and nurture herself in a caring way that no one else could ever accomplish.

Paradoxically, this new competency and balance can lead her to radiate a desirability that can result in new, healthy relationships with nonpredatory men. She may suddenly find herself moved in creative ways, painting or writing poems, songs, or stories. A community of women friends may assume new importance, especially a group that celebrates feminine spirit and generates love with each other. At this time of emerging self-understanding and self-efficacy, many women dream of a sacred marriage with "Herself," with the divine feminine forces. Ultimately, the transformation of the Rejected Lover can lead to the divine wedding. Her attachment had been to a false love; now she is free for her own divinity.

THE BAG LADY

*See, the human mind is kind of like
. . . a piñata. When it breaks
open, there's a lot of surprises inside.
Once you get the
piñata perspective, you see that losing
your mind
can be a peak experience.*

—JANE WAGNER
*The Search for Signs of Intelligent
Life in the Universe*

QUITE OFTEN, I MUTTER TO MYSELF AS I WALK ALONG THE streets on my way to the cafés where I write. People, usually men, sometimes stop me and ask me why I look so sad. "Smile," they say. "Look happy." They don't understand that my muttering and my serious look are due to an ecstatic inward dialogue. I carry parts of my manuscripts, which I write longhand on yellow legal pads and assorted scraps of paper, in a knapsack or a shopping bag. I have been known to arrive at lectures and workshops with an odd assortment of my writing bags.

Once, after such a workshop, a man referred to me as carrying the archetype of the Bag Lady. At first, I was insulted. The remark shot like an arrow into the heart of my shame as an ACOA, an adult child from an alcoholic family. It also brought up the inner complex of the Madwoman and the Judge.

I felt put down, a potential Madwoman living in chaos, the homeless one who walks the streets holding in her bag things of worth only to her. The "accuser" spoke like a man above it all, a smug judge of feminine eccentricities, a patriarchal assessor of the value of women and what we create and carry with us. But then a friend pointed out that bag ladies are survivors; they are independent, strong, do their own thing, and they don't harm others. On the inner symbolic level, I realized the Bag Lady might have a crazy wisdom needed even by those of us who seem to fit in the world. Afterward, I began to notice how frequently women would bring up their fears of becoming a bag lady. Some of these women were single and approaching forty. Others, even though married, were afraid of being abandoned and having to live on the streets, disintegrating alone in their later years.

FEARS OF THE BAG LADY

Beneath the surface of the carefully groomed woman, the highly skilled professional, the suburban housewife, the rich dowager, or the beautiful *femme inspiratrice* frequently lurks the fear of the Bag Lady. Many women are secretly afraid that they would crumble if they were completely on their own. Their worst fantasy imaginable is that they wouldn't be able to take care of themselves, materially or emotionally. They are afraid they might deteriorate, stop coping, let everything go, and end up poor and homeless. These fantasies reflect a fear of "losing it," a fear that is very real in a culture that measures success by the quantity of one's possessions, and especially one that works against the development of a strong, feminine spirit. These fears also reflect a lack of integration of the "shadow," the disagreeable parts of ourselves that we don't want to look at.

Bag Lady fears often come up when a woman is about to make an important change in her life. The change might be a physical one, such as moving into a new home, or a psychological one, such as leaving or entering a relationship, changing professions, or committing to a new way of life. Sometimes these changes are voluntary, but sometimes they are forced. In times of divorce, entering menopause, or even turning forty (or any age which a woman feels is significant), Bag Lady fears often emerge. Consider, for example, the beautiful woman who has participated in the Muse archetype, which, to an extent, all women in our culture do. When her wrinkles and lines start to show, followed by sags in the skin and jowls, an American woman especially begins to worry about her future, tying her desirability to her appearance and to her economic security, which is often dependent on a man's support. Her worries about her appearance may start as early as thirty or even in her twenties, particularly if she has seen her mother worry about aging. Some women resort to face-lifts and assume that vacant artificial look that covers the lines of experience, suffering, and wisdom to which any full female life attests. To such a woman, the Bag Lady may represent a fate she fears if she has developed neither a solid sense of herself nor, externally, a profession or economic base.

Fear of becoming the Bag Lady often keeps a woman from taking the risks necessary to having a creative and spiritual life. Sometimes her fear stems from economic insecurity, even if she is a highly skilled professional. One successful attorney named Rita, who saw her mother deteriorate before her eyes from the disease of alcoholism, feared the same fate for herself. Although her mother had died at home, Rita thought she could just as easily have died on the streets. To protect herself from such a fate, Rita developed a precise and controlled persona and was always in charge of any situation. Her amazon armor served her well in the law profession, but she really wanted to be an artist. Rita's aversion to a less strict, less secure life-style, stemming from her fear of being like her artistic but alcoholic mother, kept her from responding to the creative call. She feared that to be an artist might loosen her control, leaving her poor, addicted, and homeless.

Another woman, Donna, grew up in the Midwest in a perfectionistic family, where anything that was different from the status quo was shoved under the rug. She became a perfectionist in her own life. Donna's house was always in perfect order; she couldn't bear the chaos in the houses of friends and neighbors who were less rigid than she. Always judging others, feeling she was always right, she began to alienate others with her criticisms. Donna's worst fear was that people would pity her if they saw her loneliness and the desperate confusion that lay hidden underneath her correct persona. She judged others so as not to be judged herself, but her perfectionism was killing her because she was destroying love by hurting others' feelings.

Then the nightmares started. She dreamed she was shopping for a vacuum cleaner one day when a dirty old bag lady spoke to her as she entered the store. In distaste, Donna turned away. Months later, she had a dream that a bag lady was hanging out on the corner of the street near a neighbor's house. In reality, Donna could not get along with this neighbor, who was an easygoing musician who had many friends in and out of her house and many romantic encounters with men. But in the dream, as she passed the bag lady, Donna was attracted by the glitter of her old, bejeweled, ragged red cape.

When she told her therapist this dream, he suggested that she get to know the inner Bag Lady, talk to her, and inquire about her life. For a long time Donna couldn't bear to do this. She felt humiliated and haunted by this inner figure, yet outwardly she was obsessed and enraged at the irregular life-style of her neighbor. Then she had another dream about the bag lady. This time, the old woman was standing by the garbage can at the side of her house, as though she were going to raid it. "Matilda is my name," the bag lady kept muttering. A putrid smell seemed to remain in the air after Donna awoke from this dream. The dream came after she had had a fight with her neighbor whom Donna had criticized for her chaotic life-style. Responding with anger instead of shame, the neighbor pointed out Donna's own chaos in her finances and human relationships. This confrontation, plus the dreams of the bag lady, forced Donna to look at the dark side of her perfectionism and judgmental nature, which, paradoxically, helped her to "lighten up."

THE BAG LADY AS INNER FIGURE

The symbol of the Bag Lady was important to Nancy, a married woman who lived in a lovely suburban home; she had even written a play about a Bag Lady. Once Nancy had stayed in a fine hotel in Chicago where she noticed a rather regal, though bedraggled woman who often came to sit in the lobby. She was impressed with the dignity and freedom of this woman, an independence that she herself was trying to develop. Wandering alone and watching people, Nancy found, was a spur to her imagination. She was inspired to write a play about this Bag Lady who, she knew, symbolized a positive shadow figure in herself since Nancy was at a stage in her own

life in which she wanted to be free of unnecessary possessions, dis-
tractions, and responsibilities so that she could put her energies into
her creative work. In her play the Bag Lady brings freedom and love
into the life of a hotel manager and helps him discover a new appreciation and remembrance of his own mother, who had disappeared
and was thought to be dead.

The following dream of a Bag Lady provided a helpful image for
a sixty-year-old woman, Patricia, who was in the process of leaving
her thirty-year marriage. Patricia had also just taken early retirement
from her job and was looking for her own apartment. Never having
lived alone before, she was uneasy and anxious about whether she
could support herself with substitute work and the small craft business she had recently started. She did not want to ask for help from
others. Although she wanted to be independent and start a new life,
she was afraid of being alone and homeless, or at least alone and
poor. The night before she had the dream Patricia had signed a
lease for a new apartment.

> I am walking along a city street and meet a woman coming
> toward me who gives a general impression of being a street
> person. She looks as though she has just come from a shower,
> and I wonder if she has come from a homeless shelter. She is
> wearing a skirt and a sleeveless, low-necked shirt with shoulder
> straps. The woman is having a hard time keeping her large
> breasts inside the shirt. She stuffs as she walks, and looks at
> me and grins. I see her stuffing them down again as she gets
> nearer, and I see that one breast has two nipples.

The same night, Patricia had two other dream images. In one
she was in a car with a friendly black woman, driving around a
circular route to look for apartments. In the second she was looking
at the sky with others and saw a series of four or five rainbows that
half-filled the sky. The lowest rainbow formed a complete arc. Patricia experienced the entire series of dream fragments as cheerful
and upbeat. She felt the dream was an affirmation of the path she
was taking. Both dream figures, the Bag Lady and the black woman,
were positive shadow figures for her, symbolizing strong, independent, cheerful, and friendly women who knew how to survive on
their own. Their presence in her dream convinced her that she
could survive alone as well. The grinning Bag Lady even had two

nipples on her large breast, suggesting an extra capacity for nurturing. The rainbows in the sky suggested both the protection of the arch of the heavens and the natural beauty that emerges after a storm.

Like many women of her generation, Patricia felt she had been living according to other people's expectations all her life. She had experienced our society's negative treatment of females, particularly as she was growing up with her brother, Clark. As the female child, she always got the short share, while her brother got what he wanted. Patricia had to make do with a tricycle, even though she was the older child, so Clark could have a bike. Clark was taught to drive as soon as he came of age; Patricia learned to drive only later, after she got married. Clark was sent away to a prominent, expensive Ivy League university; Patricia remained at home and went to a small local college as a day student. Patricia knew that the discrimination that she experienced as the daughter in the family was common in her culture, and it made her angry, but to adapt she had tried to suppress her feelings. After her marriage ended, she began to have a series of illnesses. At this time she also had a series of frightening dreams in which snakes were threatening her, as though warning her to take a different path. On the conscious level she liked snakes, so their threatening appearance in her dreams caught her attention. Recognizing her frustration at having been limited by her culture and having accepted these strictures, after much inner work, Patricia decided to move out to try life on her own.

The Bag Lady dream image reveals two aspects of feminine life. As a personal shadow figure, the Bag Lady symbolizes the freewheeling, female survivor and bountiful feminine nurturer. Combined with the image of the rainbow arc, the dream suggests a beautiful and divine feminine container, since the goddess Iris is both the goddess of the rainbow and a messenger from the heavens. But the dream also brought up the external treatment of women, for both the Bag Lady and the black woman have been mistreated, and their images carry negative projections in our culture. In this sense they symbolize the rejected side of the feminine that is characterized as offbeat, peculiar, crazy, or mad and that has been scorned by our white, patriarchal society.

FACING THE FEAR: THE STORY OF DIANA

The story of Diana, a successful professional woman who consciously confronted her fear of becoming a Bag Lady and accepted this manifestation of the Madwoman as a transformative inner energy, can be a model for those of us who need to make important changes in our lives but hesitate to do so. Although Diana earned more than $100,000 a year, her line of work ceased to have meaning for her after some years as she began to change internally. In order to have the space to learn and grow spiritually, she gave up her job, sold her fast, sleek, expensive car, and began to live frugally. She cleaned out her closets and rid herself of her expensive but uncomfortable business clothes. Free of her business role and image, she felt a great sense of relief. She chose to try to make a new life for herself and enter into an exploration of her unknown inner self. During this inward and outward journey, she encountered two astonishing polarities—her fear of becoming a Bag Lady and a new understanding of sacred feminine spirit.

Diana's meeting with the Madwoman in the form of the Bag Lady was accompanied by the recognition that her life had been dominated by patriarchal values. Diana's father was a minister, and she had been brought up to conform and be a respectable Christian daughter. Whenever Diana had expressed an interest in something that didn't fit this image, her parents would say, "What will the congregation think?" The conflict between conforming to the role of a materially successful, dutiful daughter and exploring her own spiritual life kept her feeling inwardly chaotic and disconnected for several years.

As a young girl, Diana had always had a revolutionary spirit. She was a tomboy and, unlike her sisters, never quite fit the role of the minister's daughter. Her father was emotionally warm, but he required his daughters to bolster his proper public image, expecting them to be sitting in the pew, quiet and well dressed, listening attentively to his sermons every Sunday morning. Diana's mother lived for her husband, aligning herself with his image yet resenting it underneath. She had sacrificed her own needs and musical talent to remain a housewife trying to raise her daughters in strict accordance with established Christian values. Diana's mother felt martyred. A Caged Bird, she could neither nurture her daughters with feminine feeling nor empower them with womanly wisdom.

The pat answers and religious dogma that Diana received from both parents, as well as the church community in which she grew up, did not feel right to her. She knew she didn't fit in her family, but outwardly she kept up face.

Bright and beautiful, she was voted the best-looking girl in her class, while inwardly she felt invisible, miserable, even dead and had suicidal thoughts. Her family forbade her to see her Jewish boyfriend and tried to prevent her from going to a secular college. She stood up to them and left home to go to an eastern university, which she felt saved her life at the time. After graduating she worked as an apprentice, then got a high-level job in advertising in New York. Even though she was only in her twenties, she was a superb saleswoman; she had been trained by her parents in how to present the right image and how to please people. Financially astute, she bought a house and invested in the stock market. She had a secure and promising future and was on the fast, upward track of the business world.

Then, in her thirties, at the pinnacle of success, things started to fall apart inside. She had escaped from her parents, yet she wasn't happy. She felt malaise and boredom. Keeping up the pace at work, she was exhausted and confused. Feeling she couldn't maintain a false image anymore, she went into therapy. She also had her astrological chart read and immersed herself in Tarot and astrology studies. For the first time, she began to feel validated and unique.

Her dreams began to reveal that she had a great thirst for a deeper spiritual life, more related to the feminine and to the mystical sources of knowledge she had experienced as a young girl but that had been suppressed by her father's patriarchal form of Christianity. These dreams brought up an inner conflict between patriarchal religion and her own individual search for spirit. One of her first dreams in therapy showed a Madwoman, somewhat like a Bag Lady, breaking into her house while Diana tried to protect her minister father. Another dream specifically told her to read Hermann Hesse's book *After the Fall*. Diana had identified with Hesse as an iconoclastic fellow traveler on the mystical path. Hesse, who won the Nobel Prize for literature, had actually been put in a home for retarded children by his parents. Rebelling against a fundamentalist form of Christianity, Hesse later suffered a nervous breakdown in his youth. After some help from a Jungian analyst, he found his own way in writing to become one of the most influential spiritual seekers of his generation. Diana, who had been helped by reading Hesse, wondered if the dream meant that she, too, would have to go through a "breakdown" or suffer a "fall" of some kind, as part of her spiritual journey.

After entering therapy, Diana became increasingly ambivalent about her work. It no longer challenged her, nor did it give her meaning, and she felt it was beginning to obstruct her real spiritual calling. The materialistic, get-rich-quick values of her firm conflicted with her own surfacing values. She did not want to sell products that were ecologically unsound. Nor did she want to squeeze her body into tight, boxlike clothes and her feet into high heels that hurt her feet and felt foreign to her feminine independence. Moreover, she realized she needed time and space to let her spirit go where it wanted. Something compelling inside her wanted life, even though she didn't know what it was. She felt like the Fool in the Tarot who is at the edge of an abyss; she knew she had to struggle with fear and step off into "nothing." Diana quit her job and lived off her savings. Her parents disapproved of this change and particularly her new Tarot studies. From their perspective, giving up success and status and devoting herself to occult and esoteric studies seemed crazy.

However, Diana felt relieved. She loved having all the time and space she needed for her spiritual exploration—time for reading, writing in her journal, working on her dreams, and studying the Tarot. Hiking in nature, meditating, and conversing deeply with friends on the same path, she was healing herself. She felt blissful.

When the stock market crashed, Diana lost a substantial portion of her savings, and her "fall" occurred. Her fears of becoming a bag lady burst through with overwhelming force. She could imagine herself on the streets, the object of her family's ridicule, enacting the Madwoman that they already had projected onto her. Her fear and anger surfaced. She felt awful and foolish. She had lost her security, but this forced her to look at the practical applications to her life of her studies in astrology and Tarot. Later she realized that she could combine her business training with her new spiritual understanding of the feminine in order to make changes in society.

After the stock market crashed, Diana became fearful that something bad would happen to her. She dreamed of angry men attacking her. One angry man had a meat cleaver—she called him "the revolutionary in the basement." In the dream he hid in the closet of her family home, then went down a set of stairs descending into the living room to a basement, where he stood, angry and threatening. The "revolutionary" represented her own suppressed anger and revolutionary energy, which was not allowed expression in her family. Like the revolutionary underground man, Diana's first tendency had been to withdraw and hide her anger. Her father appeared in some of her dreams. In one, he had died, only to come back to life. In this last dream she had grieved over his death but didn't want people to know he was back. Her father's reappearance symbolized the threat of going back to her old life and the corporate environment. She felt confused and paranoid about the possibility of reentering the field of business she had so happily left.

In still another dream she was back in the family house. She saw a package addressed to Rev. and Mrs. X, her parents. She knew a bomb was inside and would explode if she didn't dispose of it. Frantic, she didn't know what to do with it, because no matter where she put it, the bomb would hurt someone. Finally she realized it was not her role to be the one to save everyone and deal with the bomb. Knowing she needed to leave the house, she called in an expert bomb squad that was qualified to deal with the situation. The dream showed what she needed to do—take care of herself and allow outside experts to deal with the threatening bomb, the suppressive religious system created in her family. The old family system needed to blow up so that a more healthy one could develop. The dream helped Diana realize that unconsciously she was still defending the family system and her father's image.

During this same period of uncertainty, Diana also had many dreams that revealed the feminine mysteries to be found in her descent into the unknown. In one dream she stood by an altar, investigating where the bodies of witchcraft healers were outlined in the stone by precious jewels. This symbolized the great value of her own kind of spirituality. She had many dreams of visiting ancient sites and seeing the ancient symbols of many cultures. The following dream is an example.

Walking on the beach, it feels like the turn of the century.
Many people are out playing. The mood is whimsical and I am
thirteen, walking in shorts with my hands in my pockets.
There are some tubes that open up in the sand. The other
kids want to walk in them, but I say no, they are unsafe. They
seem to be minitornado tubes that might collapse once we are

inside. Then I walk down some stairs into an underground room that has been built of bricks. The room—an Egyptian burial chamber that was hidden by the sand—is cool and solid. I see all sorts of hieroglyphics and Egyptian symbols. I like it down here and feel at home. Then I see a little boy cat crying near a tunnellike shaft in the wall. Hearing another meow from below, I realize the mother cat is farther down. I get a security guard to help get the mother cat out because I'm afraid she'll be hurt. But the security guard tells me that even if we get the mother cat out, the tomcat will still cry at that spot.

The dream revealed that, deep underground in her psyche was a source of ancient wisdom, of symbolic hieroglyphic knowledge from a rich ancient culture that she could enter and understand.

In waking life at the time of this dream, Diana had been re-searching the primitive goddess religions. She understood the im-portance of the feminine descent into the dark night of the soul to gain knowledge, as exemplified in the Sumerian myth of Inanna, queen of the upper world, who journeyed to the underworld to meet its Queen Ereshkigal, her dark sister. She also knew that mys-tics from all religions spoke of this same necessity. The dream con-firmed for her that she was on the right track to retrieving the ancient source of spiritual feminine knowledge. It also suggested she had to go down even further to avail herself of the understand-ing of the Great Mother, symbolized by the mother cat. Diana said the baby tomcat symbolized her tomboy self wanting a mother's nurturing, the care she had not received from her own mother, but she saw that she could be nourished by the maternal wisdom of the universal Great Mother deep down in the ancient psyche. In the beginning of the dream, Diana was a child walking playfully along the beach—symbolically, the place where conscious and uncon-scious meet at the ocean's edge. In the dream she is thirteen, begin-ning to come into womanhood and self-understanding. Not having been allowed to explore her own needs and questionings as a girl, exploration was essential for her now. Her dreams continued to reveal the figure of the Explorer, who descends into caves and finds ancient jewels and arcane symbols.

Diana's fears of destitution were somewhat relieved after she saw the play *The Search for Signs of Intelligent Life in the Universe.* The protagonist, Trudy, is a bag lady who hangs out on the streets of New York City. Once a successful business executive, Trudy got wise and left her job to be free. Diana felt and heard the wonderful crazy wisdom, humor, and spiritual healing that Trudy the bag lady offered. She could see herself as a profound eccentric. Although Diana still had to deal with her Bag Lady fears, she accepted her as a positive inner figure, saying, "One of the advantages of the Bag Lady is that she doesn't need anything that the patriarchy has to offer." She could see the Bag Lady symbolically as a visionary priestess of our time, trying to show the paradoxes in our collective version of reality.

Recently, to supplement her astrological work, Diana took a part-time job with a company that markets canvas tote bags, to be used for ecological purposes, instead of paper and plastic bags that destroy the environment. This work allowed her to support herself, but it was also in accord with her social values. One day a friend noticed her growing collection of tote bags and called her a bag lady. Although she was shocked at first, Diana later said with pleasure: "I have become what I feared the most—a real life bag lady, but in my own way. Realizing I was a Bag Lady was a joyous breakthrough." Diana had transformed for herself the Bag Lady image, an archetypal image with a life of its own, that wanted to be a part of her life. Now she was an ecological, independent, self-reliant Bag Lady instead of a Bag Lady called mad by the patriarchy.

CRAZY WISDOM: TRUDY THE BAG LADY

While I was pondering the meaning of the Bag Lady in my own life, someone invited me to see *The Search for Signs of Intelligent Life in the Universe*, the play that had helped Diana. The leading lady's "mad" but hilarious view of the world reveals the power-driven attitudes that drive us crazy, harden us, and make us anxious and fearful of each other. In the play, Trudy the bag lady offers gentle, crazy wisdom and healing through humor. Written by Jane Wagner, it debuted as a one-woman show starring Lily Tomlin, who portrayed Trudy as well as a variety of other female characters.

We meet Trudy the bag lady on a street corner, where she catches us turning away from her, trying to avoid her eye. She confronts us head-on about our prejudices toward her: She knows we think her voice is too loud, that she scratches too much, that her teeth are poor, and that her eyes twirl like "fruit flies." Trudy tells us that she yells because no one listens to her, and she scratches because she is on fire with creative energy. If we think she is crazy because she carries around junk, Trudy counters: "What should we call the ones who *buy* it?"[1] Trudy believes that everyone secretly asks themselves whether they are crazy. The difference between Trudy and those who think she is mad is that she acknowledges her madness: "goin' crazy was the *best* thing ever happened to me. I don't say it's for everybody; some people couldn't cope."[2] Her madness came when nothing in her life was working. It was a gift, as Socrates described: "A divine release of the soul from the yoke of custom and convention."[3] Released from "reality" in this way, Trudy now refuses to be "intimidated" by it. She thinks it is the leading cause of stress. "After all," she asks: "what is reality anyway? Nothin' but a collective hunch."[4]

Trudy feels her madness gave her a "linkup to extraterrestrial channels" and "a hookup with humanity as a whole. Animals and plants, too."[5] Her electrically charged brain now flashes on scenes from other people's lives in her trance-time, including the space aliens who watch with her. Fascinated with her shopping bags, her space chums find the weird things in them important data for research on their earth project, in which they are trying to understand the strange things we do here—like the way we measure time with clocks or wear uncomfortable and absurd-looking business suits.

Trudy and her space friends speculate that evolution may have burned out and be better viewed as survival of the wittiest than survival of the fittest. Man himself may be the missing link. Trudy's crazy hookup with humanity (the Madwoman's creative connection) could be the "jump-start" for evolution. She wonders whether going mad might even be the evolutionary mind expanding into a new shape and supposes that her "break-*down*" is a "break-*through*," and that her mind is part of a big scientific experiment to serve progress.

According to Trudy, the aliens think everything is interconnected, that we all time-share the same atoms, live under the same sky. Just as the whole makeup of the ocean can be found in every drop of water, so all of humanity's emotions are in each person. The aliens think humans' ability to delude themselves may be their method of survival. Why else do they cover up the truth as soon as they find it? Trudy reports that the aliens are doing a special study of how and when superficiality first appeared in human nature, how, from hunters and gatherers, humans suddenly became party-goers. They are also speculating about the beginning of language, which, Trudy thinks, started with our inner need to complain: When humans started to gossip, the human race became paranoid because they realized they could be talked about; paranoia started war, which started stress. Trudy points out that the aliens worry about us, knowing that other intelligent life-forms "play to play," whereas we humans play to win, thus becoming losers.

After all this research, Trudy and the aliens have developed a philosophical view similar to that of Socrates: "all we *really* know is how *little* we know about what it *all* means."[6] Instead of always trying to know the meaning of life, Trudy wonders why we don't relax "and enjoy the *mystery* of life."[7] Trudy says her greatest insight is: ". . . at the moment you are most in awe of all there is about life that you don't understand, you are closer to understanding it all than at any other time."[8]

During her trances, Trudy tunes in on and portrays other charac-ters in the play—all of whom give voice to the Madwoman within. Lily Tomlin appears as herself and worries that God has Alzheimer's and has forgotten the cosmic scheme. Agnes, a punk adolescent, confesses that she wants to have thick skin so she doesn't have to cry. Agnes feels through her skin the craziness of our world in which the very air we have to breathe is killing us. People accuse her of having contempt for society, but she knows that nothing compares to the contempt society feels for teenage punks like her. Other char-acters include Tina, a drug addict and prostitute with heart, and a community of liberal feminist friends who speak of their fight for liberation and their current state of confusion. Then there is Chrissy, who tries to overcome all her fears. Lacking focus, she works out in an aerobics club to keep fit and keeps losing and gain-ing the same ten pounds, trying to find both a man and a job. Chrissy's suicide note is found by Kate, a well-groomed woman who is wealthy and bored with life, fears chaos, and looks away in aver-sion from her "shadow sister," the Bag Lady. Finding the suicide note of a genuine woman who felt too much makes her realize the contrast with her own frozen feelings and brings Kate to the aware-ness that she has been closing herself off from her own and others' suffering. This insight allows her to catch the eye of Trudy, who offers the wealthy woman her umbrella hat to protect her from the

rain. When Kate accepts this gift, two opposite aspects of the feminine meet—the perfectionistic, critical, high society woman who
fears the Bag Lady, and the down-and-out, vulnerable, eccentric
Madwoman. Their meeting shows the possibility of feminine integration for us all.

The "mad" characters in _The Search for Signs of Intelligent Life in
the Universe_ symbolize different parts of ourselves whom we need to
meet and integrate in order to be psychologically conscious and
whole. For example, we see the Bag Lady and the Visionary through
the character of Trudy herself. The Revolutionary is present in the
liberal women and in the adolescent Agnes, who in frustration expresses herself in Dragon Lady style. Tina, the compassionate prostitute, is in her own way a Muse, while Chrissy is a Caged Bird,
hemmed in by others' expectations. Kate has been trapped in her
role as Judge and Ice Queen. It takes Trudy's gentle, zany generosity
to melt Kate's cold judgments. Trudy's departure from conventional
ideas and ways is an example of the Madwoman's creative connection that allows us to see things anew. But for us to see all of these
inner characters in relationship to one another and the fresh perspectives they bring, sometimes the mind has to break apart for a
moment. As Trudy says: "See, the human mind is kind of like . . .
a piñata. When it breaks open, there's a lot of surprises inside. Once
you get the piñata perspective, you see that losing your mind can be
a peak experience."[9]

WALKING FREE: PEACE PILGRIM

The true story of Peace Pilgrim, a woman who gave up her job,
her given name, and all her possessions to walk around the United
States for peace, is a stirring example of a physical, real form of the
spiritual Bag Lady. With only the clothes on her back and a tunic
with pockets in which she carried her necessities—pen, paper, a
peace message, correspondence, a comb, and a folding toothbrush
—Peace Pilgrim walked for peace for twenty-eight years. She carried
no money with her and was given food and shelter by people she
met. Responding to a spiritual call, Peace Pilgrim prepared herself
for her journey for fifteen years. Then, in the second half of her life,
she started her pilgrimage with the credo: "I am a pilgrim, a
wanderer. I shall remain a wanderer until mankind has learned the

way of peace, walking until I am given shelter and fasting until I am given food."[10]

Peace Pilgrim walked for twenty-eight years and over twenty-five thousand miles, back and forth across the highways of the United States, along the two-thousand-mile Appalachian Trail, and throughout the country. On average, she walked about twenty-four miles per day, depending on how many people approached her to talk. When it was cold, she walked straight through the night to keep warm. She followed the migrating birds, and according to the weather, she slept under bridges, in fields, in depots, and in cemeteries.

Walking was Peace Pilgrim's way of prayer, and she hoped to inspire people to work for peace. She walked in faith and felt protected in her humility. Walking for peace, she waited until others approached her. If they asked, she shared her message: "If you want to make peace, you must be peaceful within."

On her journey, Peace Pilgrim was often taken for a Madwoman. Arrested a number of times for vagrancy, she spent many nights in jail. She took these arrests as opportunities to share her views about peace with those she encountered, whether with policemen who arrested her or the women prisoners locked up in the same cell. After finishing her first cross-country walk, she slept in Grand Central Station in New York with the bag ladies. Sometimes, particularly in wealthy suburbs, people looked at her disdainfully. At times, her life was endangered by strangers on the road. But her inner being radiated such faith and serenity that, miraculously, aggressors stopped before they injured her.

Peace Pilgrim considered the details of her personal life to be unimportant. Although she had grown up in a poor farm family on the edge of a small town, she felt happy in her childhood because she could play in the woods and swim in a creek and had plenty of space to grow up in. She wished every child had enough space for growth. Like plants, "we need room to grow."[11] Peace Pilgrim thought the lack of formal religion she received as a child was an advantage, less "to undo from my mind later on."[12]

In adolescence, her peers looked down upon her because she refused to take alcohol or tobacco, but she knew she was choosing freedom. Born with a natural sense of self-discipline, she set priorities and led an orderly life. These qualities helped her walk her pilgrimage. For a while she pursued a conventional work life, looking for happiness in security and possessions. But then she realized that material success was not the way to meaning, and she suffered when she saw others starving. At first she searched outwardly for "God," questioning but not receiving answers. Once, after she took a long walk and reflected deeply on these questions, she went to sleep and awoke looking at the trees and the stars with a new inner belief in a sustaining creative force that motivated change and was beyond all human power. For Peace Pilgrim, this creative energy, which she felt within herself, was "God."

Her spiritual awakening came one night when she walked alone in the woods and prayed in a moonlit clearing. Feeling complete surrender and willingness to turn her life over to service, from that time on she dedicated herself to work for peace. This was the start of her fifteen years of spiritual preparation and her metamorphosis from self-centeredness to giving. During this time she experienced inner conflicts, but she strove to stop living on the surface. She believed that every person has a special part to play in the divine plan and that listening in silence is the way to hear God's guidance speaking within. To hear this inner voice, she walked in silence, appreciating the beautiful gifts of Nature.

Peace Pilgrim saw that true freedom rests on our recognition that we can be hurt spiritually only by our own wrong actions or inaction, and not by others. Peace Pilgrim believed that we would all find the way to inner peace and universal love if we could only learn to enjoy the places and people we meet in our life's journey and move on when it is time. She endeavored to rid herself of "junk thoughts," knowing that harboring resentments or bitterness toward oneself or others leads only to inner illness. Forgiveness, she believed, is the cure. She thought that most of our problems came from the "anger habit." Since suppressing anger hurts us inside, she suggested transforming the tremendous energy held in by anger into constructive tasks or through the performance of physical exercise. Fear, another big obstruction, is really fear of the unknown. To transform fear we must become acquainted with it. Otherwise, we attract what we fear to ourselves.

Peace Pilgrim worked to purify her motives so she could be of service and work for inner and outer peace. She endeavored to relinquish self-will, possessiveness, and all negative feelings. She aimed to do a small good thing each day. She devoted herself to focusing on this rather than on her "runaway enthusiasm" to solve others' problems, for this deprived them of their own journey of self-growth. Simplifying her life to its essential needs was basic to this effort. She tried to eat healthy foods and care for her body, eating to live rather than living to eat. She rested and exercised and lived out of doors in Nature as much as possible.

Through these spiritual preparations, Peace Pilgrim began to feel free. She experienced beautiful visions. Once she saw a halo and an emanation of light surrounding every flower and tree and felt the oneness that unites all beings—the oneness that, for many, is "God." One day, sitting on a hilltop in the country, she knew she was ready for her pilgrimage. She had a vision of walking coast to coast across the United States, neither accepting money nor being tied to any organization. Ready to receive food and shelter like the wandering mendicants of the East and the Middle Ages, she hoped to share her message of peace: "Overcome evil with good and false-hood with truth and hatred with love."[13]

On January 1, 1953, she began her pilgrimage and gave up her personal name, history, affiliations, and the burden of her posses-sions. Starting in California at the Tournament of Roses Parade, she thought she would be stopped or arrested by police. Instead, she was welcomed and even interviewed on TV. Eventually she was asked to speak to groups and universities. Once on trial for va-grancy, she was asked what she would do if she had to choose be-tween killing or being killed. She replied that, if her life remained in harmony, she would probably not have to make that choice un-less she was called to be a martyr by God. But if she did have to choose, it would be to be killed. When her Judges asked for a logical explanation, she tried to communicate the difference between a self-centered nature and being centered in God. Peace Pilgrim said, "I told them that in my frame of reference I was not the body. I was just wearing the body. *I am that which activates the body*—that's the reality. If I am killed, it destroys merely the clay garment, the body. But if I kill, it injures the reality, the soul!"[14] The police released her, since her pilgrimage had a religious basis. Her message was to practice "a gentle journey of prayer and example,"[15] and she saw herself as "an embodiment of the heart of the world" pleading for peace.

Peace Pilgrim was sometimes judged as a Madwoman for having such a trusting and open heart. Yet she was not naive. Knowing that humanity "walks the knife-edge between abysmal chaos and a new renaissance, with fearful, faltering steps" and that strong forces push toward destruction, Peace Pilgrim believed that the only way to overcome fear is to face it. Thus, she was willing to face chaos with the wisdom and strength of the Madwoman, whose wild courage radiates hope. Speaking with the crazy wisdom of the Bag Lady, she remarked, "This is me and all my possessions. Think of how free I am! If I want to travel, I just stand up and walk away. There is nothing to tie me down."[16] She lived like "the lilies of the field." Peace Pilgrim shared her journey up to the end of her life. Several years ago, she died instantly in a head-on collision while she was being driven to talk on peace. Her death came to her as she had expressed it—as "the glorious transition to a freer life."[17]

THE EXTERNAL DILEMMA

In *Shopping Bag Ladies: Homeless Women Speak about Their Lives,* a book of interviews by Ann Marie Rousseau and Alix Kates Shulman we are brought before the social dilemma we all face due to our neglect of homeless women. This outer mistreatment of our fellow human beings reflects the inner homelessness and rejection that many women feel. Many but not all of these women are on the streets due to poverty, old age, senility, mental disabilities, a history of abuse, drugs, and alcoholism. Often, crisis situations—disease, family quarrels, burned houses, evictions, robberies, lost checks— left them homeless and unable to cope adequately enough to find help. But all suffer from the social isolation we tend to inflict on the rejected single woman, whether she is elderly or middle-aged.

Once on the streets, the women suffer from the stress of noise and lack of privacy, from the stupor, disorientation, and confusion resulting from sleep deprivation, poor nutrition, fear for their safety from mugging and rape, exposure to the elements, and sheer exhaustion. This handicaps them further in their abilities to obtain safe housing. Some of these women have a great fear of being locked away in mental institutions or imprisoned, and they would rather struggle for themselves than depend on charity or the social system.

When interviewed, some of the bag ladies said they preferred to take their chances on the street, feeling safer outside than in run-down hotels, where they were likely to be mugged on stairways. One bag lady said she had been thrown out of a hotel because the manager had said they made more money renting rooms to prostitutes. In some cities there are shelters for men but not for women. Many of the bag ladies did not know how to deal effectively with impersonal and often rude treatment from bureaucratic systems to get financial support and shelter. As one Native American woman, who originally came to New York with her mother to earn money to send back to their tribe from the handicrafts they made, expressed it: "I went to Mary House but there was no room. They sent me to the Women's Shelter and now they say they're going to put me in a home. That's worse than being dead. I'd rather live outside than to go into one of those places."[18]

Quite a few bag ladies feel ashamed to beg and want to maintain their pride and integrity. One woman, who ended up on the streets after she left her marriage, described her husband as taking complete control of her life. He would get angry and abusive with her. "He was not used to dealing with his feelings. You could take off the lid and it was like there was nothing under it but chaos."[19] Yet *she* was the one who was considered to be "mad." Another younger homeless woman, who previously had suffered a nervous breakdown, complained about men who claimed to help her but really wanted to take her to bed: "Of course women are discriminated against and I guess that made me feel like a volcano. Everything just erupted and I went absolutely mad because I never spoke up."[20]

The social problem of the bag lady will not improve if it is ignored. This is true on both the inner and outer levels. Whether we admit it or not, the fear of being abandoned and homeless—becoming the bag lady on the streets—lurks as an unconscious fear in most of us. Unless we face this fear, we will be unable to transform it, either in our individual lives or in society. We have to learn to care for the feminine in all her forms, whether she is the isolated bag lady on the streets, the neglected Bag Lady in ourselves, or the very abused Mother Earth on which we live. One woman in a workshop gave poetic expression to the personal and cosmic plight of the Bag Lady in the following poem:

> Our Mother, the Bag Lady
> The wrinkled hose,
> The run-down shoes,
> The rose upon her hat . . .
> There she was; I watched her,

As on the beach she sat.
Her world she carried in her bags
That she'd placed by her side. . . .
Mountains high and valleys low
And seas with scudding tide.
I swear I heard the sea's roar
And smelled the forests green.
I felt the wind's chill;
I saw the snow;
Then knew that I'd been seen.
She looked at me with dark, mad eyes;
I knew not what to say
To displaced,
Dishonored Gaia.
She got up and moved away.

THE RECLUSE

The soul selects her own society—
Then—shuts the door—
On her divine majority—
Present no more.

> —EMILY DICKINSON

ONCE I MET AN OLDER WOMAN WALKING ALONE IN THE HIGH
mountains. I am an eccentric recluse myself, who
feels most at home hiking and enjoying Nature's solitude, so we recognized each other as kindred spirits, and we began to talk. Once she had lived a
typical suburban life, but after her husband died,
she found herself suddenly free to do whatever she
wished. During the summers, she spent her time
alone in a cabin in the woods where she could sing
along with the birds, follow the flight of the deer,
and watch the antics of the foxes and chipmunks.
All this play in solitude with her animal friends fed
her fantasy, and she became quite a fine poet. But
her former friends considered her a bit strange, and
sometimes she felt that way herself when she
stopped to eat alone at restaurants on her trips to
her country cabin. Although she had been content

in her former coupled life, now she was content in a quite different way living alone. Nor was she interested in remarrying. She was enjoying the new creative life she had found by living according to her own natural rhythms.

The single person who lives differently from the conventions of society is often pitied, treated with condescension, ostracized, or even considered odd and crazy by those who lead normal lives. People who ridicule the solitary eccentric may secretly be afraid, for the loner rejects and threatens their established way of life. The Recluse can be of any age—a gifted teenager, a divorcée, a person emerging from a midlife crisis, a young woman who chooses a solitary life, a bachelor or a widow, but most frequently this negative projection is onto the middle-aged or older single woman.

The female Recluse is often seen as a Madwoman, and indeed, some isolated people who shut themselves off from life, out of fear, anger, resentment, or paranoia, are mentally disturbed. The archetypal crazy old women who live in dilapidated houses with forty or so cats have their real-life and literary counterparts to spinsters such as Miss Havisham, the character in Dickens's *Great Expectations,* who rocks away in her attic room, still wearing the bridal gown, waiting for the missing bridegroom who deserted her.

Single women often share the fear of becoming an "old maid," another Recluse figure from fact and fiction. In the childhood game, getting the Old Maid card meant you were a loser. Even today, single women receive this negative projection, which can include suspicion of madness or of eccentricity. A bachelor is usually seen as free to enjoy life, while a woman without a man is often pitied. Some women still marry to avoid the social stigma of spinsterhood, even though at heart they prefer their independence. Other women choose to remain single—because they prefer it, or because they have not found the right soulmate or someone acceptable enough and would rather not make a conventional compromise. Still others are overlooked because they do not fit the collective image and are viewed as too homely or too tall, or too fat or too shy, and so on. Even among the happily married, however, women cry out for separate time for themselves and space to create for themselves; they need "a room of one's own."

The presumption that solitary women are unhappy or pitiable is not only patronizing, it usually reflects the fear of loneliness within the man, woman, or couple who makes this projection. To be alone (whether lost, unchosen, abandoned, or rejected) and unable to cope by oneself is one of the greatest fears of people who truly cherish relationships or who have not developed a rich inner life, nor achieved peace within themselves. To avoid facing the challenge of human aloneness, which all of us must face sooner or later, many people project their aversion to being alone onto the single woman.

The woman who feels lonely and has not come to terms with her aloneness may experience the negative aspect of the Recluse—isolation and paranoia. The British novelist Jean Rhys described this aspect of the Madwoman—the woman who feels alone and rejected and resents pity from others. Often other women can be her cruelest judges. In Rhys's novel *Good Morning, Midnight,* a woman in her late forties sits in a café suffering in self-consciousness as two young girls laugh at her. Muttering to herself, she expresses her rage as follows:

> Never mind . . . one day, quite suddenly, when you're not expecting it, I'll take a hammer from the folds of my dark cloak and crack your little skull like an egg-shell. Crack it will go, the egg-shell; out they will stream, the blood, the brains. One day, one day . . . One day the fierce wolf that walks by my side will spring on you and rip your abominable guts out. One day, one day . . .[1]

In contrast, Leah, a woman in her forties, identifies very much with the positive aspect of the Recluse. An independent and creative woman, she craves solitude and has lived alone more than she has coupled. Leah spends days at a time by herself doing creative work and enjoying it. While hiking, playing music, cross-country skiing, or reading, she often enters ecstatic states of consciousness; she gets high and happy from Nature and art. Reclusive life offers her the sacred space where she can go and make contact with her deepest self; it is the place where she feels soul-communion, the place where she meets spirit.

However, like many reclusive women, Leah sometimes experiences a mild paranoia about being single. Sometimes she feels so different that she feels awkward around couples and not a part of normal life. At times, her negative Madwoman Recluse makes her angry at her married friends' normality and isolates her further, out of a fear that people will want too much from her. Leah keeps to herself sometimes to protect herself from codependent behavior when she doesn't know how to regulate her own energy. Her reclusive behavior also becomes negative when it prevents her from reaching out and asking for help and when it shields her from sharing her feelings.

People who do not understand the relation between creativity and solitude also consider Leah's retreats evidence of madness. Her self-reliance often disturbs the husbands of her friends, who fear her as a powerful woman. Some husbands even consider her a bad influence on their wives, afraid that the women might be tempted by her sense of independence. As a Recluse, Leah does not like to go to parties because most often she finds the conversations superficial and a waste of time. She would rather stay at home and read. But when she does go and meets an interesting person, she may stay for hours, engaging in conversation in depth. Recovery in a twelve-step program has helped her reach out and find a balance between her inner soul-communion and her outer relationships. A statement she heard at one of these meetings—"You alone must do it, but you cannot do it alone"—emphasized the necessity to hold the paradoxical tension between her reclusive independence and her need for communion.

When Leah needs to be disciplined in order to paint in her studio, to write and study at her desk, or to practice the saxophone in her music room, she invokes in her mind a positive image of the Recluse. In this inner Recluse energy she finds the faith and power to enter her flow of feelings, energy, and natural rhythm so that she can feel and express her creative power. To counter her tendency toward distraction by external stimulation, Leah found a creative feminine model in the character of Miss Helen, a recluse in *The Road to Mecca,* an inspiring play that shows the universal human value and integrity of solitary life.

THE OLD RECLUSE: *THE ROAD TO MECCA*

The Road to Mecca tells the story of an old woman who lives alone, struggling to remain free and create—a struggle that we all face sooner or later. A play by Athol Fugard, *The Road to Mecca* was suggested by a true story he had heard about an eccentric woman living in a remote section of South Africa. The drama shows how madness is often projected onto the creative person, in this case by the towns-people, and it demonstrates the enormous strength required of the creative Madwoman to affirm her own integrity and that of her work. *The Road to Mecca* also presents the paradox between the need for solitude and the need to have one's creations appreciated by another. This process is portrayed in the relationship between two very different types of women—each a Madwoman in her own way—and the transformation of each one that occurs as an outcome of her meeting with and her confrontation of the mad Judge in the patriarchy.

In *The Road to Mecca,* we meet Miss Helen, a small frail woman nearing seventy who has been making statues that her neighbors consider scandalous ever since her husband's death fifteen years ago. Before her husband's death she leads a regular life, accompanying him to church every Sunday. She seems a meek, obedient woman and is a favorite parishioner of the pastor, Marius Byleveld. On the eve of her husband's funeral, Marius accompanies Miss Helen to her home, closes the curtains and shutters to shield her, makes her tea, offers her comforting words, and lights a candle for her before he leaves. Miss Helen sits there in the darkness, staring at the candle, waiting for it to go out and leave her in darkness. She is used to bleakness, for she has been feeling empty inside for many years, although she has hidden this from others. But that night something strange occurs. Instead of going out, the flickering candle suddenly grows brighter, and Miss Helen has a vision of a creative light to which she will become an apprentice.

Following this incident, late one Saturday night, a picture of an owl comes to her suddenly. Learning she can "see in the dark," Miss Helen knows she has to stay home from church on Sunday to sculpt the image of the owl before she forgets it. Pastor Marius sees her empty seat in church and becomes worried about her. But after that, Miss Helen stays away from church more and more often, as she creates a city of light, her own Mecca, which includes a large array of statues that she puts in her garden and her house. She sings as she sculpts, and the townspeople think she is crazy. They are shocked by the strange assemblage of camels and Wise Men facing east, the glittering peacocks, the mermaids, and the owls. She creates a Buddha, an Easter Island head, and an odd creature that is half-man, half-rooster, with his trousers only partway on. She even fashions a mosque out of old beer bottles. The townspeople talk about Miss Helen and frighten their children with stories about her "monsters." Once, they stone her house and statues.

After fifteen years of visions and sculpting, however, Miss Helen becomes frightened. New images and inspirations have stopped coming to her. Her eyesight is beginning to fail, and arthritis affects her ability to lift things and care for herself. Miss Helen is afraid that her creative process, what matters most in her life, is coming to an end. In a state of depression, she writes an alarming letter to her only friend, Elsa, a young teacher from Capetown, saying that she is in her darkest night and is losing everything. She mentions thoughts of ending her life. She tries to explain her fears to her friend:

> I have to see them very clearly first. They've got to come to me inside like pictures. And if they don't, well, all I can do is wait . . . and hope that they will. I wish I knew how to make it happen, but I don't. I don't know where the pictures come from. I can't force myself to see something that isn't there. I've tried to do that once or twice in the past when I was desperate, but the work always ended up a lifeless, shapeless mess. If they don't come, all I can do is wait. . . .
>
> I try to be patient with myself, but it's hard. There isn't all that much left . . . and then my eyes . . . and my hands . . . they're not what they used to be. But the worst thing of all is . . . suppose that I'm waiting for nothing, that there won't be any more pictures inside ever again, that this time I *have* reached the end? Oh God, no! Please no. Anything but that.[2]

Elsa arrives to visit Miss Helen and finds the elder woman nervous and apologetic, dressed less carefully than usual. Elsa, who is twenty-eight, is as strong in appearance as she is in her social philosophy. Elsa is a Revolutionary Madwoman, not a Recluse. She is an activist who is outraged by the injustices in South Africa toward blacks and women and is ready to fight for her beliefs. When she arrives, Elsa is angry and bitter about the betrayal by a recent lover whom she had hoped to marry. Even so, Elsa soon feels the magic of Miss Helen's house of colored mirrors and fantastic objects, and the old lady's sense of humor relaxes her.

The two women met by chance several years earlier. While traveling in a dusty village in the Karoo, to get away from some flies that were driving her mad, Elsa walked down a deserted road by Miss Helen's garden and peered in at the statues. She had heard about the strange old lady who was reputed to be as "mad as a hatter," although not violent. Miss Helen was repairing a mermaid in the garden and saw the young woman's astonished gaze. She asked her if she knew the direction to Mecca. When Elsa failed to answer correctly, Miss Helen pointed to the east and invited Elsa in for some tea. As the light started to fade, Miss Helen lit the candles in the room, shyly at first, because that magic room of light and color was the expression of her innermost self.

Miss Helen was accustomed to the rude gaze of the villagers, who dismissed her house as ugly, but never before had she shown anyone the interior of her glittering house of fantasy. The years of being ridiculed as "a mad old woman had taken their toll."[3] Miss Helen hadn't been able to create anything for a year, but when she saw Elsa's eyes light up in amazement, Miss Helen felt proud. So she said to her, "Light is a miracle . . . which even the most ordinary human being can make happen."[4] That night, after Elsa left, images of new statues for her Mecca flooded her mind. With joy, Miss Helen knew she could work again.

The two woman—one young and one old—became fast friends through creative play. As Miss Helen expresses it: "I trust you. That's why my little girl can come out and play. All the doors are wide open!"[5] Indeed, it was usually Miss Helen's "little girl" who came out to play first and helped the serious Elsa have fun and be a bit of a fool. When these two women "played together," the humor of the "old mad woman" joined with the young woman of social action to create a wonderful feminine relationship.

But this time Elsa is visiting not to play but to find out what is wrong with Miss Helen. Finally the older woman confesses that the church council wants her to sign herself into a home for the elderly, since the parishioners are worried that Miss Helen can't take care of herself anymore. With her fading vision and her arthritic hands, Miss Helen has had a few accidents, including a serious fire in her house. At first, Elsa is outraged that the church council wants to "put away" her friend into a "safe" church home for the aged so that she will no longer be part of the world. But then Elsa realizes that Miss Helen is allowing Pastor Marius to bully her. If Miss Helen is to survive, Elsa thinks, she will have to fight for herself. So she gives her some practical suggestions—to make appointments with a doctor and an optician to help her arthritis and improve her eyesight, and to get someone to help her take care of the house.

Putting Miss Helen away in a nursing home would be a victory for the church patriarchy, since her nonconformist life-style disturbs the parishioners. Miss Helen herself is aware that Pastor Marius is only waiting for the day when she will conform and stop creating her Mecca. So far, she has not had to fight for herself. Now, if she does not say no to Pastor Marius, she will be saying no to her very life. Helen knows this but she feels confused and needful of Elsa's strength and assertiveness. She wants Elsa to say no to the pastor for her.

In the confrontation that ensues between Marius and Elsa, Marius is alternately patronizing and cajoling in his manner to Miss Helen, calling her a harmless old lady who needs help. Elsa realizes that people are afraid of Miss Helen because she is different, however, and replies that people don't stone harmless old ladies. The townspeople are jealous of Miss Helen's creative light and fear the statues of Mecca because they express her freedom. "I'm sure it ranks as a cardinal sin in these parts. A free woman! God forgive us,"[6] Elsa says, adding that Miss Helen is "the first truly free spirit" that she has ever met and that the older woman challenged her into an awareness and responsibility for her own life that she never knew until she met her.

Then Pastor Marius's real concern comes out. He reveals his anxiety and grief that Miss Helen has abandoned the church for the "cement monstrosities" that she creates, which in another time and age "might have been called idolatry."[7] He admits that he is bewildered and jealous that she has abandoned their long friendship and that he hates that lunatic word *freedom*. Acting in the manner of the Judge, Marius justifies his own way as the only right one.

By now, Miss Helen has found her calm and strength. She tells Marius that she knew very well what she was doing when she chose to stay home from church that first Sunday and sculpt the owl. She says emphatically, "You don't break the habit of a lifetime without realizing that that life will never quite be the same again."[8] Then, speaking with authority, Miss Helen tells Elsa to light the candles, beginning with the candelabra in the center of the room. She becomes radiant, alive with her vision of Mecca—and she tries to show it to Marius. "A city, Marius! A city of light and color more splendid than anything I had ever imagined. There were palaces and beautiful buildings everywhere; with dazzling white walls and glittering minarets. Strange statues filled the courtyards. The streets were crowded with camels and turbaned men speaking a language I didn't understand, but that didn't matter because I knew, oh I just knew, it was Mecca! And I was on my way to the grand temple. In the center of Mecca, there is a temple, Marius, and in the center of the temple is a vast room with hundreds of mirrors on the walls and hanging lamps, and that is where the Wise Men of the East study the celestial geometry of light and color. I became an apprentice that night."[9]

By now, Miss Helen is ecstatic. In seeing what she has created, she finds her strength and her center. Laughing with joy, she tells Elsa to light every candle in the room. She wants to show Marius what she has learned and the magic and the splendor she has created in this room.

Look, Marius! Look! Light. Don't be nervous. It's harmless. It only wants to play. That is what I do in here. We play with it like children with a magical toy that never ceases to delight and amuse. Light just one little candle in here, let in the light from just one little star, and the dancing starts. I've even taught it how to skip around corners. Yes, I have! When I lie in bed and look in *that* mirror I can see *that* mirror, and in *that* one the full moon when it rises over the Sneeuberg *behind* my back! This is my world and I have banished darkness from it.

It is not madness, Marius. They say mad people can't tell the difference between what is real and what is not. I can. I know my little Mecca out there, and this room, for what they really are. I had to learn how to bend rusty wire into the right shape and mix sand cement to make my Wise Men and their camels, how to grind down beer bottles in a coffee mill to put glitter on my walls. My hands will never let me forget. They'll keep me sane. It's the best I could do, as near as I could get to the real Mecca. The journey is over now. This is as far as I can go.

I won't be using this *(the application form)*. I can't reduce my world to a few ornaments in a small room in an old-age home.[10]

With this affirmation of her own life and her acceptance and preparation for death, Helen returns the old-age home forms to the pastor, who at last accepts the finality of her decision. Marius, who is secretly in love with Helen, realizes they have been on separate journeys. Proudly, Elsa says to Helen: "And you did more than just say no to him. You affirmed your right, as a woman."[11]

Suddenly, Elsa breaks down. She confesses that she had an abortion and hates herself for doing it. She also feels bitterness about the plight of black women in South Africa and about Helen's aging. She resents her own helplessness. Now Miss Helen is able to help Elsa, comforting her so she can cry. The two women—one young and beginning her journey; the other old, knowing that she is at the end of her journey and in "the last phase of apprenticeship," facing the darkness of death—look at each other and laugh.[12] Their arms are open, trusting each other to make the leap of faith each needs for their respective journeys—alone and together.

Elsa and Miss Helen represent two different aspects of the Madwoman. Elsa is the bitter Rejected Lover, hiding her tears beneath her armor of anger. She is afraid to show her vulnerability. Yet also under the armor is the little girl who wants to play and who longs for personal love and acceptance. Elsa needs to incorporate Miss Helen's playful creativity and vulnerability, just as the gentle Helen needs to affirm in herself the self-assertiveness and fighting power that is so easy for Elsa to express. Elsa embodies a positive revolutionary aspect of the Madwoman in her outrage at social injustice. The Madwoman's anger fueled many of the reforms by the early feminist movement, and it is always needed to confront psychological, economic, and political inequities and abuse. Miss Helen's reclusive Madwoman energy, with its inward direction, affirms the freedom of creative expression that often is the inspiration for social action. Both women's complementary forms of Madwoman energy show what can happen in a remarkable meeting when two or more women come together.

In the figure of Miss Helen we see the transformation of the Madwoman who accepts, affirms, and expresses her creativity, even though others discount her. Although she lives a reclusive life, she is not cut off from love, as evidenced by her relationship with Elsa. Only the negative projections of madness onto her by the conformist society in which she lives cut her off from others. Miss Helen has chosen her way of life consciously, understanding that in order to be free to give form to her creations, she will sacrifice certain things. To make her visions real, her hands bend wire and mix cement to make sculptures. Through the discipline and work of giving form to the images that she receives, she shapes reality and transforms humankind, exemplified by Elsa, whose entire life was changed into one of conscious awareness and responsibility when she met Miss Helen and experienced her Mecca. Mecca symbolizes a holy place in the East—the center and goal for the spiritual practitioner. For Miss Helen it represents the purpose of her life and the actualization of her own unique personal vision—a creation of light and color and fantasy that, as she says, "even the most ordinary human being can make happen."[13] But to create her Mecca, Miss Helen had to have the courage to deviate from the conventional Christian way of life approved by the townspeople. She had to travel alone. Trusting herself, her visions and her feelings, she symbolizes the woman with the radiant inner light of feminine spirit. Miss Helen embodies the "divine madness" of creative life. According to Socrates, gadflies drive us from our static lives to search for meaning. Indeed, Elsa is driven to Helen's house to get away from the flies that are driving her mad in the hot and dusty town. As a result, her life is changed when she encounters the first truly free spirit she had ever met—a "mad gadfly" woman who tells the truth about her life through her art.

The Recluse is personified by Miss Helen, the wise old crone in all of us who affirms the value of life's journey that each of us must make alone, the passage from birth to death. Like the literary figure of Miss Helen, Rachel Carson, the reclusive biologist and writer, followed the promptings of her spirit to become a pioneer to preserve life on our planet.

HONORING NATURE: RACHEL CARSON

Rachel Carson was a Recluse turned Revolutionary. She was also a Visionary. Called by some the "Nun of Nature," she fought, in her landmark book, *Silent Spring,* against the poisoning of the earth. As early as 1962 she emphasized an ecological approach to life. Exposing the way pesticides and other toxic agents destroy Nature and the very food we eat, Rachel Carson took on, single-handedly, a battle with the chemical industry that was to change the course of history.

This shy woman who loved the solitude of Nature was attacked viciously by furious opponents for being "an hysterical woman," prone to emotional outbursts. She was accused of frightening the public by using emotionally laden words that fanned controversy. Opponents said that her book should be ignored; others dismissed it as "baloney."[14] Even horticulturists and university experts in nutrition and public health criticized and patronized her.

A naturalist and poet, a pioneer in holistic thought who was aware that every single thing we do affects the whole, Rachel Carson was concerned with preserving the living earth. She saw that the senseless and brutal tampering with Nature would ultimately destroy not only natural beauty but all life. She was alarmed at the arrogance of humankind in its assault on the environment and its abuse of living things.

Known as a modest and gentle woman, friends described Rachel Carson as dignified and intense. She was serious but had a sense of humor. Always attentive, observant, quiet, and reserved, she disliked "small talk" and was consumed with the great silence and solitude of Nature. Born on May 27, 1907, she grew up in the Pennsylvania countryside not far from Pittsburgh. She loved to explore the woods and fields and to play with the farm animals. The youngest of three children, she was a solitary child who loved to be alone "in woods and beside streams, learning the birds and the insects and flowers."[15]

Rachel said her love of Nature was a gift from her mother, who encouraged and shared with her an awareness of Nature's beauty and mystery. Her mother protected Rachel in her childhood because of her fragile physical constitution and kept her home from school if she seemed sick. A former schoolteacher, her mother tutored and read to her. Rachel loved books, and even as a young child she wanted to be a writer. At ten she won an award for a short story, and at eleven she was paid a small sum for an article on Saint Nicholas. A loner bent on her studies, she was not socially inclined and had few friendships. But peers respected her, and teachers recognized and encouraged her talents. She won a scholarship to a women's college (now Chatham College), where she majored in English literature and wrote for the school paper. Fascinated with biology and zoology, too, she studied genetics and received an M.A. in zoology from Johns Hopkins University. Later she taught at her alma mater and at the University of Maryland. She spent many summers studying at the Woods Hole Marine Biological Laboratory in Massachusetts.

Rachel was fascinated by the sea and would become its biographer *(The Sea Around Us)*, feeling her destiny was linked to the ocean. She also wanted to be a poet, and even though her poems were rejected by journals, her poetic imagination merged with her scientific passion for fact in a unique combination that created many beautiful books on nature. But her first professional writings were newspaper feature articles and radio scripts for the Bureau of Fisheries, which led to a permanent job as their aquatic biologist. During the Depression, when she was in her late twenties, Rachel's father died suddenly, and she had to support her mother and herself. The following year, when her sister died, Rachel took care of two young nieces.

"Undersea," her first nationally read essay, was published by *The Atlantic Monthly* in 1937. With a series of beautiful poetic images, Rachel described the mysterious life in the ocean. Publishers asked her to write a book, and *Under the Sea-Wind* came out three years later. The book's central character was the vast sea itself, which held the "power of life and death" over each of its inhabitants. She described the interconnections of all living creatures of the sea and their unique time, immeasurable by human "clock-time." *Under the Sea-Wind* is an exquisite description of the ocean and its creatures, but few copies sold. To her disappointment, Rachel realized that with the exception of the occasional best seller, writing books was not a way to make money. But writing was in her blood.

Rachel suffered the classic tension of the Recluse, between the joy of losing herself in writing and the pressures of the practical world. Writing late through the night, her beloved cats were her companions and possibly her Muses. Loneliness was a necessary sacrifice for the writer, Rachel said:

> Writing is a lonely occupation at best. . . . During the actual
> work of creation the writer cuts himself off from all others
> and confronts his subject alone. He moves into a realm where
> he has never been before—perhaps where no one has ever
> been. It is a lonely place, and even a little frightening. . . .
> No writer can stand still. He continues to create or he
> perishes. Each task completed carries its own obligation to go
> on to something new.[16]

But Rachel, in order to write, needed to "retire to my secret cave."[17] Despite its difficulty, isolation and solitude had their rewards. It allowed the writer to "learn to be still and listen to what his subject has to tell him."[18] Rachel needed to allow the subject to fill her and take command, at which moment "the true act of creation begins," when "the real agony of writing is experienced."[19] Enveloped in the sensitive stage of a book's process, she always tried to find the book's inner unity, its heartbeat. Her natural proclivities as a Recluse helped her in that "state of desperate determination," the torture of writing that many writers feel as they labor over a manuscript. Writers often undergo a difficult, chaotic creative process. Rachel described it this way:

> I decided that I have been trying for a very long time to write
> the wrong kind of book, and in dealing with the corals and
> mangroves and all the rest I seemed at last to fall into the sort
> of treatment that is "right" for me in dealing with this sort of
> subject. . . . The book has become an interpretation of four
> types of shore, the other chapters merely providing the frame
> for this, the real heart of the book. . . . The solution frees
> my style to be itself; the attempt to write a structureless
> chapter that was just one little thumbnail biography after
> another was driving me mad.[20]

Rachel wrote late at night with her favorite authors near at hand for inspiration—Conrad, Melville, Thoreau, Richard Jefferies, Henry Beston, H. M. Tomlinson, Henry Williams. She had wanted to earn her way by creative writing, but since she needed to support her mother and adopted nieces, she had accepted a bureaucratic job writing for the Fish and Wildlife Service. This job left her little time for her creative writing. One of the first women ever hired for such a higher-level job, she did most of the editorial work and was demanding of herself and her writing team, which provided information on wildlife and conservation, but she was also known for her sense of fun and practical jokes.

At home, her mother did the domestic duties, leaving Rachel free to attend intellectual gatherings where she could converse with like-minded people about the music, art, literature, and ideas she loved. Most of her free time was spent hiking and exploring wildlife sanctuaries. In the summer of 1946 she rented a cottage at the edge of a river in Maine. She loved the sounds and smells of Nature's solitude so much, it became her aim one day to buy a cabin in the wilderness, a goal she reached seven years later after the success of *The Sea Around Us.* The times she spent alone in Nature were her most emotional times—when ecstatic tears of wonder could flow freely in her awe of the mysteries of the wild. She felt spiritually and physically connected with each individual living being and with the vast interwoven connection of all creatures and their environment. She felt a reverence for life and awe for the "Creator and the process." She felt rage toward those who delight in killing living things, which, she said, set back humanity's progress.

Although a Recluse, Rachel had many human friends—all united through their love of nature. One was her literary agent, Marie Rodell, who accompanied her later on a deep-sea voyage to research *The Sea Around Us.* It was the first time women had been allowed on the government research vessel. Rachel learned to dive underwater, even though she was not an experienced swimmer.

The actual writing of *The Sea Around Us,* published in 1950, took Rachel Carson three years. But it contained the fruits of her whole life's work, starting with her fascination by the ocean as a small child. Her first year at Woods Hole, where she began collecting facts about the sea from reading scientific literature and by personal observation, was the book's genesis, and she acknowledged many experts in the field for helping her find and assemble information.

Finishing the book was very stressful. Family demands, in addition to her work load, left her so exhausted, she couldn't sleep. She even had to sacrifice her spring morning bird walks—the very thing that had nurtured her the most. In the summer of 1950 she submitted the completed manuscript, experiencing a sense of loss rather than relief, a feeling common to most writers. When, after some initial rejections, first serial rights were purchased by several journals and finally *The New Yorker,* Rachel's financial situation improved. *The Sea Around Us* became an immediate best seller. It sold so fast, the publishers couldn't keep it in stock, and before the year was over, it had sold over one quarter-million copies. Eventually it was translated into thirty-two languages across the globe. The book reached first place on *The New York Times* best-seller list and stayed on the list for over a year and a half.

Rachel received a lot of publicity—difficult for a recluse who valued privacy above all. She received awards, including the National Book Award, and was made a fellow of the Royal Society of Literature in England. Asked to speak publicly before large groups, the shy and introverted Recluse feared she could not do it. But she gave an inspiring public acceptance speech expressing her philosophy of life. Valuing both science and literature as important parts of life, she said their common goal was to "to discover and illuminate truth."[21] If her writing was poetic, she said, it was because it expressed the poetry of the sea, which existed in geologic time before humans came into being. "Perhaps," she suggested, "if we reversed the telescope and looked at man down these long vistas, we should find less time and inclination to plan for our own destruction."[22]

Between publicity book tours and invitations to speak, she became further exhausted. The invasion of her privacy by the public, curious about famous authors, was difficult for her to cope with. Her picture had not appeared on the book jacket, so the public began to project its own ideas onto her—often her shadow—calling her "a very large and forbidding woman," "grey-haired and venerable."[23] Hollywood was interested in the book, and RKO bought the rights to make a full-length documentary, which won an Oscar. But despite its success, Rachel was displeased with the film due to the number of scientific errors and falsifications it presented.

In *The Sea Around Us* Rachel focused primarily on the physical and geological aspects of the oceanic realm with the changing tides and on what lay unseen beneath the surface of the sea. In her next book, *The Edge of the Sea,* published five years later, she focused on the seashore, its origin, and the survival of life on the edge of that great watery world. A deluge of letters from readers, publicity projects, and invitations interfered with her writing. She had to set limits and refuse many tempting offers, even meetings with beloved friends, in order to finish her research and writing. A Guggenheim fellowship, which she later returned when her royalties accrued, enabled her to quit working for the government.

In this book, Rachel Carson studied living communities rather than simple individual entities. Her approach was ecological: "Nowhere on the shore is the relation of a creature to its surroundings a matter of single cause and effect; each living thing is bound to its world by many threads, weaving the intricate design of the fabric of life."[24]

With the royalties from *The Sea Around Us,* Rachel was able to buy a small cottage in Maine on the rocks at the edge of the ocean. In harmony with the ocean she loved, she now was living with the subject of her writing—the threshold of the sea with the ebb and flow of shore tides. Working on a documentary project for television and a book, *The Sense of Wonder,* to introduce children to the wonder of the natural world, she stressed that the child's early sense of wonder and emotional response to the mysteries of Nature are the most important ground for the later years of adulthood. Feelings came before facts in preparing the soil from which a mature life could grow; a sense of wonder was the most powerful antidote against boredom and alienation. To this end, she said, every child needs the companionship of at least one adult with whom to experience the wonder of Nature. She also wrote an article stressing the importance of saving some of the wild places on earth before "development" destroyed them. Wanting to use her own royalties to buy shoreland for natural preserves, after she died her will allocated monies to conserve wild parts of the seashore and establish a wildlife refuge on the Maine shore.

Nearly fifty, Rachel began the most difficult book of her life—a revolutionary book that challenged the technical ways we abuse the planet. It altered the course of history. Years earlier, in 1945, Rachel had written that the unwise use of DDT as a pesticide endangered birds and beneficial insects and could upset nature's delicate balance upon which all life depends. By 1958, state and federally authorized insect control planes increasingly sprayed poisons into the air, exterminating insect and bird life. Rachel wanted to write about the chemical threat to wildlife and public health, but dubious editors rejected her proposals. Seeing the difficulty of making people listen to what they did not want to hear, Rachel realized she would have to write a book about the subject, although she had no idea of how to do it. Like Cassandra, the ancient Greek seer, she predicted truths that people disbelieved because they did not want to hear them.

A superb researcher, she began to collect evidence about the perils of using pesticides, corresponding with scientists, technical experts, and pioneers in the field. She made use of the accumulating evidence about indiscriminate spraying on Long Island that killed animals and drenched commuters and children at play. She discovered two conflicting viewpoints emerging from the scientific community: Some scientists foresaw the possible dangers and advocated preventive measures, while the "positivists" held tightly to their belief that demonstration of the destruction was required before action should be taken. Rachel observed that many people, especially professional men, were uncomfortable about opposing something without absolute proof of its danger, a blindness that we have seen manifested most recently in the Reagan and Bush administrations' opposition to regulation of pollution by individuals and corporations. She saw that the need for absolute justification—to "be right"—prevented the disclosure of truth and could contribute unwittingly to destruction.[25] Outraged at humankind's harmful tampering with Nature, Rachel tapped the energy of her inner Madwoman, fueling a book that would shake the world into awareness.

The most influential person in Rachel's life died; her mother, from whom she had inherited a gentle, compassionate nature that loved all life, united with a fierce fighting spirit to combat wrongs. Although her mother was no longer present physically, her feminine spirit inspired Rachel in her crusade to preserve wildlife and human health, and to prevent "the disturbances of the basic ecology of all living things."[26] Rachel pointed out that toxins could damage the liver, the nervous system, and every living cell in the body, thus leading to cancer; they could affect newborn babies through the placenta and the milk they drank; and they could affect enzymes and normal cell division, disturbing hereditary patterns, and slowly poison the entire ecosystem. She outlined a strong case, advising the Senate to pass the pending wilderness bill.

Despite encroaching illnesses and treatments that interfered with her writing—breast cancer, iritis affecting her eyes, and infections in her knees and ankles that kept her bedridden—Rachel wrote with the fury of a mother animal protecting its young and finished the book that had obsessed her for nearly five years. Called *Silent Spring,* the title referred to the silencing of the songbirds from their death by toxins, symbolizing the theme of the entire book.

Silent Spring first appeared in serial form in *The New Yorker* in the spring of 1962, creating a sensation. Rachel Carson was vehemently attacked by her opponents. Some chemical companies threatened lawsuits, trying to suppress the work before it appeared in book form. Trade associations such as the National Agricultural Chemical Association tried to discredit it. The book was ridiculed by misrepresenting its content. She was parodied by agricultural journals and state organizations financed by chemical companies. Her book was described as more poisonous than the toxins she condemned.

The dangerous Madwoman (who tells the unwelcome truth) was projected onto *Silent Spring*'s calm and gentle author. She was patronized and described as having relied on mere feminine intuition. In magazines she was dismissed as "a bird lover—a cat lover—a fish lover, a priestess of nature, a devotee of a mystical cult."[27] One attacker claimed she was trying to lead people back into the Dark Ages, where vermin and disease would reign.

Since her health was so poor at the time, Rachel let the book speak for itself, although she did appear on a televised report. In a public address she emphasized that the pesticide issue was only a small part of a much larger problem—polluted rivers, smoggy skies, radioactive fallout. She stressed the importance of personal responsibility in the environmental revolution necessary to save the planet. One of her major concerns was that *Silent Spring* affect government policy both in the present and in the future. As a result of the book, President Kennedy requested a governmental study that ended up criticizing the FDA and other federal agencies that had ignored the problem of pesticide toxicity. This study also found that, until the publication of *Silent Spring,* most of the public had been unaware of these toxic dangers.

Rachel had never recommended the total abolition of all chemical pesticides, but she contended that these dangerous substances had been turned over indiscriminately to individuals ignorant of their devastating environmental impact. She urged that better solutions be sought and the necessity of assessing their safety before putting them out for public use. She criticized the desire for profit despite the cost to humanity. She commended the government report, adding that it needed to be "translated into action."[28] She appeared before a Senate committee, urging further study of environmental issues and legislative action to inform and protect the public. She also urged that a committee be formed to try to resolve the interest conflicts between agriculturalists and wildlife conservationists. Against the abuse of animals, she wrote to Congress urging the adoption of federal standards to protect animals used in research projects.

Silent Spring had been dedicated to Albert Schweitzer, the person Rachel admired most for putting his philosophy, "the reverence for life," into practice, and she appeared in person to receive the Schweitzer medal of the Animal Welfare Institute. Rachel received the National Wildlife Federation's award for Conservationist of the Year (1963); the National Audubon Society honored her as the first woman to receive its medal; she received the Cullem medal from the American Geographical Society; and she was elected to membership in the American Academy of Arts and Letters, one of the few women chosen for membership during its sixty-year history.

Rachel Carson was very proud to represent the contribution of women in those societies. She was a pioneer for the feminine spirit and loving heart. At the end of her life, she knew she did not have much longer to live and was thankful for every precious day of life and grateful for the vision she had channeled through her natural gifts and disciplined work, in order to be able to contribute to the fight to save the natural environment. In 1964, at the age of fifty-six, she died in Silver Springs, Maryland. In her credo, which she delivered toward the end of her life and incorporated into *The Sense of Wonder,* she shared the philosophy by which she lived.

A large part of my life has been concerned with some of the beauties and mysteries of this earth about us, and with the even greater mysteries of the life that inhabits it. No one can dwell long among such subjects without thinking rather deep thoughts, without asking himself searching and often unanswerable questions, and without achieving a certain philosophy.

There is one quality that characterizes all of us who deal with the sciences of the earth and its life—we are never bored. We can't be. There is always something new to be investigated. Every mystery solved brings us to the threshold of a greater one. . . . The pleasures, the values of contact with the natural world are not reserved for the scientists. They are available to anyone who will place himself under the influence of a lonely mountain top—or the sea—or the stillness of a forest; or who will stop to think about so small a thing as the mystery of a growing seed.

I am not afraid of being thought a sentimentalist when I say that I believe natural beauty has a necessary place in the spiritual development of any individual or any society. I believe that whenever we destroy beauty, or whenever we substitute something man-made and artificial for a natural feature of the earth, we have retarded some part of man's spiritual growth. . . .

I have had the privilege of receiving many letters from people who, like myself, have been steadied and reassured by contemplating the long history of the earth and sea, and the deeper meanings of the world of nature. . . . In contemplating "the exceeding beauty of the earth" these people have found calmness and courage. For there is symbolic as well as actual beauty in the migration of birds; in the ebb and flow of the tides; in the folded bud ready for the spring. There is something infinitely healing in these repeated refrains of nature—the assurance that dawn comes after night, and spring after the winter.

Mankind has gone very far into an artificial world of his own creation. . . . But I believe that the more clearly we can focus our attention on the wonders and the realities of the universe about us, the less taste we shall have for destruction.[29]

HEALING THE RECLUSE

Understanding the difference between solitude and loneliness is essential for the passage from the Recluse who is hostage to isolation and paranoia to the woman who values and grows from solitude. When solitude is chosen, it is the foundation of spiritual life and regenerates the soul. It has many complexions: gentleness, wild intensity, introspection and contemplation, ecstasy, serenity, awe, a silent divine energy, inner and outer peace. Solitude does not remove us from suffering; it calls forth a sacrifice of parts of the self and asks something of us in order to connect us with something greater. As the poet Rilke said, "Love is not possession." Rather, love means "that two solitudes protect and border and salute each other."[30] The experience of solitude can bring a sense of union, grounding relationships.

In contrast, loneliness often makes us feel abandoned, rejected, or lost. We feel victimized, desperate, and conflicted, a pawn of fate. A person can be lonelier in a group of people or with someone than she is by herself, when she most feels the pitying projections of other people, and the lonely child in her experiences shame. In loneliness are the seeds of its own healing, however, for anxiety and terror can be the threshold into awe as well as conscious self-understanding. This was true for Heather, a woman who was by nature reclusive.

The healing transformation for Heather occurred when she was able to make the distinction between loneliness and solitude. As a child, she didn't seem to fit in with her family. While they sat like zombies before the television set, talking about the neighbors or comparing who was most successful in their social set, Heather retreated to her room, closed the door, and read. This reclusiveness became a pattern throughout her childhood. She found the realm of imagination exciting and vital, and she had a special imaginary friend with whom she played. Among her favorite books were *The Secret Garden* and *Heidi*.

The rest of the family, all more extroverted than she, couldn't understand her behavior and criticized her for being different. They could not see why she didn't enjoy parties or become more involved in church activities like the other girls. She was most often by herself, alone in her room, reading and painting, or outside in Nature. When she went to college she had to live in the dormitory the first year and hated it; she longed to have her own apartment.

Because of her parents' criticism, and because she felt the outsider in high school and college, Heather began to wonder if something was wrong with her. She began to feel guilty about being different. Sometimes she felt as though she were hiding; often she felt isolated. She began to feel very lonely and at times was ashamed of her solitary state.

After college, she lived with a boyfriend for several years, but when the relationship broke up, she enjoyed living alone once more in a mountain cabin with her cats. Still, she longed to meet a soulmate, and she suffered from loneliness. Even though she was in her thirties and working hard in her profession, she felt judged by her parents and siblings for being single and was angry that, in their eyes, she was considered an old maid.

An important transformation came for Heather when she read May Sarton's *The House by the Sea*. Sarton, who has described not only the difficulties of being alone but also the writer's need for solitude, helped Heather to understand the difference between loneliness and solitude and to accept that suffering loneliness could be an essential part of the creative process and the call to individua-

tion. With a shift of attitude one could value solitude—being alone
and at peace with oneself. Sarton's appreciation of solitude helped
Heather feel comfortable with who she was; it helped her see that
her natural tendency to introversion and seclusion was not unhealthy, as she had feared, but rather was a rare and valuable gift
that could enable her to discover how she could contribute to the
healing of people and society. She realized that the Recluse in her
gave her a foundation from which she could move out toward others
and society. She needed solitude to know her true self, to live more
authentically from her feminine center.

"The Recluse gives me silence," Heather once said; "life in the
silence is rich. I love to wake up early in the morning and watch the
first light as it comes into my mountain cabin—to feel the sun's
warmth, to see what it touches, to see where it goes. In the daytime,
I can spend hours simply watching the path of the sun, and at night
the passage of the moon. Sometimes I spend an entire day digging
deeply into the place where the inner voice is alive. Space emerges
and gives me time to discover my genuine values. Solitude helps me
to get out of my routines so new possibilities can emerge and the
inspiration to create can find its natural channel." To develop the
appreciation of solitude and to learn to be sensitive to and direct
the new energies that come in these solitary times, she practices
sensory awareness exercises that focus simply on being; yoga to let
the body be alive; meditation in order to feel the stillness in the
body; and hiking and cross-country skiing in the snowy silence of
winter to feel the movement in Nature. Gardening connects her to
the earth's blooming and her own feminine flowering.

May Sarton stresses the importance of living as whole human
beings—neither totally isolated nor totally giving ourselves away to
others. Living in solitude means to live in this creative tension. In an
interview to commemorate her seventieth birthday, Sarton said:

> I am terribly lonely now, but I have also become enamored of
> solitude. That's my last great love. My solitude is everywhere
> and sometimes I don't speak to anyone, except just to say
> good morning to the post mistress, for days, for days literally
> in the winter. And this is hard to handle, to not get
> unbalanced and not let depression get hold of you. Everything
> becomes more intense, you see, which is partly why it's
> marvelous. There's nothing to break the intensity. The great

flow from the subconscious to the conscious is the good thing
about solitude.[31]

The transition from the woman who fears madness due to isolation or feels angry in her loneliness to the woman who knows the
wild joys, serenity, and creativity that solitude can bring us is modeled by women like Rachel Carson, May Sarton, and Miss Helen. All
three women faced the despair of existential aloneness yet took the
leap of faith to create light from darkness. Valuing solitude, each
remained true to her unique vision while accepting and bearing
with strength the tensions of creative life. Each of us is ultimately
alone in that great passage from the beginning of life until the time
when we must face death. We are alone before the unknown as we
create and at the end we must face death singly. Although we have
family, friends, children, and lovers to accompany us at various
stages on life's journey, we are alone each time we make a significant decision. Although many people in Western culture profess
Christianity, we tend to forget that Christ carried the cross alone.
Other cultures have rituals that acknowledge the essential task of
facing Creation alone. For example, the Lakota peoples stress and
honor the importance for each person to make his or her own
journey alone on their spiritual path, sometimes called the Red
Road. During the Vision Quest, the community supports the initiate
through sweat lodge ceremonies as he or she makes four stops on
the way to the place of vision, remaining alone for four days, and
then comes down to share the new spiritual knowledge with the
people. At the first stop the initiate surrenders attachments to material possessions; at the second stop she gives up friends; at the third,
family; and at the fourth, the remaining vestiges of personal identity. Then, with commitment and courage, she proceeds alone to
the place of vision where she awaits in solitude and silence to receive
the voices, visions, or whatever the greater forces offer and want her
to experience and to know in the process of dying that becomes
renewal and gives humans a relation to the greater Whole.

8
THE
REVOLUTIONARY

Anger storms
between me and things,
transfiguring,
transfiguring.
A good anger acted upon
is beautiful as lightning
and swift with power.
A good anger swallowed,
a good anger swallowed
clots the blood
to slime.

—MARGE PIERCY,
A just anger

THE FILM *THE NASTY GIRL* REVOLUTIONIZED MY OWN THINK-
ing about the Madwoman and provided an image
that could unite the opposites of gentleness and assertion, of peacefulness and combat. In a courtroom
scene, the figure of Justice is depicted as a Madwoman, huge, ferocious, and powerful. The film
dramatizes a true story of how a woman historian
was ostracized when she tried to learn the truth
about her German hometown during the Nazi era.
The English title minimizes the original German
title, *Das Schreckliche Mädchen,* which means "the
terrible or frightening young maiden." This film
provides a model of a contemporary woman courageous enough to rebel against her community's de-

nial of their Nazi guilt in order to fight for justice, a tender mother who must be relentless in her search for truth, a sensitive woman with the courage and determination of a Madwoman.

The heroine, Sonja, tells her story and the history of her model family and town in a mock documentary for German television. She begins life as a "good girl," praised for her intelligence and obedience in a parochial school, where she becomes the teacher's pet, but she also has friends among her schoolmates due to her sweet temperament and good sense of humor. As a child she is mischievous and rebellious. At her teacher's suggestion, she enters a national essay contest, winning a trip to Paris. Awarded a special medal by the mayor for her achievement, she basks in the praise.

However, circumstances lead her to become a revolutionary. In the next essay contest Sonja chooses "My Hometown During the Third Reich" as a theme, although her teachers try to discourage her from pursuing this topic. Proud of her town, a bishop's seat that basks in its resistance to the Nazis, Sonja wants to show how it kept its integrity during the Nazi occupation. Her mother cautions her to write positive things, for she comes from a respectable, upstanding family. While she is researching, Sonja learns that the townspeople don't like to talk about their memories. Puzzled by her discovery that a revered town priest was sentenced to death for trying to help the Jews, she questions an esteemed churchman who brusquely suggests that she drop the issue. Only her grandmother is willing to talk —when she tried to give bread to the Jewish prisoners, authorities told her to stop. A rebel, her grandmother continued to help the Jews and organized women for a protest march. Sentenced to prison, she was pardoned because she had ten children. Sonja's rebellious grandmother is her only model for compassion and justice.

When the essay contest is canceled, Sonja's fiancé, her former teacher, is glad because he had been feeling neglected when her energy was directed toward the essay instead of him. They marry and have two children, but Sonja cannot forget her discoveries about her hometown during the Nazi period. In order to delve deeper, she studies history and theology at the university. Researching newspaper files, she uncovers important facts that had been suppressed.

Sonja's research leads her to suspect that people are hiding the town's relationship to the Nazis to protect its current reputation.

When she asks to see the town's historical archives, her request is denied. Furious, she sues the town to release the sealed documents. Her husband calls her crazy and wants her to stop, but at the subsequent trial she is awarded access. At this moment in the film, the image of Justice is projected on a screen behind her and is shown as a powerful Madwoman holding the balancing scales, symbolizing the integration of the Madwoman's power aligned with justice.

Beleaguered by the housework and their children while his wife works on her project, Sonja's husband asks in disgust, "What does social commitment mean when a husband has to bed down the children?" He tells her she should devote herself to being a wife and mother. But Sonja is "socially committed" and continues researching. As she uncovers more, the townspeople get defensive and ostracize her. Neo-Nazi punks throw a stone through her car window, nail a cat to her door, and later bomb her house. Threatening telephone messages harass the family.

Sonja wonders if pursuing this theme is worth the threat to her children and family. But she finds she cannot give up. Her integrity forces her to continue to search for the truth. Taking advantage of a lapse in security, she gains access to files that contain incriminating evidence about the town's collaboration with the Nazis. The townspeople had projected their own guilt onto innocent people who had tried to help the Jews, and persecuted and scapegoated them. Two priests who had collaborated, now high in the Catholic echelons, were praised, not punished. One is the priest who discouraged her questions; when she reveals what she has uncovered, he sues her for defamation and slander. As she enters the courtroom, she sees an image of herself as Christ, martyred on the cross. But she wins the case. The truth can no longer be suppressed. Trying to rectify itself, the town officials order a statue of Sonja to be placed in the town hall. At the ceremony, her children in her arms, Sonja's inner Madwoman suddenly rears up when she realizes the establishment is trying to seduce her to be "one of them," to shut her up about further abuses. Refusing to conform, she becomes enraged in the courtroom, striking out at her mother who wants to quiet her.

Sonja runs from the courtroom to a sacred space in Nature, a special tree high on a hill above the town. Called the Tree of Mercy, schoolgirls hang images on its trunk and pray for their secret desires. The film ends as Sonja seeks refuge in the leafy branches of this holy Tree of Mercy, staring like a Madwoman as she holds her baby daughter in her arms. The audience is left with this image of a free-spirited, gentle woman maddened in the process of trying to honor freedom and pursue truth, seated in a symbol of spiritual refuge, the tree of life, a place of sacrifice.

This film, mixing satire and fact, draws on the true story of German historian Anja Elisabeth Rosmus and shows the way in which corrupt patriarchal judges try to ostracize and persecute a woman who insists on knowing the truth if it differs from the establishment's views or desire. It shows the positive value of the Madwoman who insists on ripping away her community's denial to uncover the facts. In an interview, Ms. Rosmus said that although her essays on contemporary history had received many prizes, when the film was released, she again became the target of hostility. Nevertheless, because she persists, her demands for truth are taken more seriously.[1] The film shows that the Madwoman and Justice can be united, even though the personal stakes are high.

THE CONSCIOUS REVOLUTIONARY VERSUS THE TERRORIST: RAISING FEMININE CONSCIOUSNESS

In *The Rebel*, Albert Camus points out that, when resentment and autointoxication take over, the rebel is in danger of becoming a nihilistic murderer: "We all carry within us our places of exile, our crimes and our ravages. But our task is not to unleash them on the world; it is to fight them in ourselves and in others."[2] The paradox between being a terrorist and a good Revolutionary confronts all women who try to understand and integrate the Madwoman. How do we fight justly? Is it possible to defend ourselves and eradicate the abuses in society without resorting to violence? Is it possible to embody the creative energy of the Revolutionary without resorting to the destructive violence of the terrorist? The Madwoman's fighting energy needs to be used to unite women rather than divide them through envy, ambition, or power plays. Instead of co-creating as sisters, women sometimes undermine each other, especially if they are governed by a dominating, power-driven masculine animus.

If the revolutionary aspect of the Madwoman gets out of control, the destructive terrorist may emerge. Whenever ego-interests begin to dominate, the Madwoman energy can destroy and blow up everything by reducing everything to her own ends—even the cause in which she once believed. If a woman fears that her Madwoman may become a terrorist, she may fail to relate to the good revolutionary force inside herself. The following dream reveals this fear of the secret connection between the Madwoman and the terrorist who wants total power, resorts to violent intimidation to gain her ends, and turns her feminine self over to her interior killer outlaw.

> I am in a chartered plane flying with other women to a special celebration of the feminine. Suddenly a woman at the front of the plane gets up, holding a machine gun. She is a terrorist and is taking us all as hostages. I recognize her as a noted feminist psychiatrist, a revolutionary in the fight for women's causes. All the women in the plane are afraid of her, although some speculate her takeover might secretly be for a good purpose. But she is hijacking the plane to put all the women in the hands of male Mexican banditos, who are hiding out from the law in a remote desert area. This female terrorist is handing over the very women whom she has encouraged to male murderers to be raped.

The dreamer, Renata, viewed the terrorist woman as a shadow figure, a combination Ice Queen and Dragon Lady. In real life this woman was remote, emotionally unresponsive and coldly aggressive, and she tended to manipulate others to get the best deal for herself. Whenever criticized, she justified herself and attacked first instead of listening. She was known among her colleagues for her tendency to accuse others in order to defend betrayed women, even though she herself sometimes hurt women through her own drive for power. Renata disliked these qualities in this aggressive woman, but she also envied her for promoting herself assertively. In the dream this woman was shown as a terrorist, turning the very women she claimed to be helping over to male bandits to be raped. She represented the divisive patriarchal proclivities of the power-ridden woman who must be first and on top. Her positive side was her self-assertion.

The personal challenge for Renata was to learn to fight for herself and to acknowledge her own mad energy and power, using it to confront the bully in men and women instead of withdrawing from them in fear. Engaged in a revolutionary project to challenge abusive patterns and make them public, Renata actually had to confront this woman herself. The dream revealed that if she was to continue her own work in the area of feminine spirituality, she would have to confront the terrorist—both the bully in the external world and the terrorist in herself who threatened her own public work with fear tactics and who isolated her, then held her hostage to her inner outlaw-in-hiding.

Another way the Madwoman energy may degenerate is through a manic excitement about a revolutionary cause without proper discipline or an effective plan of action. Getting high on the romance of a cause can result in feeling lost and confused in the chaos of excitement. Even though the cause may be important and the enthusiasm good, failing to develop the discipline and knowledge to accomplish goals can lead to embittered cynicism if results are not achieved. Resentment at the establishment, with which one cannot deal, can undercut all work toward goals and feed the outlaw rather than the Revolutionary.

The conscious Revolutionary who defends who she is and does not allow others to violate her integrity can transform her Madwoman energy to struggle for human rights and freedom. Now, perhaps more than at any other time in history, the abuses of the patriarchy have resulted in an addictive society and ecological destruction that threaten life on earth. Madwoman energy, women's anger at individual, family, societal, and planetary abuses, can fuel both personal and social transformation, provided that they recognize and learn how to use their own power. Many women need to learn to fight for themselves. Taught by culture and parents that it is not feminine to show anger, even to defend ourselves, we need to find good models for fighting for our rights. To change ourselves, our families, society, or the world, a woman has to be a Revolutionary. A modern-day model is Anita Hill, who confronted Clarence Thomas on charges of sexual harassment when he was nominated for the post of Supreme Court justice. Even though Thomas was eventually appointed, Anita Hill's courage and dignity continue to inspire women to stand up for their rights.

LEARNING TO FIGHT FOR FEMININE RIGHTS: BRENDA'S STORY

The way in which the abuses of a patriarchal system can lead to women's revolutionary action is shown by the story of Brenda, a contemporary woman who needed to integrate the positive power of the Madwoman. A historian, Brenda had always fought for social justice for minorities in peace marches and by writing articles expressing her vision of social harmony. Although she could fight for others, she had difficulty fighting for herself, for she had been brought up to be self-sacrificing and a caretaker for others. She admired heroic women in history who fought to embody their ideals, such as Rosa Luxemburg, Emma Goldman, Margaret Sanger, and Jane Addams. However, she felt sad that contemporary female models were few, and sometimes she felt resentful that, professionally, she had to identify with men.

Brenda taught in a southern university for many years. Along with other women in the academic field, she learned she was not getting equal pay or her deserved promotions. Several men in her department, who had been hired at the same time and had the same number of publications or fewer, were promoted beyond her in status and salary, while she remained at the same level for years. When Brenda began to fight back and went to the administration, no matter what evidence she presented, her requests were refused. Moreover, she was patronized and told that her major energies had to go toward her children. Yet neither her teaching nor her other work duties had been affected by parenthood.

Her department had even asked for her promotion, but the administration had turned it down. The men who were advanced had one thing in common—they were part of the "old boys" system. When a new department chairman was selected, Brenda found she was gradually being cut out of the more important teaching and committee assignments and relegated to unimportant committees. Although Brenda suspected that the chairman was a misogynist, two younger women in the department were enthusiastic about him because he seemed to have taken them under his tutelage. When it came time for their advancement, however, he sabotaged them. He exerted enough influence single-handedly to have one of these women refused reappointment; the other he diverted from meeting her publishing requirements by pushing her into campus politics and advising her to change her specialty. When she came up for tenure, she was dismissed due to lack of publications. Brenda was already tenured, so the chairman couldn't affect her on that level, but he consistently recommended the bottom salary advances for her, while the men in the department continued to receive equity raises. He also denigrated her unique approach to her subject as "soft-headed."

Finally Brenda decided to take action. She went to the dean, but he told her that "chairmen have a right to make those decisions." Shocked and angry, Brenda asked the dean to review her progress reports, but he declined. Storming out of his office in a rage, she went to the administration to begin salary grievance procedures. A quantitative study showed she was several thousand dollars below her peers, but the administration's final judgment was that there was no inequity. Brenda questioned this decision, citing the quantitative report. But the report had "disappeared," and when she asked them, the deciding group told her that they had not seen it. She wrote an indignant letter, criticizing the procedure. Then she tried to get a response from the members of her department. She wrote each person a note, describing what had happened. No one responded.

For a while, Brenda became obsessed with getting people to hear her story. She felt crazy when no one could see or hear her point of view. Eventually, she stopped fighting, feeling beaten and humiliated. She felt as if she were repeating a role she had carried as the middle, invisible daughter in her family, overshadowed by a dominant mother and sisters. Now she felt powerless before the self-justifying patriarchy, forced into the role of a second-class citizen, shamed, and lacking in self-esteem. Her new passivity conspired against her creativity and led to paranoia and isolation. When we become passive and give up in resentment, our Madwoman energy can turn against us in a destructive way, contributing to our ineffectiveness and victimization.

Brenda continued to inspire her students, and her classes were always in demand, but her skill and success in teaching did not earn her promotional or salaried reward. Inwardly enraged, Brenda kept away from departmental activities, taught her classes, then rushed home where she said she played Solitaire dementedly. Like Dostoevski's "Underground Man," she began to live below her potential since her energy was consumed in the smoldering ashes of resentment at the injustice of this academic patriarchy.

Brenda's dreams reflected her despair at the shabby way she had been treated and revealed her rage and her fears of isolation, of being labeled, of being invisible, and of being of no importance. But her dreams also revealed a powerful feminine figure whose madness could make changes. In one dream, she saw an open book with a picture of a man on the lefthand side and the title *The Grapes of Wrath*. Brenda awoke in terror at her own rage in feeling the terrible wrath and anger of the unjustly oppressed worker, symbolized by Steinbeck's novel. Another dream revealed her fear of being mistaken for a Madwoman, locked away and lost in a madhouse.

> I am looking for the history department, wandering through strange streets and corridors. Finally I reach it, and a supportive colleague embraces me. For a short time I feel happy. Soon I am lost again, searching once more for the department office. With another woman, I wander in a darkened corridor, afraid to be seen. We brush against someone in the dark. Mentally I try to alert the other woman to be still and silent so we will not be caught. Now I am alone, hiding in a toilet stall. Two psychiatric nurses discuss what they will do with the patients. I am afraid the nurses will find me and take me captive in a mental hospital, where I will become lost among the anonymity of the crazy patients. When all seems lost, I see a man in front of me—silent, foreign, smiling, eyes closed, standing erect, a headband on his forehead like a Central American Indian. Smiling, he helps me and takes my hand and tells me I can fly. As we fly away together, I am relieved to be rescued.

The dream revealed several things to Brenda. It showed her lost, frightened, confused, desperate state, and her terror at being sane yet locked away in an asylum, not recognized for who she was. This dream image reflected the crazy-making dynamics of her department. The woman companion was a shadow figure for Brenda—a Madwoman with a deceptively polite facade who, underneath, manipulated to get her way and was competitive, aggressive, and known for her poisonous barbs. This ambitious woman, who wanted to be on top, was always fighting with others and alienating them. She didn't know how to use the Madwoman energy effectively. In the dream Brenda felt that if this Madwoman spoke, she would get hospitalized. So she tried to keep her silent. Yet in reality, Brenda needed to integrate some of this other woman's aggressive energy in order to fight for herself. This woman was the first appearance of a mad, shadow side of Brenda that needed to be transformed and integrated. On the conscious level Brenda was aghast at this woman's unacceptable form of aggression. But the psyche works in strange ways. Dreams often shock us out of our captive states with figures and scenes that scare us in order to wake us up. Brenda needed to work with her inner Madwoman to learn to use that energy effectively for herself. To help her with this task, the dream revealed a friendly stranger who could help her fly to freedom, representing to Brenda a helpful, kind, inward-looking, shamanistic side of herself, not aligned with the patriarchal Judge.

In other dreams Brenda encountered similar scenes. In one dream the same woman wanted her to live in an underground house. But Brenda thought this was awful and said no. She was beginning to assert herself. This dream was followed by another in which a man wanted her to live in a cellar under the sidewalk. Again Brenda said no, telling him that he didn't see it on the inside, where it was dark, cramped, and horrible. The cellar symbolized the cramped way Brenda had been living. Both dreams emphasized her growing ability to say no, to refuse an inferior way of life. In other dreams Brenda was confronted with leaving the university, which was flooding, and with fixing an overflowing toilet. The flooding and the overflowing toilet symbolized the overwhelming feelings that Brenda had relegated to the private place of refuse but that needed to be contained and expressed. In another dream she and her sister attended a university lecture that made the audience act crazy. One woman went mad and had to be removed. Then her sister, who appeared controlled but in reality was angry underneath, started acting crazy, too, and Brenda had to take her out. In this dream Brenda had to deal with the Madwoman in the context of a patriarchal academic lecture.

Brenda's dreams revealed opposite aspects of the Madwoman. The resentful and passive or aggressive, martial modes of the Madwoman are ineffective, and in this way collude with the Judge. In contrast, a woman who can assert herself, be appropriately angry when necessary, and laugh at rigid rules can use her energy constructively.

The Madwoman began to emerge more frequently in her dreams. She dreamed she was at a party where she saw a patriarch, one of the "old boys" from the department. When she discovered she was pregnant and felt awe and wonder, he suggested she get an abortion. Suddenly, her long red fingernails shot out into angry flames. The pregnancy symbolized the potential birth of her new assertive feminine self—one that could deal effectively with the old boys. She would defend, not destroy this new self. In another dream Brenda met a humorous, free-spirited Madwoman.

> I have just received a salary raise on condition that I move to the outskirts of a large city. Not wanting to move far away, I realize my colleagues want to keep me at a distance. They also sneer that now I have new obligations. Like Judges, they tell me what to do and how to do it. Cynically I think: "The more things change, the more they stay the same." Then suddenly a strange woman appears and I ask her, "What does one do?" The woman laughs, saying, "There is no procedure. Do what you want!"

Upon awakening, Brenda felt lighter. Perhaps there was a way to deal with the critical judges of the patriarchy—not on their terms but in accord with her own feminine way. The woman in the dream was a powerful and positive manifestation of the Madwoman for Brenda—a woman who could laugh and act out of the nonlinear realm, a woman who told her she could do what she wanted in her own way—so unlike Brenda's mother, who had insisted she be the good and dutiful daughter.

After this dream Brenda felt new energy. She started to do healthy things for herself—yoga, bicycling, and building her physical strength and flexibility. She began to feel less at the mercy of others' capricious behavior. A dream showed she was now stronger. In the dream a man showed her an ugly apartment that gave her bad vibes. She refused it. Then a cultish and dangerous group of people were trying to take her hostage. She defended herself. Taking a garbage can lid as a shield and a staff as a sword, she hit them down as they tried to attack her, singing in jest Shirley Temple's song, "The Good Ship Lollipop." Now Brenda was ready and capable of defending herself. No longer would she take garbage from others; she had broken the good girl image that had been keeping her trapped.

Inwardly, Brenda was freeing herself by relating to the power of the positive Madwoman; externally, things began to change synchronistically, as is often the case when one transforms oneself. A new department chairman was elected. An honorable man, he recognized that Brenda was being discriminated against, and he wrote a letter to the dean requesting a better salary, promotion, and more responsible jobs for her. About the same time, a large group of faculty women met to discuss their condition, representing almost one-third of the female faculty. As they talked, each woman confessed she had tried by herself to do something about her unequal treatment by the men in power in the academy but had failed. Each woman had undergone a process similar to Brenda's, initially blaming herself for her low salary and lack of promotion, feeling unfit for advancement, and accepting the men's superiority and the decrees of the patriarchy. As with Brenda, anger and resentment had been boiling underneath. As woman after woman told her story of life in the university—essentially the same story of inequity, abuse, guilt, feelings of inferiority, low self-esteem—it became clear to the women assembled that they had to meet and act together. This was the beginning of their united action.

In the meantime, Brenda pursued her promotion again—to no avail. She joined a group of faculty women to discuss a class action suit to fight for their rights. In their solidarity she found reinforcement, enthusiasm, and an effective way to make an appeal, and she began to fight effectively with them for her rights. They possessed an effective aggressiveness that she had forgotten she could own in herself but that had been revealed in her dreams. Now, with hope that she could change her situation, she began to feel much better about herself. Her positive action of joining and working with others constellated a surprising new energy. Her resentment and isolation, dammed up from the patriarchal rejection, was released, and she was able to continue and finish a book that she had abandoned.

Brenda's story shows the importance of feminine solidarity in fighting back. Eventually, the women were successful in their class action suit, and Brenda received an equitable salary and the promotion she should have been granted ten years earlier. Fighting with other women against the injustices of the patriarchal Judges woke up Brenda, brought back her energy and self-esteem, and freed her from the negative projections and expectations of others. As Brenda became conscious of her inner Madwoman, befriended her, accepted her anger at being abused, and learned to turn this energy toward constructive action in solidarity with other women, she began to feel liberated. She had two wonderful dreams that showed the new psychological spaciousness she had achieved. In one dream she had placed a giant stone from Nature in her house. The huge rock air-conditioned the house and caused the air to flow free, symbolizing the natural strength, solidarity, and independence that let her breathe freely. In another dream she was at the helm of a spaceship. Looking out at the vastness of space, she was overwhelmed with wonder and awe at the beauty and grandeur of life and the cosmos.

Brenda's story shows how the energy of the Madwoman can be revolutionary and open up free spaces, both within an individual life and within the culture. Today, films are beginning to show how the Madwoman's energy can enable women to break through old identities and roles and build new lives.

FEMALE SOLIDARITY: *THELMA AND LOUISE*

The film *Thelma and Louise* depicts how women caught in sexually abusive situations that are condoned by male law can invoke the power of the interior Madwoman. In their struggle to escape the abuses of a patriarchal culture, these women become Revolutionaries rather than remain hostages to a patriarchal system that does not permit women to defend themselves.

Thelma is a Caged Bird, trapped in a confining marriage. Her redneck husband is crude and abusive, orders her around, and belittles her constantly, calling her a "nutcase." In turn, Thelma tends to be silly and spacey, confirming this stereotypical image of her, a projection often put upon women in a patriarchal culture. Men tend to use such stereotyping the more they are out of touch with their own feminine side, and the more they fear a woman's innate differences and want her to be passive. When they are afraid of female power, men often try to divide and conquer. A common tactic is to shame a woman for expressing anger, thus trying to suppress her strength. An assertive woman is frequently labeled a crazy aggressive bitch, as Thelma's husband calls Louise.

Thelma's husband abuses his wife, controlling her the way that he controls the TV with a mechanical device. He never lets Thelma be free to enjoy herself, and he shouts at her whenever she tries to initiate anything. He expects Thelma to stay at home and do housework, even though he is seldom home and dates other women on the sly. Married in her early teens, Thelma has not been with other men sexually; nor has she experienced freedom. But at heart she is a free spirit, a Caged Bird that wants to fly out of her cage.

When Louise suggests they take a weekend trip together to the mountains for fun, Thelma wants to go but is afraid to tell her husband, knowing he will yell at her and refuse. So she leaves without telling him, attaching a note to the microwave. Reflecting her inner chaos, she throws her things helter-skelter into a suitcase and grabs a gun for protection, asking Louise to take care of it for her.

Louise is older and wiser. She works as a waitress and refuses to be intimidated. Toughened from life's bombardments, including the wisecracks of men, and a traumatic past that she tries to escape and conceal, Louise tries to control her life. She has learned to fight to protect herself if need be. Opposite in character to Thelma, Louise packs her clothes neatly and puts her house in order before she picks up her friend for the trip. Driving an old 1966 Thunderbird convertible, the two women begin their vacation. In the convertible, feeling the rush of free air, Louise speeds toward their wilderness retreat.

On the way Thelma wants to stop and have a drink. They order drinks in a roadhouse, where a man interrupts their conversation, calls them cute "Kewpie dolls," and asks Thelma to dance. Louise dislikes this man's intrusion, but Thelma wants to dance. At heart, Thelma is a wild woman, seductive and sexy. Glad to be away from her bullying husband, she suddenly feels free and wants to have a good time with the man, who flirts with her as they drink and dance. Louise asks Thelma to leave so they can continue their trip, and she pays the bill. Dizzy and sick from drinking and dancing, Thelma goes toward their car, accompanied by the man, who tries to seduce her. When she says no to his advances, trying to stop him, he viciously punches her, calls her a "fucking bitch," then tries to rape her. When Louise sees this man attack her friend, without thinking she takes Thelma's gun from her purse and threatens to shoot him if he doesn't leave her friend alone. The man steps back, but when he thinks he is safe, he aggressively curses the women and abuses them verbally. Enraged, Louise tells him that if he ever sees a woman crying like Thelma, he should know that the woman isn't having any fun. He calls Louise a bitch and says, "Suck my cock," and Louise says, "You watch your mouth, buddy," and impulsively pulls the trigger, accidentally shooting him in the heart.

In a panic, Thelma and Louise jump in the car and drive away. Neither can believe what has happened, but Louise knows she is in for trouble. Thelma thinks the police will believe the truth—that the man was raping her and that he had been shot in self-defense. But Louise says, "Who's going to believe you? We don't live in that kind of world, Thelma." In a macho world, even though a woman says no and means *no!*, regardless of circumstance she is not believed. Instead, she is put down as not knowing what she wants or as having no judgment. A slogan that West Point cadets used in the sixties says it all: "The difference between seduction and rape is salesmanship." This view reduces woman to a receptacle for compliments and semen and negates her voice and her choice. But it is this "cocksman's" code that the women are up against. Louise fears Thelma will be blamed for seducing the man and that she herself will be charged with murder.

Desperate, Louise decides to try to escape to Mexico; she knows she is marked. When Thelma calls her husband at four in the morning and finds he is not home, she decides to join Louise. On the road, Thelma coaxes Louise to give a young hitchhiker a ride, and they drive to the motel where Louise has asked her boyfriend to send money. She puts it in Thelma's care while she talks to her lover, who has come against her wishes. She tells him she loves him but refuses his marriage proposal, knowing that if she stays with him or tells him anything, he will be arrested as an accomplice. Meanwhile, Thelma, who has slept with the hitchhiker, naively leaves Louise's money on the night table, even though he has told Thelma he is a robber. The next morning, when Louise discovers the money has been stolen, she collapses. All her control breaks down.

Thelma suddenly takes charge. Having lost the money, she decides to replace it by robbing a store; the young robber has described how to do it. Unaware of Thelma's plan, Louise waits in the car in despair. Thelma robs the store in a "courteous" manner and is now wanted for armed robbery. Back on the road, she threatens an officious policeman, who has stopped Louise for speeding. Thelma locks him up in the trunk of his car and tells him to be good to his wife when he pleads for mercy. Later she says to Louise, "Something has crossed over in me; I can't go back, I just couldn't live that way. Now I feel awake, wide awake. I never remember feeling this way before. Everything looks different." She has felt the "call of the wild" and likes her new feeling of freedom. Having become conscious of inequalities, slights, and abuse, Thelma will not tolerate them any longer.

When a crude and lewd truck driver harasses them with obscene language and gestures and tries to run them off the road, the Madwoman emerges in both women. Enraged, Thelma and Louise trick him into stopping. Louise tells him to apologize and asks him if he would treat his mother, sister, or wife so crudely. When the truck driver curses them and calls them crazy women, they deflate him by shooting holes in his tires and exploding his oil tanker—perhaps a metaphor for their anger at male inflation, greed and the rape of Mother Earth. Taking a stand for themselves and all other women, they will no longer tolerate exploitation by individual men or the male system.

Meanwhile, the police investigating the murder at the bar have found a file on Louise and tapped Thelma's phone. They advise her husband to be gentle to her if she calls and to act like he loves her. "Women love that shit," says a cynical FBI man, out to get these women who have rebelled against their system. Only the original investigating officer cares about them, aware that their lives are in danger due to the way the legal system abuses women. He has checked Louise's record and knows she was raped in Texas. When Thelma phones her husband, she suspects the police are there because his kindness is out of character. Then Louise calls and speaks to the one officer who believes that the murder was accidental. He asks her to turn herself in before it is too late. But Louise doubts that she will be given a fair chance. Helicopters circle overhead, police cars surround them, and high-powered telescopic rifles are aimed at the heads of these "dangerous" women, who are warned they will be shot if they don't give themselves up.

On Thelma's and Louise's journey, they have seen the beauty of Nature and felt close to Mother Earth, giving them a sense of connection that allows them to take their final journey together. Driving at night in the canyon lands, they have been moved to tears, feeling awe and ecstasy under the star-filled sky. Louise realizes that her tears had been frozen until now. Trapped at the edge of the Grand Canyon, symbolic of the abyss, Thelma and Louise know they are at a crossroads and must decide whether to give themselves up or go forward. They decide to escape; they cannot go back to the way things were. The two women look at each other and admire each other's courage. Their journey has brought them a unique love—woman friend to woman friend—a love that is rarely understood by men. Kissing each other in friendship, they agree to go on —they take the leap of faith and, holding hands, they drive the car off the edge of the canyon and soar into space. Thelma and Louise have reached a state of consciousness that will not allow them to go back to a repressive or patriarchal police state that abuses and exploits women. They choose to die for freedom. United in friendship, they fly free above the abyss as the film ends.

Unable to return to a dysfunctional society that abuses the feminine, Thelma and Louise have only one way to go—forward into the abyss, into the freedom of the unknown. Symbolically, the abyss is the place of spiritual transformation, where mystics go for divine revelation; their leap is the descent into the unconscious, into emptiness, the leap the seeker takes into the chaos of the creative unconscious to find new modes of expression. It is the bottom place into which addicts fall before recovery. The abyss is where we all must go, stripped of our preconceived ideas, ego expectations, possessions, and whatever else holds us back from making the necessary radical turn needed for personal and social transformation. To leap into the abyss appears to be madness from the conventional perspective that wants to keep things as they are, to hold on to what little security we have, to maintain the status quo, and to prevent change. In this sense Thelma and Louise have become Madwomen who have found the old boys system untenable and are unwilling to submit to the patriarchal Judges of a degenerate society. Out of their sacrifice and their revolutionary stories might emerge a new, more humane way of being for both men and women. Thelma and Louise symbolize a state of feminine consciousness that rejects and tries to leave the old system to find a new way. The storm of criticism leveled against *Thelma and Louise* for being violent is amazing in the light of the male "buddy" films in which men murder right and left. That the women were ultimately unable to establish a viable adaptation in society is less important than the fact that they chose their life statement—freedom over repression and judgment. No wonder so many women and men applauded this revolutionary film, which exposed the courageous aspect of the Madwoman in us all.

A CONSCIOUS REVOLUTIONARY: ROSA LUXEMBURG

Thelma and Louise were just beginning to discover feminine consciousness and did not have time to put their awareness into action. Another step toward consciousness—learning how to act on and instill human values into society—is needed to transform the Madwoman's energy into effective revolutionary action for humanitarian change. There are few feminine models for this kind of change. But at the turn of this century, Rosa Luxemburg, a Madwoman for justice, leaped into revolutionary action and awareness. A political spokeswoman for democratic socialism, she developed a view of radical change, believing that revolution must develop out of the growing consciousness of the oppressed via peaceful rather than violent means. Adamantly opposed to terrorism and the prevailing patriarchal view that social change must be directed from above by an elite few, Rosa believed that reformation would develop naturally from within the human community's maturing awareness of what is required for a good and meaningful spiritual life. Rosa Luxemburg proposed a humane politic coming from within a situation rather than one imposed from without by the static, absolute laws of the patriarchal Judge.

At the core of her humanistic philosophy was her moral commitment to the "freedom to think differently." Without moral virtue, there could be no human progress, she argued. The genuine aim of Marxism, as she saw it, was to restore to the people a wholeness surpassing national allegiances and uniting people at their human depths. Discrimination against women, racism, exploitation, and national domination would end with the advent of true humanistic international socialism. Opposed to artificially organized strikes, planned and controlled by party leaders, Rosa believed that the mature workers alone had the right to initiate their own struggle for freedom and that this could be done peacefully. "Harmony and solidarity" would unite individuals. In contrast to nationalism, Rosa envisioned world citizenship.

Rosa Luxemburg (née: Luksenburg) was born of Jewish parents in Zamość, Poland, in 1870. Her parents, trying to assimilate into secular Polish life, encountered anti-Semitism from Poles, opposition from Orthodox Jews, and economic difficulties. They moved to Warsaw, where they hoped life would be freer, and lived in a professional neighborhood that had only recently opened to Jews. Rosa was a bright, energetic, and happy child who was adored by her parents. When she was five, she developed an abnormal walk that left her with a limp that caused her shame.

When she entered public school at ten, she was admitted under a quota system, in which she had to score higher than Gentiles because she was Jewish. She was a sensitive child and felt humiliated by this segregation, which added to her fear that she was different. She wanted to blend in with the Poles, but her limp and her looks— she was short, with dark hair and eyes and a Semitic nose—set her apart. So did her intellectual giftedness and exceptional student record. She covered her awkwardness and feelings of inferiority by being strong, aggressive, and sometimes arrogant. At twelve, she experienced a terrible trauma—a brutal and violent pogrom raged in her neighborhood; many Jews were killed.

In adolescence she found a small underground community of students who loved poetry and literature and shared a social conscience inspired by the mystical prophet and poet, Adam Mickiewicz, who saw spiritual pilgrimage as a quest to enable justice and freedom for all peoples whose healthy instincts would lead to a natural nonviolent social revolution. Influenced by Mickiewicz, Rosa developed her humanistic philosophy of the need to nurture spontaneous revolutions that would emerge from the spiritual wisdom and healthy feelings of the common people and so result in a more humane life for all.

When she left to study the sciences, law, economics, and philosophy in Zurich—since women were not admitted to universities in Poland at that time—Rosa changed her name to Luxemburg. The ideal of the "woman-rebel" appealed to Rosa, who resisted bourgeois goals. She did not want to be a conforming, dependent housewife like her mother, nor a stereotypical Jewish woman, treated as a nonentity. Her feminine models were heroines who had sacrificed their lives fighting for the cause of freedom.

Joining a German socialist community, she met her first and major love, Leo Jogiches, a radical revolutionary. They became lovers, although he insisted their intimacy be kept secret. Rosa would be continually frustrated in her long-term relationship with Jogiches, which depended largely on writing letters, since they lived apart to work for the revolution. She believed women could both love and work to fulfill their lives, and she wanted marriage to combine emotional intimacy, physical passion, and spiritual beauty and to contribute to each partner's mutual growth as well as a just and spiritualized society. But Jogiches, who put revolution before individual human life, was threatened by emotional intimacy and resisted feelings, believing that personal life and work must be separate lest they diminish the public social cause. Rosa believed the person came first—understanding the art of human life was prerequisite to creating a better life for others. This conflict plagued their entire relationship.

Rosa desperately wanted a child, but since Jogiches was against it, her energies went into writing and revolutionary work. Her writing empowered his revolutionary vision; he gave her love when she followed his instructions and withheld it if she resisted. However, his financial support enabled her to devote herself to study, writing, and political work. As the independent Rosa's reputation outgrew Jogiches's, he tried increasingly to direct her and maintain control over her.

Rosa entered the political world publicly in 1893, speaking passionately for Polish democratic socialism at the second Socialist International congress. Brilliant, intense, passionately energetic, Rosa was charismatic, magnetic; her fiery speeches swayed the delegates. Gifted in oratory and writing, she became the influential pen behind various socialist newspapers. In this way she transformed her anger about the injustices she experienced in her own life—her handicap and her inferior status as a Jewish woman in Poland—into a polemic against political injustice and a humanistic vision of social harmony that was to affect the course of history.

Only twenty-seven years old, with a doctorate in law and political science and more than fifty articles published, her success and public recognition were growing. She became a German citizen through an arranged marriage, which was later dissolved so she could move to Berlin, the headquarters from which she wooed Polish workers in Germany with her compelling speeches about their exploitation and the necessity to fight for their rights.

Rosa became internationally known as one of the young experts on scientific socialism. Her rebellious spirit and imagination captivated her listeners, who loved her; her background in literature, philosophy, and history gave depth and perspective to the social theory she was formulating. A natural fighter for her ideals, Rosa often criticized the party and was denounced for "behaving more like a woman than a party member."[3] But her power came precisely from her feminine values. At the heart of her influence was her belief that a writer must reach deep into herself and relive emotionally the importance and truth of the subject in order to reach enthusiastically into the reader's heart.

In constant demand as a political lecturer and journalist, Rosa was influential in the socialist parties in Germany (the SPD), Poland, and Lithuania. She traveled at an exhausting pace, spoke daily to crowds of thousands, aimed her lectures at the unification of German and Polish workers, and inspired them with her speeches on universal suffrage and artistic freedom and with her political philosophy. Rosa mesmerized people with her warmth and charm, her energy, her intellect, and her depth, and she amazed and impressed the older male leaders in international socialism.

However, loneliness and depression so overwhelmed Rosa during her first years in Berlin that she began to fear she was going mad. She suffered from nervous exhaustion, severe headaches, and other debilitating symptoms. Despite her fame, her public achievements, and the love she received from her audiences, she felt dissatisfied with herself for things left undone. She also felt guilty for failing to write and visit her parents and for leaving their care to her older sister. Rosa blamed her parents for their bourgeois Jewishness. She disliked her father's lack of idealism; she criticized her mother's gentle sweetness, not recognizing her inner strength.

Rosa thought she had escaped the common lot of women despite the fact that patronizing party leaders sometimes belittled and mocked both Rosa and her friend Clara Zetkin, editor of the socialist women's magazines, as the *Frauenzimmer* ("women's room"). Although Rosa felt a separate women's movement would divide the cause, she supported women's freedom, urging her female friends to meaningful action. She criticized bourgeois women "bored with the role of doll or husband's cook," and recommended they "seek some action to fill their empty heads and empty existence,"[4] contrasting them with working-class women, who felt more deeply the inherent necessary connection between women's rights and universal human rights. Women needed to fight for equality and freedom for all oppressed peoples, Rosa believed, not merely for women alone. In 1919, when she became editor of the only socialist paper in Berlin, she planned a special edition for women, emphasizing their importance in politics. Without political influence, women could not even decide the fate of their own lives, much less that of their children or their country.

Rosa was imprisoned for being a revolutionary often during her life. In 1904 she spent three months in a women's prison in Berlin for publicly insulting the Prussian emperor. She was allowed to study, read, write, and receive guests. With time to reflect, she questioned her love for Jogiches and whether life was worth living. Tolstoy's spiritual search for meaning helped her more than Marx.

At this time Rosa criticized Lenin's advocacy of discipline and control. "He concentrates mostly on *controlling* the party, not on *fertilizing* it, on *narrowing* it down, not *developing* it, on *regimenting* and not on *unifying* it," Rosa said, and called for a "positive and creative spirit," rather than the "sterile spirit of a night watchman" (Lenin's approach).[5] She also criticized bureaucratic machinery. Against war and adamantly opposed to Lenin's proposal of armed insurrection, she felt the workers could achieve a people's revolution through raising their conscious awareness. But despite their opposition, Vladimir Lenin and Rosa Luxemburg respected the genius each saw in the other.

After Rosa joined Jogiches in Warsaw during a Polish reaction set off by the 1905 Bloody Sunday massacre in Russia, Polish police entered her room with its illegal press and arrested them the day before her thirty-sixth birthday. The antisocialist German press called "Bloody Rosa" a dangerous alien, claimed she had obtained German citizenship illegally, and exposed her affair with Jogiches. After enough money was raised to get her out on bail, a 1906 court martial found both Rosa and Jogiches guilty of trying to overthrow the Russian government. But Rosa was already in Germany.

In her midthirties, Rosa fell in love with the son of one of her best friends. Opposite in character to Jogiches, he was a romantic dreamer who loved music, poetry, and Nature. She wanted to shape the psyche of this young man as though he were her son. When Rosa told Jogiches their common-law marriage was over, he was enraged and refused to move out of the apartment; he threatened to kill both Rosa and her new lover. Defiant, Rosa challenged Jogiches, just as she challenged any abusive hierarchy that diminished human freedom, whether it was the Marxist patriarchy, bourgeois society, or an individual man.

Her conflict with Jogiches—they could not break completely due to their work as revolutionary leaders—was interrupted by another prison sentence for having "instigated violence" in a public lecture some years earlier. Afraid she would lose her young lover to a more attractive younger woman, Rosa became possessive, and he withdrew, although he remained dependent on her. Rosa agreed to a friendship that was burdened by her black moods. She used the anger over this rejection to fuel battles in the outer world with leading male Marxists and continued to criticize "central party authority." Despite her power and charisma in the public sector, as a woman in love she felt inferior. Rosa returned to Jogiches and to her work. Later, she had a more mature relationship, though a brief one, with her attorney, Paul Levi, who remained her friend and continued her work after she was assassinated.

At forty, Rosa developed her notion of socialism, differentiating it from that of Marx, Lenin, and the SPD. Marxism was not a dogma, she maintained, so to cling literally to the *Communist Manifesto* was a mistake. She became a target of abuse after she criticized the SPD establishment for justifying the use of armed insurrection and terrorism. Party editors began to reject her articles. One of the party patriarchs said of Rosa, "the poisonous bitch will do a lot of damage yet, all the more serious because she is dangerously shrewd."[6] Now stereotyped as a quarrelsome female, she felt the party was trying to silence her, and she attacked the characters of certain party members. Always the rebel, she refused to stand idle and be silenced. The revolutionary Rosa remained a free spirit fighting for her ideals, but increasingly, she became politically isolated.

Articles in journals began to attack her because she was a Jew. Her limp was cited as evidence of Jewish degeneration; she was accused of Semitic hatred of her mother country, Poland. Upset about anti-Semitism, the European Social Democrats supported Rosa as she defended herself against the attacks. Her great work, *The Accumulation of Capital,* published in 1913, came to her in four months, a time of creative intoxication that she said was the happiest in her life. It was controversial and was criticized by both the right and the left contingents of the German Social Democratic Party (SPD). The collapse of capitalism was inevitable and automatic, she argued, and its replacement by socialism could occur only through the growing revolutionary consciousness of the working class. In her next work, *Anti-Critique,* she claimed that there were no experts on Marxism, including Marx himself. Rosa always urged creativity, not dogma.

Convicted of inciting public disobedience, she put the Prussian court on trial in an appeal in 1914 by arguing that only the people, not the government, had the right to determine their destiny, and that mass strikes are only a stage in the class struggle toward human freedom and peace. Her brilliant and courageous speech made her a celebrity. Her previously banned articles were now sought by the SPD press. Rosa was sentenced to one year in prison, but she publicized her antiwar philosophy—that war could be avoided if workers enacted a general strike on an international scale, thus requiring that armies be abolished. Workers who were conscious of their power and who refused to fight could foster peace and prevent war.

Divisions in the SPD increased; when World War I broke out, the Social Democrats supported the war by voting for war funding. Rosa and others opposed the war and disaffiliated from the SPD. In despair at the outbreak of war, Rosa worked so hard that she fell ill from nervous and physical exhaustion and was hospitalized. Then she was taken to prison again. During the war, Rosa spent over three years in prison and was transferred frequently for protective custody until the war ended. In prison she wrote letters of challenge and encouragement, decrying weakness. But she also wrote letters confessing her vulnerability and despair.

Spiritually depleted, Rosa feared madness; nightmares overwhelmed her. She recorded a horrifying dream in which she was expected to sing a song while accompanying herself on the piano. About to perform, she realized she could not play the piano, and no one was there to accompany her. To have an excuse not to play, she cut her finger, then screamed in fear that she would be deserted by the friend arranging the concert. Hoping her niece could accompany her, she remembered the niece did not play the piano. The dream revealed Rosa's panic at isolation and her fear of abandonment by friends. It expressed her despair that her own singing, which symbolized the affirmation of her existence, might be impossible if she were condemned to sing alone.

Rosa was plunged into chaos, a dark night of the soul. On the universal level, she was confronted with the paradox of human existence—the mystery of good and evil—while on the psychological level, she suffered from extreme mood swings. In one of her affirmative moods she wrote: "in darkness I am smiling at life . . . and searching for the reason for that happiness . . . The deep nocturnal darkness is so beautiful and soft as velvet if one knows how to look at it. . . . One must always take everything that belongs to [life] and find *everything* beautiful and good. At least that is what I do, not guided by reason or wisdom but simply following my nature. I feel instinctively that this is the right way to live, and therefore I feel really happy under any circumstances."[7]

Nature raised her spirits. While she was in prison she was allowed to tend a garden. To see a bird, watch the growth of a plant, observe the changing weather reassured her. Finally she could permit herself to identify with her mother, who believed one could understand the songs of the birds. Allowed to read and study, she sent her friends meaningful quotations from the books she loved, informed them of concerts, and affirmed endurance and optimism. By writing she saved herself from drowning in despair, and she tried to turn material defeat into spiritual victory.

Released from prison in 1918, Rosa returned to Berlin—a city in chaos, crowds swarming the streets. Revolution threatened the country as the German government decried the danger of Bolshevism. She wrote for a newly founded socialist revolutionary paper, moved with its headquarters from hotel to hotel, pleaded in her articles for conscious action, spiritual maturity, and practical measures, and continued to denounce terrorism as socialism's ultimate perversion.

As she fought with her pen for the spiritual rebirth of the German worker, Jogiches worked with her. Older now, they were more tolerant and understanding of each other and could express tenderness. He understood that Rosa would not compromise, either toward Lenin, whose terrorist means she criticized, or toward the German Social Democrats, who had betrayed socialism by their national support of the war. Caught in the middle, criticizing both sides, she was condemned as a "female devil" who wanted to destroy the German people. Hatred and prejudice leered at her from billboards, pamphlets, and newspapers.

In December 1918 workers and soldiers fought each other, strikes paralyzed Germany, and the different factions of the SPD clashed, each accusing the others of betraying the revolution. Rosa accused the SPD of supporting the war and the emperor's army, which had turned against the workers, while she warned the German workers that they were not ready to take over the government.

Isolated, Rosa also faced her worst fear—the failure of her vision. The younger generation of socialists sought power and used violence to achieve their ends.

Government soldiers killed the uprising workers, beat them, and mutilated their bodies. The soldiers made derogatory remarks about Rosa's prediction that bloodshed breeds the annihilation of an order—a prediction that came true later, with the rise of Hitler. She blamed the leaders, not the masses, for failure.

On the night of January 15, 1919, militiamen arrested Rosa; a sum of 100,000 marks had been offered for her capture. They took her to a hotel, temporary headquarters for a division of soldiers, to the captain's room to be identified. As she was led through the lobby, rowdy soldiers jeered at her, "Röschen" and "there goes the old whore."[8] As she was taken back through the lobby, a soldier jumped out of the crowd that leered at "Red Rosa" and hit her on the head with his rifle butt, then again on the temple after she fell to the floor. Soldiers took the bleeding Rosa to a car, where an officer shot her in the temple. Driven to the bank of the Spree River, her body was dragged through the bushes and thrown into the river with the remark, "The old slut is swimming now."[9]

After her murder, various versions of the crime were reported. One German paper called her a terrorist leader and said her murder was a sentence by "the people's court of justice." But Jogiches uncovered the facts that the murders of Rosa and of Karl Liebknecht, another leading socialist revolutionary, had been planned with the cooperation of the same military group investigating the case. Jogiches was caught and shot by the military, but the publicized facts of the murders of Luxemburg and Liebknecht required a court martial. Each of her attackers received only a two-year sentence.

When her body was found months later, police tried to bury her secretly, fearing a demonstration. They knew Rosa was loved by the people, who might rebel. But Paul Levi, now head of the German Communist party, demanded a post-mortem for identification. It could not be determined whether she had died from the blows, or gunshot, or by drowning.

At Rosa Luxemburg's funeral, held June 13, 1919, a huge crowd mourned the death of a great heroine. The closing words of her last article were put under her picture on large banners carried high for all to see. She had written that the revolution would return and announce: "I was, I am, I shall be."[10] These last affirmative words coming from the feminine depths of this revolutionary heroine inspire us today, reminding us of the necessity to oppose violence and to struggle for human rights and dignity for all peoples—regardless of gender, race, nationality, or religion.

Rosa Luxemburg channeled the power of the Madwoman effectively. She faced her anger about the deprivations she felt in her personal life—her limp, her loneliness in love, her childhood, religious and gender prejudice, and the terrible social injustices she saw everywhere around her. Conscious of her madness about these issues, she took that energy and turned it to constructive action. She refused the extreme of terrorism, and she refused to be victimized by circumstances. She knew she was different, and accepting it, she opened herself to a revolutionary vision of human possibilities. With discipline and courage, with insight and diligent work, she struggled to actualize her revolutionary views of social change in the world. She sacrificed her life consciously to this commitment. What Muriel Rukeyser says in her poem about the social revolutionary artist Käthe Kollwitz describes the essence of the transformative power of the Madwoman as Revolutionary exemplified by the energy of Rosa Luxemburg:

> the revolutionary look
> that says I am in the world
> to change the world.[11]

EMBODYING FEMININE POWER

How can a woman be a conscious Revolutionary in today's world? First we must step forward and face our inner and outer fears. The Revolutionary commits to a value she believes will humanize the world, then acts to embody that value. This requires taking a firm stand and struggling for that right, if necessary. In fact, the extremes of rigid aggression and weak resistance can lead to terrorism and victimization.

The major danger for the Revolutionary is to succumb to an egotistic inflation that can degenerate into terrorism or self-righteousness, two sides of the same coin. If one becomes stuck in the energy of the Madwoman, there is a danger of coming to feel one is always right and self-justified, a patriarchal position, paradoxically. As the authors of *The Madwoman in the Attic* point out, female bonding is difficult in the patriarchy because the "looking glass" pits women against each other. If women become artificially inflated they can tend to put each other down rather than support each other. Women who fear and distrust each other are unknowingly in the service of the patriarchy, as are women who remain victimized and indulge in fear.

Facing fear by acknowledging it while courageously taking the leap of faith that something better awaits is a way to utilize the Madwoman's revolutionary energy. The Burmese Nobel prize winner, Aung San Suu Kyi, who is currently fighting her government, an unjust system, through active waiting in the name of humanity, while under house arrest, has faced fear courageously through her revolutionary stand. She believes fear is a habit that people form if they live with fear for a long time. In their hearts, she believes, people want freedom.[12] One way for modern women to overcome their fear and be Revolutionaries is to step forth and tell their stories, as Anita Hill did. Only when victims step forward and tell their stories can the denial about harassment and abuse be exposed. When women become active, take a stand in solidarity, and empowered by the constructive Madwoman energy, confront the "old boy system," they will transform themselves, find their inner strength, and be able to change the system. Women film directors like Margarethe von Trotta, who portrays women's revolutionary struggles to attain feminine wholeness in films such as *Rosa Luxemburg* and *Marianne and Juliane,* help us to learn about our strength and relationships as women.

Revolutionary assertion *requires* action that is honest, spiritually centered, and totally focused. It requires dedication to a cause and a willingness to give up one's egotistic desires, to make the necessary sacrifices, to die away from one kind of life and pursuit and into another kind of life and identity. Acting from the feminine center with other women, not against them in competition, is essential to revolutionize women's liberation. A powerful demonstration of active Madwoman power by women cooperating together occurred some years ago in Alice Springs, Australia, where a large group of Aboriginal women marched through the town. They walked powerfully, arm in arm, their ritual feminine symbols painted in color on their bare breasts, as they protested the illegal sales of alcohol and drugs to the men in their community who were demoralized from substance abuse.

The Revolutionary can utilize the Madwoman energy constructively by bringing about creative chaos from which new growth can occur. By fighting the regressive social systems that butcher feminine spirit, she can dig up dark soil in which new ideas and ways of life can germinate and grow. The Revolutionary can "rewrite" the rigid rules of the patriarch who seeks power in perfection and victory and consciously give birth to more flexible guidelines of change, discovery, and exploration, thus adding her unique feminine vision and values to the world. Already many women today are "evolutionary" Revolutionaries, like Rachel Carson. They are ecofeminists who share common goals and want to give birth to a caring and healing relation with the earth, and to envision new ways to aid ecological causes and restore balance to society and the environment.

9

THE VISIONARY

*And it occurred in the sixth year, after
I had been troubled for five years with
marvelous and true visions. In these
visions a true view of the everlasting
light had shown me—a totally
uneducated human being—the
diversity of many ways of life. . . . I
trembled over my whole body and
began to feel ill because of my bodily
weakness. For seven years I wrote
about this vision but could scarcely
complete the task. . . . I saw under
(the influence of) heavenly mysteries
while my body was fully awake and
while I was in my right mind. I saw it
with the inner eye of my spirit and
grasped it with my inner ear. . . .
And once again I heard a voice from
heaven instructing me. And it said,*
"Write down what I tell you!"

—HILDEGARD VON BINGEN

MANY INTUITIVE WOMEN ARE NOT BELIEVED WHEN THEY EX-
press what they have seen. In myth, Cassandra suffered this tragic curse.[1] An archetypal example of
the Visionary woman, Cassandra possessed the gift
of prophecy and predicted that the Greeks would
hide in a huge wooden horse outside the city gates
and attempt to conquer Troy by surprise. She was
considered mad; no one heeded her warning. Her

father Priam, King of Troy, locked her in a cell and put her under the guard of a woman attendant, whom he asked to report whatever Cassandra said. In this way he tried to control his daughter as a Madwoman yet have access to her intuitions. Many fathers imprison their clairvoyant daughters this way. Sometimes they do so with kindness, as in the case of Claire, whom we met in Chapter 2. Claire's father relied on his daughter's innate wisdom and used her as helpmate and caretaker. Husbands and employers also use women's intuitive insights to advance their own careers, although in public they may ignore or denigrate them and their way of knowing, as often happens to the Muse and the Caged Bird. The expression "the woman behind the man" shows both the power and the exploitation of women by the patriarchy.

Mothers, too, may discourage their daughters' intuitions by neglecting or disparaging them. In one version of the legend, Cassandra originally receives the gift of prophecy when, as a child, she and her twin brother are left by their parents in Apollo's temple, where their birthday celebration is being held. Drinking too much wine, the parents forget their children, who are napping in a corner of the temple, and go home to sleep. Later, when their mother, Hecuba returns for the twins, she finds Apollo's serpents licking at Cassandra's ears—the first sign of her daughter's prophetic gift. In shock, Hecuba chases the serpents away, even though she herself is related to Hecate, who as goddess of magic and witchcraft grants both visions and madness.[2] Understood symbolically, Cassandra's mother is connected to the medial arts, but she neglects to instruct her daughter in them, trying to keep her from them. Hecuba's neglect of Cassandra typifies the medial mother who does not develop her own prophetic gifts and tries to deny them in her daughter. The story of Claire in Chapter 2 and the dream of Sophie in this chapter are examples of Visionary women who are left with the fear of madness because their mothers fail to acknowledge and confront their own powers, use them, and transmit them consciously and safely.

In another version of the myth, Apollo gives Cassandra the gift of prophecy to win her love. When Cassandra refuses to yield to him, he becomes angry and curses her. Unable to recall his own gift, he tricks her and asks her for a kiss. As she raises her lips to him, he spits into her mouth, cursing her prophetic power so that she will not be believed. Women who have been sexually harassed by their relatives, employers, teachers, ministers, or therapists have experienced this combination—the promise of a secret alliance and the curse of being attacked as Madwomen if they refuse his advances, and the realistic dilemma of not being believed if they tell. When Anita Hill reported that Clarence Thomas had harassed her sexually, she was not believed and was discounted as an hysterical Madwoman, deluded by her fantasies. Like Cassandra, who suffers rape at the hands of Ajax the lesser after he drags her from her place of refuge behind the statue of Athena, goddess of justice, Anita Hill's reputation was also raped.

Later, Cassandra is betrayed by another set of elders. Agamemnon brings her to his palace as one of his war trophies. In order to win the Trojan war, Agamemnon already has sacrificed his daughter Iphigenia.[3] Outside the palace, Cassandra senses her fate—to be murdered by Agamemnon's wife, Clytemnestra, who later kills her husband and clubs Cassandra to death with an ax. Before the palace, Cassandra shrieks out that she can smell both past and future blood on the floor of the House of Atreus, the family who dishonored the feminine when Iphigenia was sacrificed. A chain of vengeful murders results. Because the House of Atreus has not honored the feminine, the Furies take over. Thus Cassandra, first abandoned by Hecuba, is later murdered by Clytemnestra, symbolizing abuse by "the mothers." Clytemnestra's anger and jealousy of Cassandra typifies the way women turn on other women and accuse them of "witchcraft," conniving, or other objectionable behavior when the offense or atrocity has actually been committed by a man.

Like Cassandra, medial women often encounter scorn of their intuitions. Women of a gentler temperament, like the introverted, intuitive, perceptive, feeling type, often fear to brave the attacks of more aggressive, judgmental thinkers. So they hide their insights, keeping to themselves, or they fail to develop ways to express the intuitions so fundamental to their nature. Others weave their visions into poems or paintings but fear to show them to the outer world.

One Visionary woman who had developed a public speaking phobia and declined lecture invitations dreamed that she had many precious jewels inside her. But the jewels—her visions—were stuck in her throat and threatened to choke her to death. Her fear of critical judgment and immediate censure—by men or women—was keeping her from voicing the truths she saw. She needed to connect with her inner Furies, the Madwoman's power, to risk rejection and put her gifts forward.

Another reflective practical woman, who was always looking ahead to see the possible outcomes of a decision, described the way she felt. When she would express the results she foresaw, she was usually told, "You worry too much," or "Forget about it. You can't think of everything that will happen." Consequently, she felt misunderstood, since her legitimate concerns were not considered realistic. Angry inside, she would grit her teeth in frustration, especially when her predictions came to pass.

Still another woman who felt akin to Cassandra said she felt betrayal when others disbelieved her at crucial times. In adolescence she was molested, but her parents had discounted what she said. So it especially hurt her when, as an adult, she shared her intuitions in relationships with men who didn't believe her and minimized her mode of knowing. Later, when she shared the vision of a book she planned to write, people tried to discourage her, saying, "You're wasting your time. There's no market for such a book. Who would buy it?" Through all these experiences she had to have faith in herself and keep working to embody her vision until her book was published.

The Visionary woman who is intuitive and sees into the future reveals messages—sometimes dark prophecies, sometimes visions of light—and is suspect to the rational mind. Her knowledge and perception come from mysterious sources that transcend logic and empirical methods. Since her visions cannot be comprehended by rational thought alone, she threatens hierarchical thinking and is feared, ridiculed, and even condemned for her access to a realm that many refuse to experience. Poets, mystics, saints, shamans, artists, actresses, teachers, and healers, including some psychotherapists, are some of the traditional and contemporary channelers of visionary wisdom.

The Visionary receives knowledge directly from the unconscious through images, dreams, inner voices, words and titles, ideas, or bodily sensations that come to her suddenly, sometimes shocking her, sometimes inspiring her with ecstasy. She is like a medium who has a direct channel to a psychic spring. Toni Wolff, Jung's colleague and Muse, first called this way of feminine knowing "medial."[4] The medial woman, she said, is immersed in the collective unconscious; she has a special gift of vision for the good of human-kind—for wholeness and harmony in the world. Since her relation-ship to the psyche exists primarily on the universal level, however, her personal life may suffer. Moreover, the medial woman who is not aware of her special relation to the unconscious may unknow-ingly be overwhelmed by the power of the unconscious and become its agent, acting out what is "in the air." She may then become the scapegoat who carries the negative projections of those who deny what she sees in them or in the culture. As carrier of dark aspects that can disrupt prevailing values, the medial woman becomes a threat to others. Joan of Arc was such a visionary scapegoat, yet she brought hope for an entire culture and became an icon and symbol of salvation.

The Visionary seems dangerous because she sees things from the "other side." If her visions seem mad, it is because they turn ex-pected routines and assumptions we take for granted upside down into chaos. Visions cut through either/or formulas and superficial solutions to show the depth of meaning behind the obvious. Be-cause such people see beyond the material realm, they may feel out of touch with others. Due to the different nature of intuitive percep-tion, which allows reception of new and unusual insights, Visionaries often fear going mad themselves. Drifting away from earthly life via dreams and visions is a danger—one that can end in madness. Some Visionary women are so ephemeral and fragile that others are afraid to interrupt their fantasy world, like the character of Laura in Ten-nessee Williams's *The Glass Menagerie*.[5]

While the Visionary's talents and nature are often regarded as esoteric, intuition is an inherent human quality, which can develop to a certain degree. Most people have moments of vision, flashes of awareness that can change their lives, or prophetic dreams that point to necessary realizations and changes. The "normal" woman needs to learn to recognize her intuitive potential and honor it in small ways in herself. In the film *Resurrection*, Ellen Burstyn portrays an ordinary woman who becomes a visionary yet remains grounded and humble. After a near-death experience as a result of an auto accident, she starts having visions and gradually discovers she has the gift of healing. First she uses it to heal her own paralysis that resulted from the accident. Then she finds she can heal others by empathizing with them in their pain through her love, and she holds public healings. Because she maintains she does not know

where her gift came from, only her deep love helps her in the process, she is branded as evil by a Christian fundamentalist who wants
her to say her gift came from God and His word, and her life is
threatened. When she realizes that her gifts of healing are too
threatening to be used in public ways in her community, she leaves
and works at an ordinary job in a secluded gas station in the desert.
Unrecognized by the people she helps, she continues to use her
visionary gift for healing out of public view. At the end of the film,
she heals a young boy from terminal cancer, without saying anything
about it to him or his parents. She manifests the miracle through
simple human love.

In former times, many women hid their intuitive nature so that
they would not be persecuted or tormented or ostracized as strange.
Some suppressed it; in others, it was repressed early, when they were
young girls, a result of harsh criticism by parents. Women who denied their intuitions usually suffered the consequences. Unused,
their psychic abilities turned against them in the form of fears, resentment, guilt, anger, illness, and madness. Yet when women revealed their visions they were often persecuted as witches: Joan of
Arc; Jezebel, wife of King Ahab, who was called a dangerous seduc-
tress by the Old Testament patriarchs who disapproved of her pagan
worship of the Mother Goddess: and the Russian poetesses Anna
Akhmatova and Marina Tsvetayeva, who were silenced and forbidden to write for decades by the Soviet regime. Her suffering and
persecution were too much for Marina Tsvetayeva, who managed to
escape in exile but later committed suicide. Anna Akhmatova, who
survived, preserved her poems for years by memorizing them, until
the ban on her writing was lifted, and she was lauded as the high
priestess of Russian poetry. Still other visionaries were sent to the
madhouse for their revelations.

When women do not accept their innate intuitive talents, they
can experience manifestations of madness. Their children bear the
brunt of their mother's unused potential. This is illustrated in the
following dream of Sophie, a woman who experienced her mother
as mean and mad. Sophie's mother always picked an adversary, then
started an argument.

My mother is trying to explain to my brother and myself why
she has been so mad and crazy and mean to us. She tells us
she had been given a supernatural power to know what was

happening at a particular moment in various places, as well as the power to predict the future. Fearing this special knowledge as dangerous, she tried to suppress it. To assure that her psychic knowledge would not burst out unexpectedly, she remained a housewife and withdrew from worldly activities. As a result she felt mad and irritable and on the defensive most of the time, she tells us. My brother and I look at her in astonishment and say: "Don't you realize your power could be used for good and transformation?" What a waste, I reflect, that my mother hasn't used these special powers.

Sophie said that her mother was depressed most of the time and was often sick. Sophie felt that if her mother had acknowledged and developed her intuitive and medial powers and used them in a creative way, her energy would not have erupted into irritation with her family. Instead, her mother functioned like a Dragon Lady, trying to possess her children, especially devouring her daughter and resenting her creative energy. Intuitive herself, Sophie consciously worked on forming and grounding her own medial powers after she had a warning dream that she had married her mother. This dream was actually a nightmare, emphasizing Sophie's fear that she might become like her mother or else be dependent on her. Heeding the dream's message, she entered a creative writing program in order to develop ways to articulate her intuitions.

Because the medial woman can feel unexpressed emotions around her and gain knowledge in this way, she often senses what is happening in the environment, even though she may not be aware of it. For example, if the interactions in her family group or community are dysfunctional and crazy-making but are taken as normal by others, she may think she is the crazy one. She may pick up the stress of the family and act it out. Feeling weakened by the chaotic force of the unconscious contents that she mediates, and by the negative reactions of those around her, she can become isolated, hysterical, and paranoid and even sink into madness. Or if she identifies with her powers or with the contents she transmits, she may feel inflated with power and think she personally deserves credit as the source of the new ideas to which she gives voice. She then may be tempted to glamorize and romanticize her role as prophetess. On the other hand, feeling used by a force beyond herself, she may feel deflated and become angry at her fate. If she does not understand her role as mediatrix, "she will become the first victim of her own nature."[6] For example, if she regards the ideas or archetypal contents that she should communicate to the culture as her own personal possession, she may succumb to the bewitching power of wanting to be a guru.

The spiritual challenge for the medial or Visionary woman is to become conscious of her gift and to value and appreciate her unique potential to receive and mediate her visions. She needs to learn to discriminate between intuitions that refer to her own personal life and those that relate to the environment around her. Some of her visions arise from the collective unconscious and are demanded by the psyche's urge for wholeness. Such visions refer to new ideas and feelings that require expression in society. Since any gift requires the sacrifice of conscious development, the medial woman has a special task before her: She must be able to distinguish consciously the personal from the impersonal, or in Toni Wolff's words, "to become a mediatrix instead of a mere medium."[7] This means she must actively prepare herself not only to receive the visions but to communicate them. If she consciously chooses to do this, "she consecrates herself to the service of a new, maybe yet concealed, spirit of her age."[8]

Toni Wolff, herself a medial woman, described this feminine mode of knowing in 1951. Now, in the last decade of the twentieth century, modern women are becoming aware of their visionary gifts and want to deal responsibly and consciously with intuitive knowledge. Rooted in the feminine center—whether it is through their relation to the goddess cultures or to ancient matrifocal roots, or grounded in Mother Nature—they are trying together, as sisters of the earth, to envision and create a world in which feminine values are respected. But in order to honor the Visionary woman, her paradoxical nature and the conflicts from which she suffers must be understood. Otherwise, she is likely to continue to be dismissed as a Madwoman.

THE VISIONARY'S CONFLICT: PERSONAL DESIRES VERSUS TRANSPERSONAL SERVICE

The medial woman must reconcile her gifts with her desires. As a Visionary, she is called upon to serve the greater transpersonal forces and to transmit messages to the community. Yet as a human being with personal longings, she may want to lead a "normal" life and have a love relationship that may conflict with her medial duties. She has to learn to reconcile her personal life with her call to service.

One reason the Visionary feels caught in this terrible paradox is her worry that by accepting her potential for prophetic vision, she will lose personal love, since the medial quality is often feared and even condemned. Thus, trying to hide or deny her unique way of knowing, an intuitive woman sometimes puts all her psychic abilities into concrete relationships. Misplacing her gift for knowledge, she may advise her lover, children, and friends or comment on their weaknesses. When an irritated lover gets angry at this unsolicited advice, in shock the medial woman cannot understand what happened. In fearful anticipation of being rejected for her intuitions, some women even avoid committing to relationships, suffering the agony of loneliness. Others, resentful that they are losing out on life, refuse to put their intuitive potential in the service of the divine or the human community. Still others enter into relationships with men for whom, through their intuition, they may help solve difficulties in an existing relationship, only to find themselves thanked but left alone. For example, one woman I know recently realized she has a tendency to get into relationships with married men. As she got to know these men, she would see how they miscommunicated in all their relationships, and she would tell them about it. But her wild intuitions would scare her lovers and attract their negative projections and judgments. One man told his family about her, and they turned on her as a witch figure who had been causing all their troubles with this man. By focusing all their anger at her, they were brought together against a common enemy, and she was rejected and abandoned. In therapy she works on developing more realistic relationships, has realized her tendency to reveal her intuitions prematurely, and works to become more conscious in the way she communicates.

In contrast, other intuitive women choose to serve something beyond themselves. They may be called by religions into positions as priests or nuns, or they may be inspired as artists. If they choose this path consciously, they will not feel any resentment. But if they feel pushed by outer forces onto this demanding path, they may have a sour, martyred, separate feeling about their life that can turn to despair. For example, one woman faced the choice of marrying the artist with whom she was in love or remaining single. She decided she would not marry, because it would have meant that she had to sacrifice her own creativity to the life he wanted them to have together, for she would have had to be the grounding force in their relationship. Thus she suffered from her lonely longing for a personal, romantic relationship.

Some women live in defiance, refusing service to their creative call because they resent their fate as Visionaries. Maria Callas suffered this conflict between her call as high priestess of opera and her longing to be Onassis's wife. In her personal life she played out the tragedy of the great druidic priestess in the opera *Norma,* who betrays her call as Visionary priestess to be with a human lover who later leaves her for another woman. Norma throws herself into the flames of a funeral pyre when she realizes the enormity of her self-betrayal.

The following dream of a Visionary who felt unfulfilled in her romantic life shows this conflict between personal longing for romance and the role of priestess to which her dream was guiding her.

> Two men take me as a hostage in an open car to a high mountain community in the Andes. The people there are awaiting my arrival, since I am supposed to be the oracular priestess for their celebration. They lead me to the center of the circle to give me the herbs that will put me into trance. Afraid, I escape to Paris, where I had lived in my twenties. I awaken in fear, knowing the two men will return to take me back to be the oracle.

Paris was the place where she had experienced romance as a young woman. Now older, she was being called to share her visionary wisdom in the community. Her resistance to being central to the community as the oracular priestess was interfering with the creative call she felt to write a novel, her form of visionary expression.

The Visionary is often thrust into a paradox that confuses her and throws her into a negative pattern of behavior. Some women may be called to serve the creative forces by being alone and silent at the heart of Nature in order to receive and reveal the mysteries of Mother Earth. Yet the Visionary's flesh and feelings may yearn for the touch of human love. Morgaine LaFay, as described in the novel *The Mists of Avalon,* suffers from this conflict. As a priestess of the Great Mother, she belongs to the Goddess. She must sacrifice the tie of marriage and any other love alliance with a mortal man for personal fulfillment to the Goddess's greater designs. Morgaine, who is a priestess in training to study holy things and prepare herself to receive the gift of healing, has been chosen by Vivianne, the Lady of the Lake, to replace her as High Priestess of Avalon. But Morgaine is tempted when she falls in love with Lancelot. Later, the gods direct her to unite sexually, in a sacred ritual that honors the divine union of man and woman before the Goddess, with a man whom she does not know is her brother, Arthur. Morgaine has heard and responded to the call of the Goddess—a voice that she cannot misunderstand and from which she cannot hide. But on the personal level, when she learns what she has done, she is angered at this incestuous union that defies all human mores. In despair and defiance at the brutality of the Goddess's will, she steals away from the otherworldly Avalon to live in human society at her brother's court. Morgaine feels afflicted by her "sight" and oracular destiny. Yet when she is set in human society, she knows she has betrayed her task as priestess. Not destined to belong to the human world, Morgaine fears she will lose her visionary sight as well.

Then Vivianne, the aging High Priestess of Avalon, goes to King Arthur's court to ask him to protect Avalon—its old laws, the ancient forms of Nature worship, and the sacred groves, which the lesser kings are despoiling. Morgaine fears the Christian priests will drive the old pagan priestess out of court as a Madwoman. But worse than that happens: Vivianne is murdered—in the name of Christ—as an evil sorceress by a man who wants to rid the land of all the pagan ways of Avalon. The murder of Vivianne shocks Morgaine into recommitment to her true destiny.

Morgaine wonders why humans have come to identify the creative force with the vengeful father of battle rather than with the loving mother of the growing fields. Morgaine knows that the Mother Goddess has her dark side, too, and contains the Madwoman within her own manifold mysteries. The Great Mother is not only the Green Lady of the fruit-bearing earth; she is also the Dark Lady of the Seed, hidden in the winter soil, and the Lady of Rot as well.[9] Morgaine herself experienced this darkness when she was sent to lie with her brother. She observes that the Goddess has been driven out as "Madwoman" by the Christian priests who understand neither the flow of Nature nor that all divine forces—light and dark, Christian and pagan—are really one. Because people do not want to struggle for enlightenment or bear the suffering of the mysteries that are too difficult to grasp with reason alone, they want a God who will protect them and make things easy. So the priests attempt to obliterate the divine paradoxes that permeate human purposes; they give definitions that deny the unfathomable holiness of Nature's sacred flow.

In the end, Morgaine proceeds alone to retrace her steps, to reenter Avalon, and to reclaim the role of priestess that she renounced. Knowing she cannot escape her fate as priestess and that she will be called to perform the Goddess's tasks wherever she goes, Morgaine finally accepts the sacrifice and suffering of her calling —that she must forgo her own will and follow the way of the Goddess.

HONORING THE VISIONARY

In our culture we have lost our awareness of the importance of oracular knowledge, and we fail to honor or even listen to the Visionaries who mediate visions. We have forgotten to revere the ancient mysteries; we have discarded the rituals that allow the mysteries to unfold and be revealed. In ancient times the role of priestess was central to human life. At Delphi, for example, the oracular priestess was consulted for her wisdom. The very word *sibyl* (a title for the priestess) derives from the Greek words *sios (theos)*, meaning "God," and *bola*, meaning "advice." The sibyl was believed to receive the words of God directly in a consecrated ritual. After purification, the sibyl received the oracular message down in the bowels of the earth in a dark cave. She went into a trance, her body would writhe, and her shrieks would come forth from below. She might utter the revealed knowledge vocally or she might write it, communicating via hieroglyphics or symbols.[10]

The priestesses were chosen very carefully, while they were still children, for their pursuit of wisdom, beauty, and purity. They underwent rigorous training, education, and initiatory trials, requiring death and rebirth. To receive the divine inspiration and to reveal it to the hearts of others, they had to be chaste and pure. Great sacrifice was required of them, and they owned no personal possessions. Some reports say they had to bear within themselves the shaking of the changing, cyclical earth. When possessed this way, they were close to death or madness, and their bodies would writhe in agony as the illumination passed through them.

A guide to the underworld, the sibyl helped journeyers to interpret what they learned there and to return. She advised the Romans to consult the triple goddess of the underworld, Hecate, who sits at the crossroads where three paths meet. She helped Aeneas enter the Underworld via a dark, primeval forest to find the hidden Golden Bough, which had to be presented to Persephone before he could return to earth. In Ovid's version, Aeneas calls the sibyl a goddess, offering to build a temple to honor her. But the sibyl declines, saying that she serves the divine forces as a priestess but is not herself a goddess.

The sibyl was seen as an aged but mighty priestess. Michelangelo painted the Cumaen sibyl on the ceiling of the Sistine Chapel as a huge, powerful, massive figure with alert eyes gazing out from under furrows of wrinkled flesh. He believed that the sibyl's prophecies revealed the world's destiny. Among the Cumaen sibyl's prophecies were the rise and fall of Rome and the birth of Christ.

The consequences of dishonoring the ancient seer are shown in the following legend. One day an old woman from Cumae came to Rome to see Tarquin, the Etruscan king. She offered to sell him nine books containing the destiny of the world in exchange for three hundred pieces of gold. The king refused this strange offer from the old eccentric woman, thinking she asked too much. The old woman left but returned to Rome a few weeks later. This time she offered to sell him only six books but for the same price. The king refused again, saying the price was too high. Much later, the old woman returned for the last time, offering three books to the king for the same price. At last the king consented to buy the books and asked about the others. The old woman said that she had burned them. After reading the three books, which spoke of the destiny of the world, he asked the old woman (who was the Cumaean sibyl) to rewrite the other six books, but she refused. The three books revealed much of Rome's rise to become a world empire. But its ultimate destiny remained unknown, due to the king's failure to recognize and honor the old woman who was the High Priestess of Cumae.

The Cumaean sibyl and the Delphic pythia received their divinatory powers from the earth. The earth and the sacred sites where the oracular temples were located inspired them.[11] Inspiration could occur through a dream or an ecstatic trance. When the human soul joined with the divine soul in a sacred wedding, then the message from the deity could be transmitted. Thus, when asked to read the oracle, the Delphic pythia wore a white gown, dressed as the bride of the god before entering Apollo's temple. She was still a priestess of the earth. Named for Pytho, the dragon that Apollo had slain, she spoke from a dark, underground cave on the side of a dark abyss, a fearsome chasm through which earthquakes reverberated. Within this gorge a waterfall fed the purifying waters of the Castalian spring.

Worshipers who wanted to consult the Delphic oracle had to undergo special sacramental rites: fasting, seclusion, purification, wearing ritual robes, and providing an offering. Walking along the Sacred Way, a steep winding path of hallowed stones to the great megalithic entrance of the temple, they entered from the east, where Greek temples faced to honor the source of light. Then they passed by the eternal flame of Hestia's hearth and proceeded through the darkened temple to the rear, where a gold statue of Apollo stood. To consult the high priestess, the worshiper had to descend to an underground waiting chamber. Lower yet was the sacred prophetic cavern where the dragon priestess, the pythia, sat on a tripod, a three-legged stool, perched above a deep fissure in the earth. From this dark abyss rose vapors inhaled by the pythia, who fell into a trance. In this state the high priestess relived the great dramas of the earth and humankind and uttered her prophecies. The scholar of mythology Mircea Eliade notes that Mother Earth herself was the original oracle at Delphi, revered by all.

The oracular priestess at Delphi received her knowledge via divine revelation and appealed to the intuition of those who posed questions. "Know thyself" was her precept. She recognized Socrates as the wisest person on earth because he acknowledged what he did not know. A sense of measure, an acceptance of the finitude of being, and a commitment to one's chosen journey were her guiding principles. She honored poetic truth especially, because poetry honored the mystery of existence and expressed the relationship between the visible and invisible worlds.

After the Goddess cultures were dishonored and Apollo was separated from his Dionysian and feminine aspects, the priestesses became subservient to patriarchal values and interpretations. The sibyl was exploited.

RAGING AT GOD: *THE SIBYL*

Because the Visionary's destiny is to reveal the universal truths of existence that encompass not only the beautiful but also the terrible, and because her revelations sometimes frighten the conservative public that denies them and calls them mad, she finds herself set apart, cast out even, from the normal course of life. Sometimes she explodes in rage, feeling exploited by both divinity and humans. The following passage from Pär Lagerkvist's mythic novel *The Sibyl* expresses the Visionary's fury:

But I shake my fist at him who treated me so, who used me in this way, in his pit, his oracle pit—used me as his passive instrument—raped my body and soul, possessed me with his frightful spirit, his delirium, his so-called inspiration, filled me with his hot breath, his alien fire, and my body with his lusting, fertilizing ray so that I had to bear this witless son, who is a mockery of man—of reason and of man—a mockery of me who had to bear him. Who chose me to be his sacrifice, to be possessed by him, to foam at the mouth for god and to bring forth an idiot. Who has exploited me all my life; who stole from me all true happiness, all human happiness; who bereft me of all that others may enjoy—all that gives them security and peace. Who took from me my love, my beloved; all, all—and gave me nothing in return, nothing but himself. Himself. Who is in me still, filling me with his presence, his unrest, never giving me peace because he himself is not peace; never forsaking me. Never forsaking me!

I shake my fist at him—my impotent fist![12]

Revealing her despair at the conflict between her role as priestess and her longing for love, Lagerkvist's sibyl rages at the god who has used her voice, then punishes her when she accepts the love of a mortal man. Once a great priestess of the holy temple at Delphi, she uttered prophecies that had been revered like those of no other. As a young peasant girl, she felt alone with her visions. Growing up in the countryside where her parents, simple farmers, worship at the earth goddess Gaia's modest shrine, she experiences the holy presence in Nature. Her father offers gifts to the goddess at a turf altar he has built; her mother honors the mysteries by drinking from the holy waters. The trees and the springs are sacred places, where the girl prays with them. As she enters womanhood, she is troubled with visions and voices, and she feels alienated from others. Terrified by the violent turn of her psyche, she fears that the chaos in her mind might mean she is mad. But she also experiences ecstasy and is seized with longing for the wonder of divine presence that she experiences from the visions.

When she is chosen to be the vessel for the holy spirit at the temple of Apollo, she hopes to be lifted up into the light by the god. But instead she is consigned to sit in a dark, suffocating cavern, on a tripod above a deep hole in the ground that reeks of goat stench. Perched above this abyss, the sacred serpents of the god slither by as she inhales the smoke of burning laurel leaves, which dizzies her. Falling into a trance, her body writhes in torment as the wild spirit of the god fills her. Hardly able to bear the agony, yet consumed with ecstasy, she becomes possessed by the god, crying out in pain with his messages to the priests, who interpret her strange screams to the people. When she awakens from the trance, she wears a bridal gown, wed to the god who always leaves her alone and abandoned, yet longing to be filled with the wild bliss once more. For many years she lives this way, revered from afar as pythia, yet avoided by the people who fear her close contact as oracle for the divine. She feels like an outcast and is treated by the priests with condescension. For it is they who interpret her wild shrieks; she is merely the vessel. Yet she cannot live without the oracle that holds her hostage. She also learns of the corruption surrounding the temple. The townspeople live off and profit from the licentiousness of those who come to the temple festivities to hear her utterances.

On the day her mother lies dying, the sibyl is sent home in her ritual garb. She looks so strange, her mother barely recognizes her. Allowed to stay on at her childhood home for a time, she goes one day to the holy spring where she sees a man drinking its pure waters. As they talk, she falls in love, and for the first time she feels human warmth. They make love by the river, where later he is drowned for daring to take the god's bride as his own. When their union is discovered, she is condemned by everyone for betraying her virginal vow as priestess. Although the raging mob wants to stone her to death, they are still terrified of her and allow her to pass by. She climbs to the safety of the wild mountain outside town, where she lives as a recluse, cast out by the people. There she learns she is pregnant and gives birth to a child who she thinks is born of the union with her human lover.

But the events surrounding the birth are strange. The sibyl's son is born several months late, and she is awakened from labor by goats that lick the birth blood from the baby. This reminds her of her last ritual union with the god in the oracle pit. At that time she felt the wild god in her in the shape of a black goat, violating her with its ruthless power. As her son grows up to be an idiot with a leering smile, she herself falls into mad despair. How cruel that the fruit of such wonderful human love is destined to this terrible fate. Worse yet, she sometimes wonders if she conceived on the ritual day at Delphi, when she was raped by the god. Could this idiot be the god's son? Possessed by bitterness and resentment at the cruelty of the ineffable to whom she has sacrificed her youth, her home, and her parents and who has deprived her of human love—feeling exploited, mocked, raped, horrified—she drifts into mad brooding.

God is merciless. Those who say he is good do not know him. He is the most inhuman thing there is. He is wild and incalculable as lightning. Like lightning out of a cloud which one did not know contained lightning. Suddenly it strikes, suddenly he strikes down on one, revealing all his cruelty. Or his love—his cruel love. With him anything may happen. He reveals himself at any time and in anything. . . . The divine is not human; it is something quite different. And it is not noble or sublime or spiritualized, as one likes to believe. It is alien and repellent and sometimes it is madness. It is malignant and dangerous and fatal. Or so I have found it.[13]

The sibyl grows into old age, an outcast living on the wild slopes above Delphi. Her only companions are her middle-aged idiot son and the wild goats surrounding their mountain hovel. She has told her story to a stranger who is also cursed by the god and came to her hoping to understand the meaning of his own despairing life. As the ancient seer tells him her strange story, he feels that her deeply furrowed face has been "touched by fire" and that her eyes truly have "seen god." When she finishes, she notices her son has disappeared. Like a wild animal, unencumbered by her age, she follows her son's tracks up the mountain until they disappear into the boundless, snowy moonlit mists above. By the time she returns she realizes the idiot is the god's son, born in incomprehensible form, returning to his father as mysteriously as he came to her. The ancient sibyl finally sees the inscrutable mystery, the divine paradox encompassing good and evil, light and dark, bliss and annihiliation, rapture and agony, consuming fire and devouring abyss—the divine riddle that exists to keep us questioning. Her old eyes look inward and she turns to the stranger and says:

> The most incomprehensible thing about him [the divine] is that he can also be a little turf altar where we may lay a few ears of corn and so be at ease and at peace. He may be a spring, where we can mirror our faces and drink sweet, fresh water from our hands. He can be that, too, I know. Though he was not that for me—I think he could not be.
> For me, he has been a wild chasm which engulfed me and all that I held dear. A glowing breath and an embrace without safety, without peace, but for which I longed nevertheless. A hot and alien power which ruled my ways.[14]

Realizing that the stranger's fate, like hers, is a blessing that binds them to the infinite mystery to keep them searching, she tells him that his hatred of the god is itself an experience of the divine. Then the ancient sibyl continues to sit alone above Delphi, gazing out, seeing all things with her old eyes.

The sibyl's story shows the transformation of a Visionary who rages at the god because of her exploitation. Placed on the tripod and given drugs by the priests, it is they who report and interpret her visions by their own masculine rules and needs. She accepts her treatment as a purely passive receptacle and does not know what she herself has seen. After she begins consciously to suffer her conflict between divine and human love, she lives alone in the wilderness, cast out by the townspeople, symbolic of the collective crowd who are afraid of the sibyl and her visions, especially when they are not controlled or harnessed by patriarchal rules and customs. People fear the unknown, the ineffable, the powers and visions they cannot understand, and they seek to dilute them through formulas handed down by the patriarchy. A modern-day example is the fear some people have of women's reproductive powers and their attempts to harness sexuality.

Alone in the wilderness, the sibyl must look at her despair and feel her rage at the god. Telling her story to the stranger helps him to understand his quest, and it allows her to see her own life in perspective. Learning to accept life's ineffable mysteries, she realizes she has borne the divine child (symbolic of the divine inner child in all humans, no matter how idiotic this looks from a rational perspective). Transformed, she sees for herself, and she knows her visions without outer influences. Masculine priests no longer interpret her life to and for her. Rather, she looks directly at the mystery of existence. She can gaze at the divine paradox of the terrible and the beautiful and accept this ineffable union as she accepts all things. This is the ultimate challenge for the Visionary—to accept responsibility for what she sees and to be able to give her visions embodied form, expressing them no matter how strange and enigmatic they seem.

PRIESTESS OF POETRY: ANNA AKHMATOVA

Anna Akhmatova, one of Russia's greatest twentieth-century poets, suffered from the conflicts of the Visionary. Called by some the "high priestess of Russian poetry," her lyrical, personal poetry was vilified by the Stalinist totalitarian government. Along with Boris Pasternak, Osip Mandelstam, and Marina Tsvetayeva, she was one of the four great Russian poets in the twentieth century who came to represent Old Russia.[15] In contrast to many other Russian poets, she chose not to emigrate. Loving the Russian soul and soil as she did, she felt it would be a betrayal to leave. As a young woman, Akhmatova lamented her fate as prophetess, which kept her from enjoying the warmth of human love. Eventually, she chose to bear witness to her gift and to her fate as a Visionary through her writing. Foretelling the destruction and doom of war, like Cassandra, Akhmatova was not believed by some; her voice became too threatening to others. For twenty years, she was silenced by the Soviet regime.

Born near Odessa by the Black Sea in June 1889, Anna's family moved north to Tsarskoe, where she grew up in a town lush with green parks and meadows, where the poet Pushkin had lived as a youth. In summers, the family returned to the Black Sea coast, where she fell in love with the ocean. Her early relationship with Nature was mystical and informed her poetry. Writing of her childhood, she said:

> I grew up in the patterned silence
> In the cool nursery of the young century
> And people's voices were not dear to me
> But I could understand the voice of the wind.[16]

When she was ten, she suffered from a mysterious illness; she became delirious, and it was feared she might not live. After she recovered, she began to write poems. Later, she believed her writing was connected with this childhood illness. Death and illness marked her family: A younger sister died when Anna was five; and her mother, another sister, and other female relatives suffered from tuberculosis, a disease that plagued Akhmatova herself later in life. But her pagan joy of life was not diminished; she was at home in the water—the ponds of Tsarskoe and the Black Sea.

It was with this image of Anna as a mermaid that the poet Nikolay Gumilyov fell in love, later immortalizing her in his poetry as the moon girl, as the water nymph with sorrowful eyes, and as the Beatrice who inspired Dante. At first, Anna did not return Gumilyov's infatuation, and he made several suicide attempts in his despair at her rejection. Years later, after they were married, the Muse became a "witch" in his eyes, as he described her in one of his poems. At that time, Anna wrote many poems expressing the agony of her suffering.

In 1905, Anna faced death on several levels—on the personal, when Gumilyov first attempted suicide, and on the national, when the Japanese destroyed the Russian fleet. Then her parents separated and money became scarce. The earlier death of her little sister also cast its shadow, but she continued to study and write poetry.

Her early poems honored the young girl who is at one with Nature—the medial girl who can call the fish and the sea gull to her. This young girl sits on the shore, rejecting her earthly admirer while she waits for a prince who never comes. In her poem "By the Sea Shore," these images combine with a "shadow" image of a young sister who is lame but who understands sorrow, death, and the deeper meaning of life. In these early poems, the Muse comes to Anna in dreams, appearing as a slender girl, a stranger who bathes with her in the sea, who teaches her to swim, and whose words "fell like stars on a September night" with "the voice of a silver pipe."[17] Upon awakening, Anna, unable to remember her words, asks the mysterious Muse why she took away the vision. Much later, Akhmatova stressed the essential importance of remembering one's visions, a task she had to accomplish actively during the long years of her censorship, when she committed her verses to memory.

For Akhmatova, the Muse was feminine, a pagan daughter of Nature related to the Russian Mary. A deeply religious and passionate woman, Anna tried to heal the split between spirit and bodily desire—a split from which women of her time suffered. Through her poetry, she tried to give a voice to women to show they are whole human beings and courageous, integrated heroines. For Anna, poetic inspiration was always a gift, whether from the Muse, or from Nature, or from the miraculous grace of God. She linked the pagan Muse with the Christian pilgrim women as she linked poetry with prayer. When the poetess's voice is silent in grief from withdrawal of the word, her sister, the pagan muse can relieve her suffering through her creative relationship to Nature.

> Your hair has grown grey. Your eyes
> Have grown dull and misty through tears.
>
> You no longer understand the birds' song,
> Notice the summer lightning or the stars.
>
> For long now the tambourine's not been heard
> Yet I know you are frightened of silence.

I have come to replace your sister,
By the high fire in the woods. . .[18]

When Anna married Gumilyov in 1910, they honeymooned in Paris. Later in Paris, she met the artist Amedeo Modigliani, with whom she sat in the Luxembourg gardens reciting Verlaine and wandered in the moonlight in the old bohemian quarters of the Left Bank. A dreamer and a romantic, Anna was a medial woman who could intuit other people's secret dreams and yearnings.

Gumilyov was away much of the time, and Anna began to write seriously. Her poetry appeared in journals and expressed the belief that the divine God is present here and now on earth, that poetry is organic, and that life is a gift to love and be lived. No matter how harsh the reality of the world, she wrote, escape is not the answer; the poet's purpose is to bear witness, embodying truth through the word. Akhmatova's first collection of poems, *Evening*, was published in 1912 to favorable reviews. Her poems poured forth personal feelings, especially those of the woman who feels unloved or has been abandoned by her lover and is driven mad through suffering the pain of love. At these times, even "the Muse" seems to withdraw her divine gift, the "golden ring" of inspiration.

In 1912 Anna gave birth to a son, Lev, but her marriage was failing. She lived in a way that affirmed her freedom and independence as a woman while her husband insisted upon his own independence and on continuing affairs with other women. Both shared a passionate love for poetry, but as Akhmatova expressed it later, each lived on secret heights. They shared a spiritual bond, but they could not sustain a day-to-day relationship. So they separated, and Anna gave over the care of her son to her mother-in-law.

With her striking appearance, graceful gestures, and musical voice, Akhmatova soon became part of St. Petersburg's bohemian literary scene and was a Muse for other Russian poets. To the poet Osip Mandelstam, she was a "black angel" touched by God's strange stamp; once he even called her a "Cassandra." To Aleksander Blok, her beauty was so great, it inspired terror. To Marina Tsvetayeva, she was a "heavenly fire" to whom the tragic poetess dedicated a volume of her verse. Tall and slender, gray eyes framed by straight dark hair and a fringe of bangs, dressed in black silk, adorned with a shawl and an oval cameo at her waist, Akhmatova's charismatic presence inspired Modigliani, among other artists, to draw her portrait. Yet while her poetry was lyrical, personal, and confessional, she herself was reserved.

With *Rosary,* her second collection of poems, she became one of Russia's most popular poets in the early part of the twentieth century. Although Anna lamented over the "bitter fame" that had come to replace the warmth of love and the joy of youth, in *Rosary* she emphasized that love is eternal and can transcend ordinary time and space, surpassing finite partings and separations. She believed that poetry enabled the suffering lover to survive abandonment despite love's torment, and she pointed to peasant women who live this philosophy by their simple hope and faith, understanding that life brings suffering and is a trial through which humans can find their source of strength.

When war broke out in 1914, it disrupted Russian life for many years. Instead of the patriotic dreams of glory that excited many Russians, Akhmatova intuited the bitter years of blood ahead. During the war years, her separation from Gumilyov was finalized, and she left their house in Tsarskoe. From this period until the end of her life, she missed having a home since she was always living in others' houses. In 1918, when she married again, it was to an opposite type of man—a scholar named Vladimir Shileyko, who was possessive and jealous, a stern tyrant who destroyed her poems by burning them in the samovar. This marriage lasted only a few years—difficult cold years, when Akhmatova's Muse was mainly silent.

Despite the despair in her personal life, her most profound suffering came from war, which she saw as a wounding of Christ's body and of the living land. In her poems she often spoke through the voice of the pilgrim woman, and she felt her own duty as a poet was to chronicle the tragedy of war as she saw it. Like the young girl originally maddened by the loss of love, the older Akhmatova was now maddened by the horrors of war. While her first impulse was to ask God to take her as a sacrifice, she knew her duty as a poet with the secret "gift of song" was to stay and bear witness to the bloody battle. Thus, in *White Flock,* her third collection of poems which was published in 1917, she added the motif of war to her previous preoccupation with the theme of love.

Akhmatova was beginning to accept her fate as a poetess and prophetess. Earlier, she had devoted many poems to lamenting that the bittersweet fame into which she had been plunged was no compensation for the loss of personal love. Fame was "a trap where there is no joy or light!"[19] But now, she began to accept her strength and authority as a poet and the responsibility incumbent on her. She was prepared to surrender her dream of the prince and her identity as romantic Muse in order to accept her role as priestess and pilgrim-wanderer.

> No, tsarevich, I'm not she
> Whom you wish to see in me
> And for long my lips
> Have prophesied, not kissed.
>
> Don't think that in delirium
> And tortured by pain and grief
> I loudly court disaster:
> It is my profession.[20]

The years of revolutionary strife within Russia brought terror into her life. Gumilyov was arrested and shot in 1921 as an anti-Bolshevik conspirator. Anna was becoming isolated by the revolution from many of her friends and from the main literary circles, but she continued to write. The volumes *Plantain* and *Anno Domini MCMXXI*, published in the early twenties, expressed her grief and horror of war. They were the last to be published until 1940. During this period, Soviet literary critics turned away from the classic piety of old Russia, which Akhmatova represented, and toward the revolutionary poems of the Futurists. Akhmatova was dismissed as a relic of the past, as a poetess of "indoor intimacy," and as an aristocratic anachronism of Russia's old religions. Her poetry was criticized for its mysticism and eroticism, its limited scope of personal emotions, and its lack of revolutionary vision. Marxist critics dismissed her poetry as unworthy of serious literary attention, and it became difficult for her to publish. In 1925, further publication of her work was banned, via an unofficial party resolution.[21]

During this period, Anna became seriously ill with tuberculosis. Most of her literary friends had emigrated from Russia by now, and she was cut off from her readers. She felt mysteriously bound with Russia's suffering and had a prophetic sense that her voice, though stilled at the moment, reflected that of many others. Remaining in Russia to endure its chaos and torment, and to bear witness when she could to its rebirth, she was considered by some to be a Madwoman seeking martyrdom.

Stalin's reign of terror was now beginning to descend upon writers. People were arrested and executed in large numbers. At this time Akhmatova moved in with Nikolay Punin, the art historian. Accommodations were difficult to find, and Punin's former family lived with them. Anna's son, Lev, now sixteen, joined them. Her relationship with Punin, who flirted with other women and treated Anna badly, was cold and lonely, and Anna was extremely poor. She still looked striking, however, even in old clothes. She wrote few poems but studied Pushkin in depth and did translations. She explored the lives of women heroines in history and the Bible, which she later embodied in poems. During this time she lost confidence in herself, but she knew it was a time of testing. It was also a time when Punin, Lev, and her close friend, the great poet Osip Mandelstam were arrested. By the 1930s, as conditions in the Soviet Union became progressively worse, Akhmatova had learned to survive. Yet fear was in the air, and describing what she saw after a visit to Mandelstam, who was executed shortly afterward, she wrote:

> And in the room of the disgraced poet
> Fear and the Muse take turns on watch.
> And the night goes on
> Which does not know of dawn.[22]

Lev was arrested again, sentenced to death, then exiled, and later released to fight in the war. Anna could not earn a living from her poetry and became very ill from a diet of black bread and tea without sugar. While she waited outside the prison in the long lines of people, hoping to see her son, she composed the poems in *Requiem*. She and her women friends memorized them to preserve them, for a poet could receive a death sentence if a written verse was found.[23] If she wrote a few verses down, she burned the scrap of paper immediately after memorizing them.

Akhmatova's ability to formulate things via words, to bring order out of chaos, made her a prophetess for the people. As prophetess, she was able to see horror and not run away. She could verbalize the unspeakable and cut through the masses' denial of destruction. In *Requiem* she dedicated her own sorrow and suffering to speak for all other women who were confused and alone, standing outside the prison in long lines of terror to see loved ones, but who continued to survive and live on.

Anna saw the journey of the solitary woman suffering for her loved one as universal, linking herself and other women archetypally with the mother, Mary, who suffered for the crucifixion of her son, the Christ. By opening the door to death and passing through madness, a woman could gain new strength. "Already madness with its wing / Has covered half my soul,"[24] said Akhmatova, who felt we must look directly at horror with open eyes and, passing through this madness, not forget "the old woman's howl like a beast that was hurt,"[25] the cry of horror, the shriek of rage from the woman whose loved ones were taken away to prison or execution. *Remembering* the suffering one has lived through is essential so that it will not be repeated. The poem "Requiem" is her cry of rage at the horror occurring in her country, a mad scream to keep us from forgetting.

The ban against Akhmatova's poems was lifted in 1940, but only for a short time. Some of her poems were allowed to be printed in magazines and in book form. But a few months later, authorities declared that the publication of her book happened by mistake, and it was withdrawn from libraries and from sale. She feared she might succumb to madness, but although she suffered from the abuse of Soviet authorities and the fear of madness, she finished *Requiem* and wrote "The Way of All Earth," a poem in which the heroine, originally from a heavenly city, Kitezh, is called back from her earthly stay, having faced the horror of madness and the desire for death, to journey "right in the path of bullets" to her real home with God.[26]

When Hitler invaded the Soviet Union in 1941, the Russian people could unite against a common enemy. This relieved the alienation of individuals set against each other in fear during the reign of terror. Akhmatova was allowed to speak once more, and she addressed the women of Leningrad on the radio, reminding them that they were strong enough to protect their city, to help the wounded, and to survive through a difficult time. Despite her frail health, she stood in defense of the city during air raids. Then the Communist party ordered that she be evacuated to an outlying place. Eventually Akhmatova, with a friend, moved to Tashkent, in South Central Asia, where she remained for several years, until 1943. During this period she was shaken by the suicide of a sister poet, Marina Tsvetayeva, who hanged herself in 1941. The two women had first met in secret the year before, sharing their admiration for each others' poetry.

In 1942 her poem "Courage" was published by *Pravda* and was read often to wartime audiences to give them strength. Akhmatova acknowledged her role as a poet-prophetess for Russia. She accepted her own suffering as a fate from which she could generate a vision, a feminine strength that included the ability to shed tears yet not submit to defeat. Living became a way to find meaning in a time of war, although Anna was herself not immune to fears and periods of weakness. Because she had been able to pass through the madness during the time of terror, however, and bear witness to the strength for herself and others in her poems, her own words testified to her ability to survive and record the courage and strength of humankind.

In Tashkent she found herself among friends once more, and a volume of her poems was published. But her health declined again, and she came near death with typhus. After this time, her appearance changed. No longer looking the thin, stylish Muse, she changed her hairstyle and gained weight. When she was able to return to Leningrad in the spring of 1944, she found that the man with whom she had hoped to live had married without telling her. Again, her fate seemed not to live a "normal" life but to be consecrated to poetry "where every step's a secret / And there is an abyss to left and right / And fame, a withered leaf, lies underfoot—."[27]

Despite personal disappointment, suffering, and age, Akhmatova reaffirmed her acceptance of her fate as poet. She wrote:

> As if I were a river
> The harsh age changed my course
> Replaced one life with another,
> Flowing in a different channel
> And I do not recognize my shores.[28]

Still she would choose her life: "Who can refuse to live his own life?" she emphasized with her inner authority.[29]

Before her poems were censored again in 1946, Anna had a reprieve from her suffering. Her son was released in 1945 and returned home to be with her. A collection of her poems was scheduled for publication, and she was visited by Isaiah Berlin, of the British Embassy, an admirer of her work from abroad. But this visit from a foreigner was dangerous; in previous years, it would have been considered on a par with treason. Anna felt that the subsequent 1946 censorship of her poetry as "empty, apolitical poetry" and "harmful" to the education of the young was a consequence of this visit. The Communist party resolution again criticized her poetry for its mysticism, eroticism, and sense of doom. Her spiritual affirmation was called a leftover from the old days of aristocracy, and she herself was decried as "a harlot nun whose sin is mixed with prayer."[30] Anna's poems in print were destroyed, and she was expelled from the Union of Soviet Writers.

The Soviets treated Akhmatova as though she were a mad Muse, relegating her to the time of past romanticism and disregarding her prophetic perceptions of the war. The censorship was publicized abroad as well as in the Soviet Union, and Akhmatova became more isolated as a result of this new witch hunt. She was required to show herself twice a day at her window so the guards in the street could report that she had neither committed suicide nor escaped. Abuse from literary critics was aimed at her during these postwar years of Stalin's unpredictable furies—it was the Cold War, a time of ferocious attack upon artists.

In 1949, both Punin and her son, Lev, were arrested again. In an attempt to save her son's life, she wrote in 1950 some verses, *In Praise of Peace,* in which she praised Stalin and others. Akhmatova considered them to be poor poems and later asked that they be omitted from her collected works. But her son's life was saved. Meanwhile, Akhmatova was quietly working on one of her greatest works, "Poem Without a Hero," which took her twenty-two years to complete (1940–62). In one section she acknowledges her link with other Madwomen, herself silenced as a crazed prophetess just as Cassandra was imprisoned.

> Just ask my contemporaries:
> Camp women, prison women, martyrs
> And we will tell you of numb terror,
> Of raising children for execution
> At the block, or back to the wall,
> Of raising children for the prisons.
> Pressing our blue lips together
> We who are like crazed Hecubas,
> Like Cassandras from Chukhlomy,
> Thunder out in silent chorus

(We, who are crowned with shame for ever)
We've crossed Hell to the other side. . .[31]

After Stalin's death in 1953, conditions eased for Ákhmatova. For her translations of Victor Hugo she received money—the first in a long time—enabling her to pay off debts to friends. As a translator, once more she could be regarded as a writer and was even allowed a small *dacha* (forest cabin) at a writer's colony near Leningrad. Her son was finally released in 1956. Much later, she wrote a poem expressing the horror and abuse she had endured and the way she was cursed, then dismissed as a Madwoman.

They took me out to the very brink
And for some reason left me there—
I will roam the silent squares,
As if I were the town's mad fool.[32]

In the last years of her life, Akhmatova received recognition and even honor for her work. Starting in 1956, her poems began to be published once more. Younger poets, including Joseph Brodsky, visited her, and she encouraged and tried to help new writers. Soon she received letters of thanks from devotees of her poems who thanked her also for her existence as a model of strength and integrity. Foreign admirers visited, including Robert Frost. In 1963, "Requiem" was published in Germany. Honored abroad, she received an Italian prize for literature in 1964 and, in 1965, an honorary doctorate from Oxford University, where she was compared to Sappho.

Twice, toward the very end of her life, there was talk of her nomination for the Nobel Prize. But in March, 1966, suffering from a longtime heart condition, the great poetess died at the age of seventy-five. Hundreds of admirers came to honor her at the church in Leningrad where she lay in state. She was buried where she felt at home—in the pine forest graveyard at the writer's colony near Leningrad.

The themes of Akhmatova's last poems emphasized love's ability to transcend the finite separations of time and space, affirming the immortality and sacredness of spiritual relationships and the prophetic nature of dreams, which link us to the other world. She valued the gifts of life we receive while we are "guests on earth," such as the wonder of music and the fragrance of a wild rose. She maintained that standing at the foot of the cross marks the place of human transformation. To be a seer, she emphasized, requires embodiment in a world containing both beauty and inhumane horror —a paradox that she dared to face. She came to see her wandering and homelessness on earth as a suffering necessary to bear for her fate as poet. She learned to serve the Muse by putting her visions into words, thus expressing the paradox of human life and death. Although she had wanted to be a womanly Muse to a man, she learned instead that she had to serve her own Muse and accept her fate as poetic prophetess for her country. Having lived in a mad time of terror, sneered at as an hysterical female who still believed in God, silenced for her visions, Akhmatova survived to become the "living conscience" of literature, bravely facing darkness and chaos as a poet in a time of war.

GLENNA'S STORY: RESOLVING THE CONFLICT

Glenna's story exemplifies how different patterns of the Madwoman can surface in one person. In a midlife crisis, after having experienced many of the patterns of the Madwoman, she had the following dream of a seer. The dream emphasized the importance of her Visionary side at this time in her life, when she had just turned forty.

I am in an audience in a large hall or cathedral. I recognize some of the people, including an older couple. The audience is waiting for the presentation. A tall, handsome man steps forward. He is dressed in clothes that are impeccably tailored; he is from high society and looks like a god. The audience has been assembled for the formal presentation of the woman who is his fiancée.

Behind the scenes, the woman, a blond Barbie doll debutante type, is being prepared for the presentation by a small group of women. To my surprise, they put her upside down in a washing machine. I can see her legs sticking out. When the group of women take her out, I am shocked. In the course of preparation they have grafted another woman onto the top of her body. From behind the blond debutante towers a tall, exotic, Oriental woman—a seer. The blond Barbie doll woman who was to be the fiancé seems disoriented and dizzy that she is carrying this oracular woman, whose presence dwarfs her. The curtain opens for the presentation. It is the oracular seer, not the debutante, who is presented to the audience.

Glenna awoke in awe and dread that the oracular woman was so prominent and that this exotic seer was presented to the world to be married to the bridegroom instead of the blond socialite. To Glenna, the blond debutante represented one of the beautiful people leading a conventional life—a "normal" woman who is likely to be chosen to be a wife. Glenna wanted to marry, but she could never adapt herself to the status quo. She was always traveling about on a quest for transformation. Her intense spiritual need to move on had led to the breakup with her last lover, a sensitive man whom she had hoped to marry.

A striking image in this dream is the behind-the-scenes preparation ceremony in the washing machine by the group of women, a ritual Glenna alone had seen. At first, her association to them was the "Stepford wives"—a group of conventional women wanting to normalize the bride-to-be and adapt her to society. But she had witnessed the reverse. The group of women became more like Madwomen who were attendants to an uncanny ritual. Are they hairstylists or alchemists, she wondered to herself, not realizing at the moment that symbolically, hairdressers are the shapers of feminine identity.

Washing, or "the bath," is a symbolic purification ritual for the sacred marriage, for the alchemical divine wedding of masculine and feminine energies within each person. In accord with the transformation by the Madwomen, this preparation was shown in the dream as chaotic. They put the initiate upside down in a whirling washing machine, much as the ancient Maenads whirled in a frenzy during their dances to Dionysus. Was the godlike man appearing in impeccably dressed form really Dionysus, god of the vineyard and of drama, to whom the Maenads—creative artists, Visionaries, and medial people—are devoted?

Glenna woke up in wonder and confusion. The dream had revealed several things to her: "Things are not as they seem." Her concept of the bride-to-be had been turned upside down. The bride-to-be was not the Barbie doll debutante but the strange oracular Oriental seer. Glenna was presented with her medial side, and her vocation was presented as a call to be embodied in the world. The seer is about "seeing," Glenna mused to herself. Her work in the world was to see what is and to embody her vision.

Glenna had always felt herself to be a rebel. A tomboy and the only girl in the family, she was a companion to her father and a young playmate to her brothers. She learned to fish and hunt and to be at home in the outdoors. But her father, a blue-collar worker, felt inferior to his more educated wife. He didn't like his job, yet he took on extra work, hoping to help his children get the education that had been unavailable to him. Consequently, when he was home he was not fun to be with. He did not know how to play; everything he did was goal-oriented. Underneath his external appearance of strength, however, he felt passive and suffered from a lack of assertion. He wanted his daughter to be happy, but he did not understand her.

Glenna's mother had always longed for a daughter, and she had felt her dreams were answered when Glenna was born. She was ill during her pregnancy with Glenna and sickly throughout much of her daughter's childhood. A Caged Bird, she was a woman of intelligence trapped in a marriage and in a religious and cultural milieu that pronounced that she had to remain at home, a good and dutiful wife. Her way of coping was like that of many Mad Mothers of her generation—she became sick and addicted to alcohol. Still a pawn of her orthodox Catholic beliefs and her midwestern, bourgeois upbringing, Glenna's mother wanted her daughter to be a normal girl who would marry and lead a conventional life. She could not see Glenna for who she really was; nor did she try to unravel the puzzle of this daughter who was an enigma to her. Consequently, Glenna felt like a caged bird in her home and longed to get away from her family.

At home, Glenna experienced chaos; her brothers often fought among themselves and with her father. Her mother, secretly drinking her unlived life away, locked herself in her room, pretending to be sick. Her oldest brother was artistically talented but also drank and took drugs; often he would come home drunk and stoned and become violent, adding to the family madness. Although Glenna admired this creative brother, she feared his destructive tendencies. Later, when he became a street person, she discovered her own underlying fear of becoming a Bag Lady.

Bored, afraid of the mad chaos at home, feeling trapped like a Caged Bird, at seventeen Glenna left home for the first time. She became an exchange student and went to Africa. Excited about learning and travel, she wanted to study at a university that held classes on a ship that traveled around the world. But her parents said they could not afford it, although they had tried to help her brothers go to good schools. Her parents wanted her to be educated, then to marry; so, they reasoned, a junior college would be sufficient. This was a blow to Glenna, who, as a result, became passive about her education. Following the pattern set by her father, she felt inferior about her potential for a professional life, so she settled for a college not of her own choice. This set a pattern for the next seven years of her educational life, the time it took her to graduate. She would attend college for a semester or two, then drop out to travel. Periodically, she would return to school, finally finishing up in a field that did not inspire her.

A natural questioner, Glenna had started rebelling against authority in high school. She had stopped going to her church because the priest was preaching sermons in favor of the Vietnam war. During the late sixties, she transferred from her local college in the Midwest to the University of California at Berkeley. She became a Revolutionary and continued to protest the war in peace marches. She demonstrated for the cause of the "People's Park" and participated in an underground healing clinic to help nurse the wounded Revolutionaries so they wouldn't have to go to public hospitals, which could lead to their eventual arrest. For a while she lived in a house with members of the Black Panthers. Her revolutionary Madwoman burst out. She was enraged at the Berkeley police for firing tear gas and shooting at the young rebels who were fighting injustice and protesting for peace. Glenna was reduced to shouting and screaming in the streets and hurling tear gas canisters back at the police.

One of the lucky ones, she did not get arrested. But she became cynical about society and the "American dream." She dreamed that she was homeless on the streets, a bag lady wheeling a shopping cart down Telegraph Avenue. She dropped out of school and traveled to Europe and behind the Iron Curtain. There she saw other forms of political corruption. Was there no place on earth safe from corruption and injustice? she wondered.

While at the collective level she was dealing with injustice via her Revolutionary activities, she suffered a severe violation at the personal level when she was nineteen. In a rare moment of peace on one sunny morning, she was walking through a beautiful grove of eucalyptus trees. From behind, a man attacked her and tried to rape her. When she fought back, he beat her up and started strangling her, trying to choke her to death while attempting to rape her at the same time. While she was fighting back, his erection failed him. At some point in the struggle she dropped to the ground unconscious. When she regained consciousness, he was gone, probably thinking she was dead. Some students found her and rushed her to the hospital, where she stayed ten days, fighting for her life.

Between the rape and the failed revolution, Glenna became very depressed. Her gentle and vulnerable feminine side had been severely injured, as had her fighting feminine spirit. In the grip of a "night sea journey," a descent into the underworld of the unconscious, a journey which took her into the depths of the abyss to die and be reborn, she went inward for healing. From a Revolutionary, Glenna became a Recluse. To heal herself, she went to the Greek islands for a month-long meditation retreat. She spent a year in this way, recovering in the solitude of Nature. She learned to sail, and to earn money, she made jewelry, macramé, and other crafts, which she sold to tourists. She emerged feeling centered but aware that she had to learn to fight effectively. She hopped a freighter to Brazil, where she was exposed to native healing techniques, and she studied a Brazilian form of martial art. In this way, she began to work to integrate her inner Madwoman. She finished her degree at Berkeley and went to another university, where she got a master's degree and taught school abroad for a few years.

In the minds of her more conventional peers, Glenna was still a dropout, a Bag Lady Madwoman. When she saw the French film *The Vagabond*, directed by Agnes Varda, she identified with the protagonist, a young, homeless adolescent girl who hitchhikes around the countryside with only a knapsack and eventually freezes to death by a river, hungry and wounded. Glenna knew the dangers of drifting, yet she also knew there were lessons to be learned—experiencing other cultures, wandering freely in Nature, surviving, learning to fend for oneself. During her travels she consciously evoked her Madwoman, using the martial arts effectively in several different instances when she and her traveling companions were attacked. She learned she could survive outside the "system," the "American cage." She signed up as a crew member to sail the seas for four years. She learned to provision, repair the sails, and splice lines; she scuba dived beneath the boat to check moorings and repair the anchor lines. Experiencing many cultures, she felt the freedom of the oceanic wild woman. Both marriage and society represented the "cage" of the American dream.

By this time Glenna was thirty-five and was in a relationship with one of the sailors, who had become addicted to opium, easily available at the ports where they docked. Although sailing around felt adventurous and liberating, she began to have a series of tidal wave dreams, which shocked her into awareness. Tidal wave dreams often warn the dreamer that he or she is in danger of being overwhelmed by the unconscious, and they emphasize the necessity to become more grounded. Heeding the message of these dreams, she knew she had to change her life. Synchronistically, she learned about a conference on healing and decided to attend. The conference opened up a whole new world for Glenna—the interconnected realms of symbolism of the psyche and of Nature.

Then Glenna fell in love with a man who inspired her, and she became his Muse. But there was a snag in their relationship: He was married with a family. Although he knew his marriage was destructive for both himself and his children, he couldn't bring himself to take the necessary step of divorce. Nor, later, was he able to commit himself fully to his relationship with Glenna. When Glenna confronted him and set a limit, he wavered, unable to respond fully at the time. Feeling rejected, Glenna ended the relationship, much as Camille Claudel had ended hers with Rodin. But unlike Camille Claudel, Glenna did not descend into paranoia and madness. Depressed, she suffered from the mad Muse and Rejected Lover patterns for a time. But, knowing the healing power of the Recluse in solitude, she continued her inner work.

She decided to start therapy with a wise, sixty-year-old woman who became her first feminine model for an authentic life. With the help of therapy, she decided to apply to a doctoral program in counseling. The conference had opened up a path for spiritual growth and healing to which Glenna wanted to commit herself—her first real commitment to a professional area.

In graduate school Glenna suffered another rejection and betrayal: She was assigned a woman supervisor who overstepped her bounds and intruded on Glenna's privacy, asking her to reveal confidentialities inappropriate to this teacher-student relationship. Glenna confronted her and told the supervisor that she was not her therapist; she already had one. Not seeing Glenna for who she was, this power-ridden but insecure woman (a Madwoman of the Dragon Lady variety) took revenge and wrote a letter accusing Glenna of being shallow and mentally unstable and recommending that she be ousted from the doctoral program. The committee in charge dismissed Glenna and later "buried" the letter. Rejected both in her relationship and in her profession, Glenna was in despair. She considered dropping everything and sailing out to sea again. But her therapist reminded Glenna of this dropout pattern and, since protest would have been futile, encouraged her to seek training elsewhere. Her therapist also accepted Glenna's rage at the betrayal by the supervisor but helped her see the necessity of transforming the rage into creative work. Glenna studied elsewhere; she found a teacher who recognized her ability in this field, affirmed her in it, and encouraged her to reapply to the same program. Glenna's therapist supported her in this reapplication. In the meantime, another committee was in charge; Glenna was accepted and completed the program with honors.

Although she had felt betrayed by both her teacher and her lover, Glenna's inner Madwoman helped her fight for her own integrity rather than be devoured by power struggles and revenge. Nor did she succumb to the despair of being the victim. She remembered the Native American saying: "Appreciate your enemies because they make you strong." Understanding the value of these words, she remained loyal to her values and commitments and fought for herself in an honorable way.

It was during this period of dealing with betrayal that Glenna had the astonishing dream of the oracular priestess. The dream awoke Glenna to the central importance of this new feminine visionary side of herself that needed expression. A year later, Glenna had another dream affirming the importance of the priestess as an inner feminine value she needed to affirm in herself and in her outer life. In the dream she saw a beautiful, stately woman with a necklace of triangles, crescents, and circles embossed in her flesh, near the throat chakra. This reminded Glenna of the pictures of necklaced

Egyptian priestesses. While her first "seer" dream had shown a conflict between the oracular and the ordinary sides of herself—there were two torsos separating from her waist—this dream image showed she was at one with the priestess in herself. Today, grounded in the authenticity and power of her feminine center, she serves the Visionary in herself through her work as an established member of the healing professions. Glenna has learned to use her intuition in her work as a therapist, to guide her in the way she works with clients, as she integrates this visionary knowledge with the discipline of timing and containing the boundaries necessary to the therapeutic relationship.

EMBODYING THE VISIONS

If a woman is truly a Visionary, she must live in accordance with her visions. An inspiring example is Minnie Evans, an African-American folk artist from the South who, in a vision, was commanded to paint or, it was predicted, she would die. Choosing to paint, she remembered her ancestry, saw the colors of her people's spirits in dreams and visions, and painted them as illuminated, rainbow-colored angels' wings. Some called her crazy, but by the end of her life, she had painted a chronicle of her people's heritage, as a witness to her spiritual origins.

The Visionary is gifted with seeing what others cannot see ordinarily, and her task is to reveal these visions to her community. She must not only see but remember and record what she has seen. To see and then forget is to leave oneself open to ambiguity and disparagement by skeptics because one is not giving expression to the mysteries. Living in accordance with the gift of vision requires training. This is why the ancient priestesses underwent years of spiritual preparation and discipline before they participated in the rituals. In our time, artists and writers train themselves to remember their visions by recording them in words, paint, musical notes, or movement. They work for years at their craft, learning to revise, to paint out and over. Similarly, it is important for Visionary women to seek out a reliable teacher who can guide them in learning the mysteries.

Some women don't know where to start. There are so many paths, so many choices, it is easy to become confused about which way to go. Taking the first step on one path is necessary in such cases and will help ground this type of woman. Grounding is essential for the Visionary. Visionaries often emphasize the importance of ritual work in grounding. Beating the drum, folding clothes in ritual preparation, caring for sacred objects and places, writing poetic verses, digging into the earth to plant seeds—all are ways of bringing the Visionary down to earth. Living the sacred in our ordinary lives is essential.

The Visionary must learn to distinguish those visions that should be expressed from those about which she should remain silent. There are times when it is important to honor the mysteries through secrecy (lest we make light of them), until we feel them dance in our very blood. Visionaries of all kinds must temper the revelation of what they see with finely tuned judgment. Timing and method—knowing when and how to express a vision publicly—are essential. This is as true for the practical woman whose intuitive perceptions focus on her family and friends as it is for the seer who is mediating a message to society.

Some women often do not actualize what they see for fear of losing the vision. As a friend of mine, a woman writer, expressed it this way: "Pulled into the flesh, the flicker may go out. But if a woman lives only in the sky, she has no edges or shadow or weight." When we try to put our visions into words or colors—to embody our visions—we fear we may lose the experience. Nevertheless, we must dare to give flesh to our visions, while accepting our limitations. The Russian philosopher Nikolai Berdyaev said that we can never fully embody the divine vision due to our human finitude. But our task is to devote ourselves to our crafts and bear the creative tension between the transcendent vision and the limits of the embodied work. A Visionary who is flaky and spacey is not really working to embody the vision in herself and the world. Caring for our own bodies and for the earth and paying attention to the needs of the society and the sensate world are important to ground the Visionary so she has the strength and substance to do her work responsibly.

The Visionary must also be conscious of pride and egotism that interfere with her task. Although she is the vessel for the medial power she transmits, she is not herself the power. Pride often leads to ambition, envy, and jealousy, wanting to be first or to be the guru —all dangerous to her Visionary calling. Doubt and fear, too, interfere when they prevent a Visionary from expressing herself and put her at the mercy of those who would belittle her. Many visions are fearsome simply because they come from the unknown. Using the Madwoman's assertive energy in a positive way can help us fight off unnecessary fears and learn how to protect ourselves, our limits and boundaries—when to say yes, and when to say no.

A major issue for the Visionary is how to deal with the power that comes from her visions. Inflation (acting superior to others; "I know it all!") is a great temptation for a Visionary woman. Its opposite, deflation (feeling inferior and lowly, like a fraud) is another danger, especially for the woman whose intuitions are discredited by others. A woman who has come into power via her visionary nature (as do many therapists, spiritual leaders, teachers, public speakers, authors, and entertainers) must be especially careful to avoid the pitfalls of both narcissistic inflation (which would feed a power drive) and deflation (which could keep her from speaking out and giving voice to her wisdom). *"All women indeed are sisters under the Goddess,"* observes Morgaine in *The Mists of Avalon.*[33] Thus a woman who succumbs to hubris, who regards herself as superior to others, and who wields her visionary power over others for her own ends abuses her gifts. To use visionary gifts to try to force things to bend to one's own will is a form of black magic that wreaks havoc on the soul.

To be a Visionary takes faith and trust that the cosmos is "a spiral dance" and wants us to be there as revealers and revelers. Ultimately, visionary powers are available only if we have reverence for them and work seriously with commitment. Paradoxically, the Visionary must be vulnerable and open to receive new images, yet strong, skillful, and decisive enough to express them.

Visions are mysterious gifts. We get glimpses in transcendent moments, for example while listening to music, looking at an artwork, or walking on a mountain trail and seeing a fragile columbine. Once I was trekking in Alaska, trying to see the great "Denali," Mount McKinley. I waited for two hours while the clouds occasionally opened, revealing for a moment different faces of the majestic mountain. Seeing just a few of the mountain's multitude of mysteries overwhelmed me and reminded me of my humble place as part of the greater whole. But this experience emphasized my path—to share the importance of the truths about feminine mysteries that I had seen.

We cannot honor the Visionary adequately if we do not respect her vulnerable, receptive mode—looking inward and listening in the dark temple of the earth to the deep silence. The poet Rainer Maria Rilke reminds us in *Sonnets to Orpheus* that there is a temple in the ear, just as there is a temple in each of the senses as well as in the "third eye" of the Visionary. The meter of music and poetry, and of our feet as we walk along Nature's trails, can put us in a receptive trance to see, to smell and touch, to hear and record the voices of the angels as we travel between the visible and invisible worlds. To travel between the "worlds" and mediate the messages from the spirit to the community is the Visionary's path of divine ecstatic "madness."

10

THROUGH

THE MADNESS

The great sea
Has sent me adrift,
It moves me as the weed in a great
river,
Earth and the great weather move me,
Have carried me away,
And move my inward parts with joy.

—ESKIMO WOMAN SHAMAN

SHARING OUR STORIES OF OUR JOURNEYS THROUGH MADNESS or chaos and our rebirth as creative women is essential to freeing feminine spirit in ourselves and others. Discovering the ways that different women have returned from their descent into madness can give us hope and courage to meet and transform the Madwoman within us. New Zealand writer Janet Frame, for example, has shared her journey in her novel *Faces in the Water* and in her autobiography.[1] Artist Leonora Carrington has described her suffering of madness in her fictional work *Down Below*. By writing and painting her inner characters, Carrington said, "I try to empty myself of images which have made me blind."[2] In her novel *I Never Promised You a Rose Garden,* Joanne Greenberg emphasizes the importance of accepting the suffering of psychosis together with returning to the world. In this fictionalized autobiography, Deborah, the protagonist, escapes into her own imaginary world due to a trauma she experienced during surgical operations when she was only five years old to remove a tumor in her urethra. This trauma was compounded by the doctors' deception about the reality of pain, denial by her family, prejudice because she is Jewish, and taunting by schoolmates because she is different. Retreating into fantasy helps at first but later isolates Deborah from others. Her later return to health is facilitated by discovering that her female psychiatrist is neither afraid nor horrified by her trouble, but only genuinely angry at the abuses and lies from which Deborah has suffered. Greenberg emphasizes the necessity of integrating the imaginal and the outer worlds in order to return to society as an actively contributing participant. "You have to take the world first, to take it on faith as a complete commitment. . . . Then, on what you yourself build of this commitment you can decide whether it is a decent bargain or not. . . . Contributing is building the commitment. . . . Health is not simply the absence of sickness. We never worked this hard just so that you might be unsick," Deborah's therapist tells her.[3]

The Madwoman's destructive aspect can be transformed into creativity. To do this we need to change the conditions that have led to the madness. Sometimes a woman naturally outgrows some destructive aspects. For example, a Muse, as she grows older, may realize that the outer appearance of youthful beauty that was once so important to her life fails to give her meaning now. As a woman passes through menopause, Nature forces her to confront her Madwoman. If she fails to confront directly her anger at aging, she is likely to become bitter and resentful. She may be jealous of her daughter's youth and deflate her enthusiasm or try to compete with her. Or she may become depressed, aging even faster, dwindling away without sharing her wisdom. But if she can accept the mad crone within her—the inner Hecate who sits at the crossroads of life and death—she can share with us her own unique perspective and oracular wisdom.

The aging sibyl was finally able to see the whole of life and death and, accepting its paradox, look out over all things in serenity. So a woman who accepts her inner Madwoman and learns to relate to her can come to affirm the tragicomic paradox of life. To do this requires appealing to a greater spiritual part of herself that transcends her individual ego desires and emphasizes the importance of sharing her wisdom with the community. Letting go of outmoded projections and wishes frees us for group action and service to humanity. Transforming society is inherent to transforming the Madwoman, but that revolutionary change has to start within each individual woman. This requires learning the value of being alone, that is, integrating the Recluse. Older women often find the Revolutionary side of their Madwoman and devote themselves to political action, trying to effect social change. Some women free their energy to create artistically—writing or painting their unique story.

When the Madwoman is transformed from destructive paths and embodied in creative ways, a woman will *not* give up her vision. Rid of the resentments, paranoia, and isolation that result when her anger is suppressed or goes unrecognized or unacknowledged, she will be free to create. Her vision will be clear and congruent, and she will have the courage and wisdom to embody it in the world.

The conscious journey to meet our interior Madwoman entails many challenges and can be facilitated by a skilled guide who gives us reassurance that there is value in our descent into chaos, that something creative can come out of the darkness, that we need not end up in the locked ward of isolation. Here the process of psychotherapy can be invaluable. It can help us recognize the different patterns that hold us hostage and consume our creative energy. By having a safe place to communicate our secret fears, to recognize our rage, to learn to turn its energy in constructive directions, and to allow our tears to flow, we can make the voyage into the heart of darkness, into the wilderness of our inner nature. We can find new sources in ourselves and discover the deep well of spirituality and creativity that would remain unexplored had we remained only on the surface of our conscious lives.

As we meet our interior Madwoman, we will learn that we can project the Madwoman image onto others. We can act her out, *or* we can use her energy as a transformer. If we project the Madwoman onto others, it is usually due to our feelings of fear or envy. We may fear her power, if we don't acknowledge the power within ourselves, and we may use it negatively against other women. We also split apart the feminine energies in ourselves, leaving ourselves feeling helpless and confused. When the Madwoman is isolated and cut off from the whole, whether on the internal or external levels, the resulting dislocation tears things apart, as the Maenads of ancient Greece tore apart people they did not recognize in their anger and frenzy. If we remain unconscious of our different energies or deny them in ourselves and condemn them in others, we fail to develop as whole women. When we unconsciously act out the Madwoman energies and give in to destructive acts of anger and frustration, as in the case of Camille Claudel who destroyed her artwork and ended up in the madhouse, we also fail to come to terms with the shadowy sister energies within ourselves.

Meeting the Madwoman plumbs the inner depths of our self-knowledge and suffering. If we do not face our inner selves, our dark sides, if we do not come to know ourselves, we can get trapped in a vicious circle, becoming prisoners of the Madwoman patterns we try to avoid. A Caged Bird like Mrs. Bridge, a Rejected Lover like Maria Callas, or a mad Muse like Camille Claudel becomes lost or self-destructive, never reaching her own authentic feminine center. By choosing to confront the Madwoman and the source of her strength, the situations or frustrations out of which she emerges, and by choosing to acknowledge, work with, and transform them, we learn to recognize and honor the Madwoman's dark feminine energies as part of a greater whole.

In the process of confrontation and transformation we can go through a stage in which we descend into the abyss, experiencing a kind of chaos and confusion. This can look and feel like madness, or be a temporary experience of it. Most of the women who share their stories in this book, as well as the historical models, experienced this kind of psychological and emotional upheaval. Some even feared they might go mad, like Rosa Luxemburg and Anna Akhmatova. Each felt the anguish and unpredictability of her situation and individual tragedy but chose to face her inner Madwoman, to reshape her unique self, and to find her authentic voice. Life itself is chaotic, changing, and unpredictable. Life is "mad"—"weird at the edges and wild at heart," as the protagonist of the film *Wild at Heart* reflects. The madness of emotional upheaval can be a healing process if we open ourselves to its lessons, integrate them, and try to communicate to others what we have learned. If we do not attempt to share what we have learned with our community, we become isolated and fail to fulfill our human destiny.

The journey through chaos to meet the Madwoman can be a creative process, for the Madwoman connects us to creativity. Just as Ereshkigal, Sumer's dark goddess of the Underworld, was mad, suffering from labor pains while trying to give birth, and needed empathy and compassion, so does every woman experience a mad time as she tries to give birth to a new way of being, whether she brings forth an artwork or her new feminine self. The very image of a woman in labor, crouching to bring forth the new being passing through the birth canal, conjures up a picture of the Madwoman. This image brings us back full circle to the Mad Mother, for in the end we must all give birth to ourselves.

The following story of a contemporary woman, an artist, shows a journey through madness that culminates in giving birth—both to her new feminine self and to her artwork.

MOIRA'S JOURNEY

Giving birth—embodying creativity in the world—is a major problem for many women with external, natal Mad Mothers. It can seem to these daughters that the embittered, hostile mother does not want her daughter to surpass her. Imprisoned herself in a cage of cold rage, the Mad Mother who refuses to face her own fury at the frustrations and limitations in her life resents her daughter's potential for growth and often tries to stifle it. Moira's story is a testament to the way a woman can transform the madness passed on by her mother and put that energy into creative expression in the world.

Moira came from a lineage of Madwomen. Three generations of mothers were embittered because they had been deserted by men. Her great-grandfather had left home to join the silver rush in Nevada. Her grandfather, who was an alcoholic, was killed in an automobile accident, leaving her grandmother to fend for herself, while her mother had successively married three alcoholic men and drove away each with her ire. Moira, too, was abandoned by these fathers and left to live with her wrathful mother.

Moira's mother was abusive to her on all levels—physical, emotional, and mental. Often her mother would go out with men, leaving Moira alone at night when she was little. Sometimes her mother would bring the men home to their house. In the middle of the night, Moira's mother would wake her up, slapping her face if she sucked her thumb in her sleep. She would beat Moira with wire coat hangers, sticks, paddles—anything within reach. Once she beat her so viciously on the ear with a belt buckle that she left a lasting scar.

As a child, Moira was so afraid of her mother that she always hid her hurts for fear she would be punished. When she was six, while she was playing, she stepped on a thumbtack and had to hide the pain. She was more afraid of her mother's angry spanking than the wound in her foot. Later, in preadolescence, she was sexually molested for an entire year by a distant family member, but she feared telling her mother about it. Venturing to tell her grandmother, the old woman chided her for making up such bad stories. This made Moira begin to doubt her own sense of reality. Denial was a madness raging within her mother and her grandmother. Both refused to look within, remaining trapped in their own lives and limited views of life.

In school Moira was an excellent student, and she tried to win her mother's love this way. But her mother put her in a double bind. Demanding perfection, her mother threatened to double any spanking she might receive for misconduct at her Catholic school. But when Moira won honors for public speaking, her mother ignored her at home and did not attend the performance. When Moira was chosen to be a cheerleader, her mother made her quit. The same thing happened when she won a place on the varsity swimming team; again her mother demanded she quit the team. School was Moira's haven; her teachers loved her because she was a good student, but her mother constantly threatened to take her out of school. The older Moira got, the more jealous her mother seemed to become of her bright and pretty daughter.

Multitalented, Moira was gifted in several of the arts, and she continuously experienced a flow of creative images and ideas. Her mother's jealous threats led to a pattern of quitting any endeavor she began. Gradually, she became afraid of success. Following her mother's negative response to her public speaking achievements, Moira suddenly went blank during one competition and could not bring herself to speak onstage again. She began to feel crippled in the world at large. During those years she had repetitive nightmares in which her mother pursued her with a knife. The dreams were so frightening that she was afraid to go to sleep. In waking life, her mother often ignored her by sitting like a zombie in front of the television set and not speaking to her. At other times, her anger would explode into physical violence.

For most of her adolescence, Moira felt like the figure in Edvard Munch's painting *The Scream*. Toward the end of her time at home,

Moira finally expressed the force of these feelings when her mother hit her. Moira screamed so loud and long and powerfully that her mother never tried to hit her again. Having experienced the power of the mad cry, soon afterward, at eighteen, Moira left home never to return again. Many years later, she was able to articulate her feelings about this through a poem, "Sadly Sixteen."

When I was sixteen,
my mother lost her sex
She would have been happy for me
to have lost mine as well.

To leave me virginal
to my toes. Dry,
untutored and artless
in the ways of love.

A frustrated vixen.
Acidic. And smelling of vinegar.
Yes,
this would have fed her jealousy,
nourished her cruelty.

When I was sixteen
I had a woman's desire to be filled
with sweet passion:
a man's hot white blood.

I wanted it.
She lost it.
Mother and daughter
traded guilt
for hatred.

For Moira, the two major areas of injury resulting from her life with this Mad Mother were her relationships with men and her willingness to show her creative work to the world. With men, Moira tended to repeat her mother's pattern—the only feminine model she had seen. Her mother was vicious, bickering, jealous, and possessive, accusing the men in her life of causing her troubles. Moira suffered from a dichotomy in her own personality—she was a sweet, affectionate woman most of the time but also had a dark, terrible Madwoman side like her mother. Fearing abandonment in relationships, Moira was always looking for the father she never had. She tried to hold on to men through her charm and sexuality, but she would inexplicably become terribly jealous and accuse her lovers of infidelity. She quarreled with a lover when she learned he had talked with his ex-wife. Afraid he was going out with his former wife on the sly, she tore up the ex-wife's photograph and threw the pieces into the toilet. Another time, with another lover, she found one of her paintings that she had given to him as a symbol of their union hanging over the bed in which he slept with her as well as other women. In a rage she grabbed the picture, tore it in half, and rubbed the red and black chalk pastel colors over his brand-new white couch. These were only two of a number of mad episodes with men in which the Madwoman suddenly broke through in a frenzy.

After some therapy, Moira realized she had internalized the Madwoman modeled on the personal level by her mother. Afraid of this fierce feminine figure, she also knew that the Madwoman is a universal symbol and holds creative power in the collective unconscious. An avid reader, Moira had delved deeply into world mythology and recognized the various guises of the Madwoman in feminine figures like the Hindu goddess Kali, the Greek goddess Hecate, the Polynesian volcano goddess Pelé, and the Sumerian underworld goddess Ereshkigal. By looking within at the developmental patterns inherited from her personal legacy of Mad Mothers, and by looking beyond the personal to the archetypal realm through her readings in world literature and her knowledge of art history, Moira knew she had an essential task before her—to face the Madwoman and to change the negative patterns she had learned from her mother by utilizing the creative power of this dark feminine force.

Moira's inherent creativity fired the process of her transformation. In her late twenties, images came to her through her dreams in a great flood, and she spontaneously painted a series of larger-than-life-size pieces that she later called the Demon Paintings. At the time she was in art school and in Reichian therapy, both of which temporarily helped her face the power of these paintings. The first painting revealed two significant figures: a huge and threatening Demon Lover and a small, submissive, powerless woman (the female victim that Moira had experienced all her life in her mother and that she had felt in herself). In the middle was a large red cross, revealing the inner crucifixion she was feeling. As soon as she painted this picture, which she described as emerging spontaneously from her unconscious, she knew it was meaningful, for it suggested the Catholic iconography with which she had been raised. Next came a painting that she called *The Virgin and the Whore*. To her shock, the third painting was of a woman sitting on the lap of a demon who masturbates her while a nun, with the face of a Madwoman, frowns. For Moira, this symbolized the personification of her guilt. Her next painting showed another woman, mad with jealousy, holding an anatomical heart, green with envy. Next she painted a red-haired, red-lipped woman who was masturbating, her leg lifted up in the confessional. In this painting the father confessor cannot hear the woman because he was Death itself, and the demon was leering over her shoulder as she tried to make confession. Other paintings followed, including *Death and the Devil*. This painting frightened her with its awful possibility of suicide; she feared that freedom from the demons might come only through her own death. The final painting in this series she entitled *Resurrection*. Moira is on the cross this time, but instead of a demon there is a pregnant woman standing in front of her, symbolizing new life.

After she finished this series of paintings, Moira felt an overwhelming sense of euphoria. She had been able to give form to these images that came from the chaotic unfathomable realm of the unconscious. Through her art she had been able to make the "invisible" visible. This was important to her because it was a way of communicating her inner visions to others. She knew the paintings were archetypal and expressed forces inside many people, and that they would speak to a large audience. But she herself felt she was in the throes of the demon, and the immense power of the paintings frightened her. She lacked a container for these energies. Mistakenly, she thought that destroying the paintings might free her from the grip of these grotesque figures so, with the help of a friend, she performed a ritual to exorcise these demonic figures. She took the huge paintings by truck deep into a forest, where she ripped them from their frames and tore them apart by hand, one by one. At the same time she destroyed a painting of the dark goddess, whose black eyes and flagrant sexuality disturbed her. Then she buried the pieces. The process took hours. After this ritual she had hoped for relief, but instead she felt torn inside. Too late, she realized this destruction was not the way to get rid of her disturbing inner psychic forces. She became aware that the paintings were like her children, as artworks are to artists, regardless of the content. They were also potential museum pieces, something confirmed later by others when she showed slides that she had made of the paintings. A dream she had later spoke to this issue.

> I am giving birth, in primitive fashion by squatting on the earth, with the help of a midwife who is the same woman who helped me perform the ritual of destroying the paintings. Another shadowy female figure stands behind me. As I push the infant out, I realize in horror that it is dead. Then there are more labor pains, and another baby comes out, also dead. This continues until I have given birth to twenty-four dead fetuses, each smaller than the last.

Much later, after reflecting on the shocking dream, Moira wondered if the female figure behind her was the Madwoman preventing her from giving birth, aborting her creations. Then Moira had another Madwoman dream that demanded her attention:

> I am in a darkened room with an oriental rug on the floor. Underneath the rug I see an illuminated rainbow-colored snake. She looked at me straight in the eyes and even seemed to look like me. Although the snake was very small and not threatening, I started stepping on it madly. The little snake seemed indestructible and peeked at me from underneath the rug. Once more, I stamped on every part of the rug like a Madwoman to get rid of it.

After some reflection, Moira realized that stamping on the translucent rainbow snake symbolized the way she had destroyed her creativity, as she had her paintings—from fear. In reality, Moira was afraid of snakes, but she also knew the snake was an ancient goddess symbol and represented the divine feminine. The Rainbow Serpent is the feminine creatrix for many of the Aboriginal peoples in Australia. Since snakes shed their skins every year, it suggested that potential transformation and creativity were hiding under the rug and trying to come out and get her attention. But like a negative

Madwoman, she tried to destroy the very symbol of feminine transformation and creativity.

These dreams terrified Moira and eventually forced her to go
back into therapy. In this way the nightmares came to be healing
dreams, helping her realize that she had to deal with the childhood
wounds to herself and later to her creative process. These wounds,
coming developmentally from her embittered mother, who had
made her quit any successful venture, had been interfering with
both her relationships with men and with putting her creative projects forth into the world. She had destroyed both her relationships
and her paintings out of fear: "Because the wound stood between
me and life, I couldn't get anything out into the world. I couldn't
pass through that wound."

Moira said this about a relationship with a man whom she loved
deeply and that had ended partly because her inner Madwoman had
gotten out of control. This man was controlling, but also protective
and nurturing. Moira had refused to let herself be controlled by
him and became unpredictably emotional in many of their interactions. Later, she felt she had driven her lover away by getting hysterical and saying horrible things: "I also had a needy little girl inside
me that developed as a result of living with the Madwoman enacted
by my mother and grandmother. It felt like someone else was inside
me—the Madwoman. Even my voice would change." She alternated
between being a needy little girl, an angry and possessive witch-
bitch, and her responsible mature self. Although her lover was attracted to her Aphrodite side, to her sense of play, and to her
intellectual and artistic side, he left because Moira was too much
like his own mother, so emotionally unpredictable that he never
knew how she would respond.

When the relationship ended, Moira went into a depression so
disturbing that she knew she had to seek help. She became inertial
and couldn't get out of bed. She could not "be." Feeling suicidal,
she became obsessed with thinking about methods of killing herself.
But deep within, Moira knew she would never commit suicide. From
a former marriage, she had a grown son to whom she could not
leave this horrible legacy. Moira desperately wanted to transform
the negative relationship she had experienced with her own Mad
Mother. Even though she had experienced so much turmoil in her
life, she had learned to be a positive, loving mother. Her love for
her son was deep, and she experienced it as a divine love that held

at bay the demonic power that wanted to destroy her. Loving her son was the beginning of learning to love herself in this unconditional way.

Unlike her own mother, Moira consciously chose to probe the depths of her misery to change the pattern of the Mad Mothering she had received. She finally went into therapy with a woman who was emotionally supportive and a positive feminine model. Moira experienced this period as a consciously chosen descent into the underworld to encounter the Madwoman, much as Inanna, the Sumerian goddess of the upper world, consciously chose to descend into the netherworld to meet her mad sister Ereshkigal, goddess of the dark realm. Like Inanna, who had asked a female aide to assist her in the descent, Moira had enlisted the aid of her therapist, as well as a long-term friend steeped in the knowledge of this feminine journey. But the journey was Moira's alone, and it took extraordinary courage and faith for her to live through the chaotic period of breakdown that followed.

During this period, Moira lived alone on the top floor of a house nestled deep in a canyon. Her windows looked out onto the green leafy trees that she felt as a healing presence. She began writing in her journals, and she said that writing saved her life. She also walked on the earth, which she felt radiated through the soles of her feet. "Through much walking, meditating, and writing poetry amid the trees, I found my true natural Mother, the Earth, which healed me," she said.

Her breakthrough came shortly before the winter solstice. One afternoon she was feeling depressed and fell asleep. When she woke up she heard a repeating refrain: "I am caught in a web of misery." To the sound of this refrain she walked and wrote. Words and images poured out for about six hours. She stayed up all night, trying to make sense of all that had come forth on the exact date (11/11/88) of the card of the High Priestess in the Tarot.

Two weeks later, on Thanksgiving, she had an unusual experience. Over a period of several hours, while driving to her friend's house for Thanksgiving dinner, she found three dead but perfect bodies of barn owls lying along a country road. She knew the owl carcasses were a beautiful gift, and she picked each one up with care and put it in her car. She saw the owls as a synchronistic reflection of her internal state, similar to the experiences of shamans in all cultures for millennia. When she arrived at her destination, upon seeing the owls, the friend who was helping her through this period spontaneously confirmed this, saying, "The three barn owls symbolize the maiden, the mother, and the crone." These are the three aspects of the mother-daughter relationship: youth (daughter), middle age (mother), and the old woman (grandmother). Her friend also said, "This is Lilith."

Immediately, Moira knew she was being offered a feminine mystery that could help her in her quest for personal transformation. Like the paintings that had come to her, she didn't know what this mystery meant at the time, but she trusted that it was important. Taking the three owl carcasses home to her canyon retreat, she cleaned and skinned them and kept the feathers in her room, and she felt their healing presence.

For the next two months, Moira did much research on owls and on Lilith, discovering that the owl was a companion to Lilith. Both had vision and could see in the dark. She learned that the biblical Lilith had been the first wife of Adam, made from the same dust rather than from his rib. Unwilling to be his inferior, she had refused to lie beneath him. She learned how the story of Lilith, like that of most women in biblical history and mythology, had been abused and twisted by both the Jewish and the Christian patriarchies. For this reason Lilith was called "the Woman of the Night who murders children." Moira associated this with her dream of the twenty-four dead fetuses, as well as the dream in which she had stamped like a Madwoman on the beautiful rainbow snake. She also related all this to the fact that since she had destroyed her paintings (her creative children), she had been unable for some time to create in her former deeply connected, authentic way. She felt she had desecrated the gift of her own creativity and the gift to read her own soul. Moira saw how she had repeated her mother's repudiation of creativity by dishonoring her own creativity through the destruction of her paintings.

Finally Moira felt ready to create again. She fashioned an artwork—an assemblage—that she called *Lilith, Snake Dance Through the Night*. The creation of *Lilith* was the breakthrough for her. In this work, she honored the Madwoman in herself by honoring Lilith, a dark feminine form of the Madwoman. She made a mask of herself and wrote a prayer on a piece of metallic, reflective paper, placing it underneath the face of the dark feminine figure. In the prayer she asked that her creativity be returned "on all levels, in all areas, and

forevermore." In the complex assemblage of *Lilith,* she placed the
barn owl's wings, the head, the tail, and the talons, as well as a large
snake skin, a gift from the friend who had helped her. She also
included the poems she had written during her descent, along with
a portrait of the Buddha, which symbolized her devotion to the
spiritual path. In this way Moira reunited with creativity, and she
found that union through Lilith the Madwoman—the divine but
dark, chaotic creative mother who would not subject herself to the
judgmental patriarchy.

For Moira, to create in this way was a form of prayer and a
celebration. Through honoring Lilith she herself became the creative mother. As if to confirm the entire process, on one of her
walks shortly afterward, she found a dead great horned owl on the
ground. She kept the head, wings, and talons of this great and awe-
some being that had been offered to her by Nature. Looking into
the eyes of the great horned owl, she saw maggots, and she knew
this was life too. It was neither offensive nor disturbing to her. She
knew that some people might see her response as madness, but she
found the maggot-eyed owl utterly beautiful—it was part of the
whole—the cycle of life and death.

Her creation of *Lilith* broke through the Mad Mother complex
that was disturbing and inhibiting her. Moira turned to face the
Madwoman directly and to honor her by expressing her nature
through a powerful artwork—one that she will never destroy but
that hangs on her wall as an ever-present reminder of the mystery of
creation. Since then she has had several wonderful dreams of giving
birth to little girls who are beautifully formed. She also had the
following dream that suggested she had transformed the Mad
Mother in her psyche.

I am in my home and my mother is with me. It is night time,
and I'm in my bed, which is situated next to a table where she
is sitting staring at a candle. At first I think, "Oh, my poor
mother is mad!" I surround her with peace, love, and
blessings and go to sleep feeling perfectly safe and unafraid of
her, as I had been as a child. The following morning my
mother rushes up to me with a radiant smile on her face and
declares, "You didn't call the police!" I say, "What do you
mean?" And she responds, "You didn't call the police and tell
them I'm crazy." She seemed genuinely grateful. When I look

up on the wall I see a beautiful, expensively framed painting, and I think, "Isn't that like my mother, who hasn't any money, to go out and buy a beautiful and expensive work of art?" I feel great tenderness and admiration for her and a deep *acceptance* that she is my mother.

In a recent dream, Moira was onstage accompanied by a little girl who was performing confidently and by a wise older woman who embodied the creative energy of the Madwoman for her. This dream displayed the union of the three feminine aspects—maiden, mother, and crone.

This is a story of how one woman transformed her childhood isolation and abuse and sought to understand how the complexities of good and evil manifested in her life. Today, Moira is a successful artist and published writer. The Madwoman continues to inspire her with upcoming projects for books, films, and life.

INVITE HER TO LUNCH: THE MADWOMAN AT YOUR TABLE

How can a woman transform the Madwoman's energy so she can free herself from the fears that keep her from her fullness? Before transformation can occur, we have to learn to identify how the Madwoman manifests herself in our own lives. In order to gather in the Madwoman's energy, we need to recognize her.

As we learn to recognize and work with the different patterns of the Madwoman energy, we will see that all exist within us at one time or another, even though one or two predominate. Learning to enter and use the creative side of each will enable us to express ourselves more fully as women and as human beings. But to avail ourselves of the creative energy, we must learn to live within the paradox each pattern presents. For example, the Ice Queen can offer us the sense of distance and objectivity we need for clear perceptions, as well as a sense of limit and boundary. But her aloofness and frozen feelings can cut us off from life. The Dragon Lady emanates fiery passion that ignites the flame of transformation and creativity, but her unpredictable rages can explode and decimate, burning up herself and others in the process. The Saint can nurture, love, and care for others with her generosity, but if she fails to look within at her dark and difficult side, which includes her own desires and needs, she is likely to harbor resentment and become a martyr who criticizes and fends off angry energy in others. If the Sick Mother can acknowledge and accept her pain, she can become a wounded healer who contributes to the passage from illness to health; but if she confines herself in a closed cell of sickness, she paralyzes herself and others by manipulating them to live around her.

The Caged Bird can offer domestic comfort and nesting in a safe and secure abode, but she may sacrifice her own freedom and adventure and resist change in her family and herself. The Muse can inspire us to create and honor beauty, and to reach places beyond our ordinary dreams, but if she stays on the pedestal of adoration, she usurps the energy that belongs to the divine. While her lyrical charisma can lure us to spiritual growth, she can also seduce us like the sirens, only to crash our ideals from inflation to deflating cynicism. If the Rejected Lover learns to survive the ordeal of abandonment and betrayal, she can learn from her suffering and grow beyond victim to strong heroine. Her rejections can be the very spur to action to find new and better opportunities for growth. But if she falls into seeking revenge she will hurt others, while if she remains the victim she will sink into stupor and passivity.

The Bag Lady can be a symbol for the free spirit beyond the clutches of material possession. Her crazy wisdom can offer fresh perspectives and provoke innovative ways of life. But as a dropout from the system, she can be victimized, and she fails to contribute to society. The Recluse knows the value of solitude and of honoring sacred time and space. By valuing aloneness she learns how to make the inner voyage, and if she comes out of her seclusion, she can share her knowledge of that journey with others. But if she isolates herself from friends and community, she can fall into paranoia and even the hatred of humanity.

The Revolutionary can show us the risk and courage we need to create a better world. But if she wields her power over others, and claims that the end justifies the means, she can become a terrorist, threatening our very existence. Also, the Revolutionary sometimes parades her moral righteousness, thereby aligning with the patriarchal Judge.

The Visionary can show us new ways of being through her clairvoyance and guide us through the sacred mysteries that give life greater meaning. But if she becomes so esoteric and ethereal that she fades into the mist, she cannot ground her vision and we remain untouched. Or if she identifies in inflation with the archetypal energy, she may think only she is carrying the needed knowledge for the whole society. If she seeks power over people, she can be a false prophet or a guru, claiming she is the "chosen one" while devaluing others' contributions. The Visionary can also use intuitions to hurt other people and hold them hostage or harass them.

Working with our dreams—a way in which the Madwoman is revealed—is one way we can get to know her. My own dream of the Madwoman, mentioned in the Preface, caused me to confront her by writing this book, which has been both a creative and spiritual task.

Identifying the Madwoman in our interactions is another way to see how she relates—when and how she presents herself. How does she interfere, and how does she help us? For example, in relationships, one partner often assumes the role of the superior Judge while the other reacts to the craziness of perfectionistic demands by acting out the Madwoman. Once we recognize these warring opposites in ourselves that are acted out unconsciously in relationships, causing them to go awry, we can work to change them into effective agents of communication.

The Madwoman often emerges through the course of bodywork. While she was working on a woman's diaphragm, one bodywork therapist had a vision of a Madwoman who seemed to be leering from her client's eyes. When asked what she was experiencing, the client said she was remembering a fight with her sister in which she had not expressed her anger effectively. She had suppressed this anger, which went underground, turned into resentment, and affected her breathing. Just as she had been unable to release her anger adequately, neither could she breathe freely. Recognizing this by actually feeling it in her body helped her to expand her repertoire of emotional expressions and live more fully. Art therapy and dance therapy also elicit the Madwoman's energy because they invite us to be active and experience our feelings in the body.

Once we have identified the Madwoman in ourselves, we can talk with that figure. We can ask her what she wants and what we are doing to arouse her ire. What does she look like? In your mind, create her—give her form. Describe her in a poem, or paint a picture of her. Does she like a special color? Does she have a favorite animal? Where does she live? Dance with her. Find out how she moves. If we know more about her genuine needs and desires for expression, we can integrate this new information in constructive ways in our lives.

Ritual is another way to work with the Madwoman energy. Other cultures understand this much better than those gripped by rational bias and Western technology. For example, in the ancient African religion voodoo, the ritual of making a voodoo doll was performed to help a person get into their madness and release it. From sunrise to sunset, for eight hours, practitioners would make a doll—which represented their own interior mad perception. The creator of the doll would stew in his or her own madness. If the dollmaker hated someone, forming the doll could force her into realizing she was making her own perception of the enemy. One of the rules of making a voodoo doll was to put a piece of one's own hair (symbolizing one's own thoughts and energies) on the right side of the doll. By sitting actively with those negative feelings for a contained period of time, the perception could be felt and released. The ultimate aim was to turn the mad perception into compassion.[4]

After recognizing her own patterns of madness, one woman decided to fashion a Madwoman mask. After she put on the mask, she could hear the shriek of rage lurking within her own voice. She decided to sit in a circle of chairs and give voice to a memory of her madness. Feeling release, she sat in each chair in the circle, consciously voicing every incident of anger she could remember but had failed to express. She found she had to go around the circle many times, as forgotten moments of unexpressed anger arose in her. Later, she went back to her women's group and shared this experience with them. The women decided to ritualize the experience. They lay on the ground in a circle, each a spoke of a wheel, her head in the center. Feeling their sisterhood, the women started to dance in their minds with the Madwoman who had been locked inside them. Getting up and painting their faces, they danced, yelled, and screamed like wild banshees, feeling their own primal mad energy. One woman painted a beautiful group portrait, expressing their experience in the form of many wonderful and exotic Madwomen, each peering through the green vines of a primeval jungle.

As I finished writing this book, I, too, had a vision of many Madwomen—all uniting in love, in work and play, with hope and joy for peace and harmony on earth. I would like to share my vision and follow the suggestion of the shamaness from Bali: "Invite her to lunch"—invite, that is, the transformed Madwoman in all her blazing creative fire. Imagine Rachel Carson, Rosa Luxemburg, Anna Akhmatova, and Peace Pilgrim conversing at your table, or in my own fashion, all hiking together through the autumn leaves of an ancient Appalachian forest. Allow them to hike with you up to Eagle Point—a great rock lookout from a clearing in the forest. Perhaps Frida Kahlo, Zora Neale Hurston, Harriet Tubman, Indira Gandhi, and Golda Meir will journey with us, too. We will set out a picnic lunch on Mother Earth's *feminine* philosopher's stone, Nature's embodiment of the solid center of the female self. Sitting on Psyche's stone we will dip our feet into the rushing river flowing by us—the ever-changing river that flows via different channels into the sea. Each of our lives is like the myriad streams, changing directions and carving out a unique course. Journeying together, we will sit on the same rock, remembering the great waters from which we came and to which we will return. In the meantime we will talk together and even laugh with tears streaming from our eyes. On this Indian summer day, we will plant our seeds of wisdom in the rich dark soil and know they will be resting deep beneath the winter snow, to burst forth suddenly in the amazing glory of spring. Our mature fruit will offer new blossoms to our younger sisters. Our different colors and vibrant visions will join in endless combinations that change unceasingly as we roll and romp among the crimson, gold, and copper leaves on the ground, playing like young girls with our mothers and grandmothers and our daughters and sisters, delighting in the ecstasy of our communion, rustling the brilliant autumn leaves that carpet our great common Mother Earth.

NOTES

CHAPTER 1

Meeting the Madwoman

1. See Merlin Stone, *Ancient Mirrors of Womanhood: Our Goddess and Heroine Heritage* (New York: New Sibylline Books, 1979) and *Larousse World of Mythology,* Pierre Grimal (New York: Excalibur Books, 1981).

2. See Sandra M. Gilbert and Susan Gubar, *The Madwoman in the Attic: The Woman Writer and the Nineteenth Century Literary Imagination* (New Haven: Yale University Press, 1979).

3. For a detailed description of the Judge, see my *Witness to the Fire: Creativity and the Veil of Addiction* (Boston: Shambhala, 1989), chap. 9.

4. Euripides, *The Bacchants,* in *Ten Plays by Euripides,* trans. Moses Hadas and John McLean (New York: Bantam Books, 1988), pp. 281–312.

5. See Carolyn G. Heilbrun, *Toward a Recognition of Androgyny* (New York: Harper and Row, 1973), p. 7.

6. See Carolyn Heilbrun's, *Writing a Woman's Life* (New York: Ballantine Books, 1988) for a book that shows facets of feminine spirit.

7. Quoted in Betty Cannon, *Sartre and Psychoanalysis* (Lawrence, KS: University Press of Kansas, 1991), pp. 249–50.

8. John Weir Perry, *The Far Side of Madness* (Dallas: Spring Publications, 1974), p. 6.

9. Evelyn Underhill, *Practical Mysticism* (Columbus, OH: Ariel Press, 1942).

10. For working with women's dreams, see Karen Signell's *Wisdom of the Heart: Working with Women's Dreams* (New York: Bantam Books, 1990).

11. For active imagination, see Robert Johnson's *Inner Work* (San Francisco: HarperCollins, 1987).

CHAPTER 2

Mad Mothers, Mad Daughters

1. Codependency is an addictive disease in which one looks for one's center outside of oneself. Codependents tend to focus on the problems of others —whether through pleasing or controlling—rather than on their own lives. See my *Witness to the Fire: Creativity and the Veil of Addiction* (Boston: Shambhala, 1989) for further analysis.

2. Ingmar Bergman, *Autumn Sonata,* trans. Alan Blair (New York: Pantheon Books, 1978), pp. 61–62.

3. Ibid., p. 19.

4. Ibid., p. 51.

5. Ibid., pp. 57–58.

6. Ibid., pp. 61– 62.

7. Ibid., p. 63.

8. Ibid., p. 79.

9. Ibid., p. 84.

10. See my discussion in *Witness to the Fire,* pp. 115 – 64.

CHAPTER 3

The Caged Bird

1. Muriel Rukeyser, "Kathe Kollwitz," in *No More Masks: An Anthology of Poems by Women,* ed. Florence Howe and Ellen Bass (New York: Doubleday Anchor Books, 1973), p. 103.

2. Marilyn Frye, *The Politics of Reality: Essays in Feminist Theory* (Trumansburg, N.Y.: Crossing Press, 1983), pp. 4–7.

3. See Phyllis Chesler's analysis in *Women and Madness* (New York: Avon Books, 1973).

4. I have analyzed the way our fathers cage us in *The Wounded Woman: Healing the Father-Daughter Relationship* (Boston: Shambhala, 1982).

5. See Robert Bly, *Iron John: A Book about Men* (Reading, MA: Addison-Wesley, 1990), and Sam Keen, *Fire in the Belly* (New York: Bantam Books, 1991).

6. Jeláluddin Rumi, *The Ruins of the Heart,* trans. Edmund Helminski (Putney, VT: Threshold Books, 1981), p. 25.

7. Evan S. Connell, *Mrs. Bridge* (New York: Viking Press, 1959), p. 35.

8. Ibid., p. 202.

9. Ibid., p. 173.

10. Ibid., p. 246.

11. Charlotte Perkins Gilman, *The Yellow Wallpaper* (Old Westbury, NY: Feminist Press, 1973), p. 36.

12. Quoted in Ann J. Lane, *To "Herland" and Beyond: The Life and Work of Charlotte Perkins Gilman* (New York: Pantheon Books, 1990), p. 121.

13. Ibid., p. 99.

14. Ibid., p. 182.

15. Ibid., p. 188.

16. Charlotte Perkins Gilman, *Women and Economics* (New York: Harper and Row, 1966), pp. 43 – 44.

CHAPTER 4

The Muse

1. Quoted in Karen Monson, *Alma Mahler: Muse to Genius* (Boston: Houghton Mifflin, 1983), p. 151.

2. Ibid., p. 44.

3. Ibid., p. 145.

4. Ibid., p. 155.

5. Ibid., p. 279.

6. Ibid., p. 288.

7. Ibid., pp. 309 –310.

8. Ibid., p. 318.

9. Camille's pregnancy and abortion have not been documented officially, although they seem likely to have occurred. Reine-Marie Paris, *Camille: The Life of Camille Claudel, Rodin's Muse and Mistress,* trans. Liliane Emery Tuck (New York: Henry Holt, 1988), pp. 13–14.

10. Ibid., p. 21.

11. Ibid., p. 22.

12. Ibid., p. 60.

13. Ibid., p. 67.

14. Ibid., p. 135.

CHAPTER 5

The Rejected Lover

1. See the Ghostly Lover chapter in my *On the Way to the Wedding: Transforming the Love Relationship* (Boston: Shambhala, 1986).

2. Fay Weldon, *The Life and Loves of a She-Devil* (New York: Ballantine Books, 1983), pp. 186 – 187.

3. Euripides, *Medea,* in *Ten Plays by Euripides,* trans. Moses Hadas and John McLean (New York: Bantam Books, 1981), p. 38.

4. Quoted in Arianna Stassinopoulos, *Maria Callas: The Woman Behind the Legend* (New York: Ballantine Books, 1982), p. 101.

5. Ibid., p. 21.

6. Ibid., p. 106.

7. Ibid., p. 166.

8. Ibid., p. 191.

9. Ibid., p. 198.

10. Ibid., p. 206.

11. Ibid., p. 282.

12. Ibid., p. 284.

13. Ibid., p. 324.

14. Ibid., p. 332.

15. See the chapter on the Demon Lover in my *On the Way to the Wedding: Transforming the Love Relationship.*

CHAPTER 6

The Bag Lady

1. Jane Wagner, *The Search for Signs of Intelligent Life in the Universe* (New York: Harper and Row, 1986), p. 15.

2. Ibid., p. 17.

3. Ibid., p. 18.

4. Ibid.

5. Ibid., p. 21.

6. Ibid., p. 201.

7. Ibid., pp. 202–203.

8. Ibid., p. 206.

9. Ibid., p. 19.

10. *Peace Pilgrim: Her Life and Work in Her Own Words* (Santa Fe, NM: Ocean Tree Books, 1991), p. vi.

11. Ibid., p. 1.

12. Ibid.

13. Ibid., p. 28.

14. Ibid., p. 37.

15. Ibid., p. 27.

16. Ibid., p. 56.

17. Ibid., p. xiv.

18. Ann Marie Rousseau and Alix Kates Shulman, *Shopping Bag Ladies: Homeless Women Speak about Their Lives* (New York: Pilgrim Press, 1981), p. 82.

19. Ibid., p. 53.

20. Ibid., p. 115.

CHAPTER 7

The Recluse

1. Jean Rhys, *Good Morning, Midnight* (New York: W.W. Norton, 1986), p. 52.

2. Athol Fugard, *The Road to Mecca* (New York: Theatre Communications Group, 1985), pp. 26 –27.

3. Ibid., p. 25.

4. Ibid., p. 22.

5. Ibid., p. 21.

6. Ibid., p. 61.

7. Ibid.

8. Ibid., p. 63.

9. Ibid., p. 67.

10. Ibid., p. 68.

11. Ibid., p. 71.

12. Ibid., p. 75.

13. Ibid., p. 22.

14. Paul Brooks, *The House of Life: Rachel Carson at Work* (Boston: Houghton Mifflin, 1972), p. 297.

15. Ibid., p. 16.

16. Ibid., p. 1.

17. Ibid., p. 113.

18. Ibid., p. 2.

19. Ibid.

20. Ibid., p. 158.

21. Ibid., p. 3.

22. Ibid., p. 129.

23. Ibid., p. 132.

24. Ibid., p. 176.

25. This is the destructive aspect of the Judge.

26. Brooks, *The House of Life*, p. 244.

27. Ibid., p. 303.

28. Ibid., p. 306.

29. Ibid., pp. 324–326.

30. Rainer Maria Rilke, *Letters to a Young Poet*, trans. M. D. Herter Norton (New York: W.W. Norton, 1963), p. 59.

31. May Sarton, *A Self Portrait*, ed. Marita Simpson and Martha Wheelock (New York: W.W. Norton, 1982), p. 22.

CHAPTER 8

The Revolutionary

1. Anja Elizabeth Rosmus. *Should German Movies Look Back? The New York Times* (October 21, 1990.)

2. Albert Camus, *The Rebel*, trans. Anthony Bower (New York: Random House, 1956), p. 301.

3. Quoted in Elzbieta Ettinger, *Rosa Luxemburg: A Life* (Boston: Beacon Press, 1986), p. 88.

4. Ibid., p. 113.

5. Ibid., p. 120.

6. Ibid., p. 173.

7. Ibid., pp. 215 –216.

8. Ibid., p. 245.

9. Ibid., p. 246.

10. Ibid., p. 244.

11. Muriel Rukeyser, "Kathe Kollwitz," in *No More Masks: An Anthology of Poems by Women*, ed. Florence Howe and Ellen Bass (New York: Doubleday Anchor Books, 1973), p. 100.

12. Aung San Suu Kyi, *Freedom from Fear*, ed. Michael Aris (New York: Penguin Books, 1991), p. 234.

CHAPTER 9

The Visionary

1. See Robert Graves, *The Greek Myths*, vols. 1 and 2. (London: Penguin Books, 1960) and *Larousse Encyclopedia of Mythology*, Pierre Grimal (New York: Excalibur Books, 1981).

2. After the fall of Troy, Hecuba herself was said to have been transformed into one of Hecate's black bitches after she was put to death for cursing Odysseus and the Greeks for their barbarism.

3. Unknown to her parents, Iphigenia was saved at the last moment by the goddess Artemis to serve as her priestess.

4. Toni Wolff, "Structural Forms of the Feminine Psyche," trans. Paul Watzlawik. Monograph privately printed for the Students Association, C. G. Jung Institute, Zurich, July 1956, pp. 9ff.

5. Laura in Tennessee Williams's *The Glass Menagerie* is an example of the fragile medial woman drifting into fantasy. I have described this as the Girl of Glass pattern in *The Wounded Woman: Healing the Father-Daughter Relationship* (Boston: Shambhala, 1982).

6. Wolff, p. 9.

7. Ibid., p. 10.

8. Ibid.

9. Marion Zimmer Bradley, *The Mists of Avalon* (New York: Ballantine Books, 1982), p. 399.

10. See Norma Lorre Goodrich, *Priestesses* (New York: HarperCollins, 1989), pp. 288–323 and the book throughout for a sourcebook on the priestess culture.

11. Ibid. p. 223. Pythagoras claimed that these revelations of wisdom arose from currents that met at holy intersections in the depths of the earth. Hence the underground domain of the pythia's oracular chamber.

12. Pär Lagerkvist, *The Sibyl,* trans. Naomi Walford (New York: Random House, 1958), pp. 137 –138.

13. Ibid., pp. 136 –137.

14. Ibid., pp. 149 –150.

15. Osip Mandelstam was arrested during the Stalinist purges and died in a camp in 1938. Marina Tsvetayeva went into exile, later trying to return. After her husband was executed and her daughter sent to a labor camp, she hanged herself in 1941. See Amanda Haight, *Anna Akhmatova: A Poetic Pilgrimage* (New York: Oxford University Press, 1976), p. 153.

16. Ibid., p. 7.

17. Ibid., p. 11.

18. Ibid., p. 36.

19. Ibid., p. 54.

20. Ibid., p. 54.

21. Ibid., p. 80.

22. Ibid., p. 96.

23. Ibid., p. 98. Nadezhda Mandelstam and Lidiya Chukoskaya were among the good friends who memorized verses to preserve her poems.

24. Ibid., p. 105.

25. Ibid., p. 107.

26. Ibid., p. 117.

27. Ibid., p. 138.

28. Ibid.

29. Ibid., p. 119.

30. Ibid., p. 144.

31. Ibid., pp. 153–154.

32. Ibid., p. 164.

33. Bradley, *The Mists of Avalon.* p. 285.

CHAPTER 10

Through the Madness

1. Janet Frame, *An Autobiography* (New York: George Braziller, 1991).

2. Leonora Carrington, *The House of Fear* (New York: E. P. Dutton, 1988), p. 21.

3. Hannah Green (pseudonym for Joanne Greenberg), *I Never Promised You a Rose Garden* (New York: Holt, Rinehart and Winston, 1964), pp. 248 – 249.

4. New Orleans Historic Voodoo Museum.

INDEX

PERMISSIONS

Books and articles quoted or cited in the text under the usual fair allowances are acknowledged in the notes. The author is grateful for permission to use more extensive quotations from the following sources:

A Self-Portrait by May Sarton, Edited by Marita Simpson and Martha Wheelock, by permission of W.W. Norton & Company, Inc. Copyright © 1982 by Marita Simpson, Martha Wheelock and Ishtar Enterprises.

Letters to a Young Poet by Rainer Maria Rilke. Translated by M.D. Herter Norton, by permission of W.W. Norton & Company, Inc. Copyright © 1934 by W.W. Norton & Company, Inc. Copyright renewed 1962 by M.D. Herter Norton. Revised Edition copyright 1954 by W.W. Norton & Company, Inc. Copyright renewed 1982 by M.D. Herter Norton.

The lines from "The Muse as Medusa" are reprinted from *Selected*